CRIME SCENE DECISIONS:

INVESTIGATION, ANALYSIS, EVIDENCE, PROOF

Eric Golembiewski

Crime Scene Decisions: Investigation, Analysis, Evidence, Proof.

ISBN Paperback 978-0-9993151-1-8
ISBN ebook 978-0-9993151-0-1
First edition, first printing, 2017
Publisher's Cataloging-in-Publication Data
Golembiewski, Eric
Crime Scene Decisions: Analysis, Evidence, and Reports / Eric Golembiewski. –1st ed.
p. cm.

1. Criminal investigation—Handbooks, manuals, etc. 2. Evidence, criminal—Handbooks, manuals, etc. 3. Crime Scene searches—Handbooks, manuals, etc.
I. Title.

363.25
2017

To the seekers.

Acknowledgements

Thank you for reading this book. We live in an era of limited time, and your choosing to spend some of it with *Crime Scene Decisions* is a compliment.

Every officer, lab technician, attorney, judge, and jury I have ever met has imparted some knowledge to me on how to build better investigations. Thank you all for the lessons.

My family members encouraged me throughout the writing of this book. Thank you for giving so much room and support

The archetypal cases of this book occur in jurisdictions everywhere. The cases presented are based on actual events, but should not be considered actual cases. Every book has limits, and *Crime Scene Decisions* presents one method of preliminary investigations among many.

This book does not provide legal advice, and nothing in here should be considered instruction in the law. There may be a difference between technological and legal possibilities. Laws change all the time, and it is impossible to predict what is allowed in any particular jurisdiction. The reader is responsible for learning about the legalities of cases.

This is a book of ideas. Investigation can have risks to health, safety, and liability. The reader chooses actions and is responsible for his or her own actions. The author and publisher assume no liability for how this book is used, and the outcomes of actions taken by people who have read this book.

Contents

Introduction

Deciding How To Investigate.

The Way of Preliminary Investigation

The primary goal of an in investigator conducting a preliminary investigation is to prove who did what. The secondary goal is to provide as many evidence based facts as possible to prove parts of a case, like trying to prove the components of presence and action. The first goal is absolute, and will not always be achievable, but the second goal is gradual and should always be met.

Unfortunately, a lot of investigators do not always reach the point of proving who did what, nor even proving details within the body of the case. I embraced the goals, but I noticed my investigation outcomes were not always consistent with my goals and maybe I could solve more cases by making changes

I wrote *Crime Scene Decisions: Investigations, Analysis, Evidence, and Proof* to help improve preliminary investigations. My goal is to show how investigators can investigate cases to the full extent in the earliest phases.

This introduction starts with common and obvious investigation problems. The precursor to problems is methods from training, and the mechanics of crime itself. The method in *Crime Scene Decisions* is explained by evidence, and how evidence fits into a scene-based, evidence centered approach built on decisions.

Decisions are the best teacher because analysis precedes the decision, and action follows it. The decision-making investigator creates investigations made of proof, rather than to prove or disprove someone else's ideas. The basic method to investigate cases to prove who did what is to start with scenes, and end with evidence. Evidence proves presence and action, and is the result of interacting scenes.

Symptoms of Problem Investigations

Successful investigations able to prove who did what only come from finding evidence to prove who did what, even if there is little proof. Failure, on the other hand, has many routes falling under the headings of not understanding the case, and not understanding the investigation. Regardless of route to failure, there are four common symptoms of investigative failures:

1. Incomplete investigations.

2. Poorly supported conclusions.

3. Awkward reports.

4. Too many court cases.

The four failure symptoms share the common origin of the investigator's choices. The first three failures might be clear to anyone scrutinizing investigations, but court provides an external check of investigations as the place of accountability for the accused and investigation itself. Decisions in court come down to evidence to prove who did what. Cases with decisive evidence, (much or none) tend not to go to court. Indecisive evidence leads to court appearances. Court cases often include enough evidence to convince a district attorney to charge a case, but not convince a defense attorney.

All four of the symptoms of problem investigations arise out of investigator decisions about how to conduct an investigation based on bad processes. Most of the problems overlap, but the ideas include:

1. Lack of basic skills competence or adequate equipment can derail an investigation. Bad decisions in collecting, processing, and storing evidence can destroy a case. Failure to isolate the scenes and start with a good assessment leads to uninformed work.

2. Rushing to judgement or oversimplification limits an investigation by blocking recalculation of decisions based on infusions of new information. This is bad process based on the investigator's desire to be right, and not change. Simplification treats the crime process as an inevitable form of history. A strict linear checklist doctrine hamstrings removes critical thinking, presenting everything in an oversimplified, predetermined order.

3. Getting caught up in the emotional aspects of a case from impressions based on involved persons' analysis. This leads to what people want to believe, rather than what is supportable. This is bad process where the

investigator follows the involved person's approach rather than an independent evidence based approach.

4. Cognitive bias when an investigator goes not follow a logical path based on evidence and facts, but chooses an irrational path toward looking for patterns based on a subjective perception of reality. This is bad thought process based on the investigator's approach, partly out of a desire not to be wrong, and looking for a shortcut to find answers. Profiling is formalized cognitive bias used in investigations. Only the facts solve cases, and it is better to have an investigation of few facts than a lot guesses seasoned with facts.

5. Confusing luck with skill, and incorporating luck into process. Detailed statements should not be mistaken for proving a case.

These are not problems to be solved by more work. The solution lies in removing these practices which are based on habits from training and experience, developed over time.

Training Before Investigations

Training and experience for investigators starts in academies. The training anticipates the officer will respond to a scene, stop the emergency, and start the investigation with limited resources. The form is a logical and linear method:

1. Get statements about what happened.

2. Determine what laws have been broken.

3. Obtain the evidence to support or refute the first two points.

4. Create the report.

The form works, and is easy to teach. It is a majority solution because it covers the majority of situations the instigator faces. Knowing those steps I considered the functional impact of training doctrine on investigations. I investigated my own investigation method and found four outcomes correlating with the steps:

1. Statements drove overall investigations.

2. Crime types guided evidence efforts.

3. Evidence became a binary tool to prove or disprove the first two points.

4. Writing the cases was the reflection period, often post- investigation when little could be done to alter the path.

The four steps are conducted in linear fashion, and the method relies on the investigator to be thorough and get true and accurate information from persons before evidence work. The method builds in a simplifying strategy of using evidence to either prove or disprove the statements and laws. It reduces work by limiting the requirements to proving or disproving statements and laws.

The method is effective in solving many cases, but no amount of work will solve cases where the method is mismatched to crime where parts of the crime process are unknown to be investigated. Investigation is nearly impossible when an investigator does not know what he does not know. The solution to creating a method lies with making the method applicable to what is knowable in a case. The crime process of creating the circumstances which an investigator investigates should inform and drive the process of investigation.

Crime Process Before Training

Crime is a process more elementary than issues of right or wrong; it is a defined action, series of actions, or outcomes. All crime has three colliding parts, as any non-crime event involving persons:

1. Persons with thoughts who are present and take action. These are transitory.

2. Opportunities for the thoughts to become actions of scenes coming together. These are often transitory.

3. Scenes where the action took place. These are often changed as a result of action, and continue to bear evidence proving interactions.

The first two parts of crime are rarely witnessed by the investigator, but the scene is often seen by the investigator as outcomes. Evidence and scenes are the constants in all investigations. Scenes are the only part of the crime process to hold evidence, and scenes should have a broad definition of any entity. I thought about the broadest approach to scenes and crime:

1. Everything (entity) is a scene, it is a just a matter of scale.

2. Crimes take place at scenes by process.

3. Evidence results from the process of scenes interacting.

Classic thought defines scenes by their evidence bearing ability. The reverse of the formula is scenes define the evidence. Scenes come first in the crime process, and should also come first in the investigation process.

Scene-based, Evidence-centered Investigations

Investigators work to prove presence and action of persons in the form of who did what. Why would an investigator focus on ephemeral thoughts, actions, and opportunities to find evidence when the scenes have the evidence?

The scene-based, evidence-centered investigation has three related ideas based on the crime process at scenes:

1. Scenes hold evidence.

2. Investigations must be conducted by process to obtain evidence.

3. Evidence can be reverse-engineered to show what scenes interacted, and how.

These three ideas are addressed from the two approaches of scenes and evidence. Since almost every case an investigator's contact with scenes precedes evidence, the method is more direct, but in order to get useful evidence, the investigator must know about it, and what goes into it.

Evidence Function Decisions

Evidence was, is, and always will be the way to prove who did what. The *Crime Scene Decisions* method starts with scenes and ends with evidence because evidence processing is unrevisable action, so the decisions driving action must be on target.

The most basic idea about evidence in *Crime Scene Decisions* is evidence comes from scenes interacting. The initial work on the idea comes from Locard's Principle, expressed as, *every contact leaves a trace.* This book covers the most common evidence types, how they work, and what they can do in detail both as skills and within the context of different scene types.

The evidence skills an investigator chooses are ways to obtain evidence to prove facts. The evidence must meet the standards set forth by Daubert or Frye. Daubert is the federal standard which supersedes Frye, but Frye is still used in some states. Evidence processes must be accepted by the scientific community, and the results repeatable. This is why DNA identification is accepted in court (assuming it was correctly done), and clairvoyant statements are not.

Evidence can be defined in many different ways. Direct evidence requires no intervening process and proves a fact. Circumstantial evidence requires a person to conclude something based on multiple issues. Evidence is not limited to proving guilt. Inculpatory evidence proves guilt, whereas exculpatory evidence exonerates the suspect. All types of evidence work have common elements, making decisions more predictable and the investigator more productive.

Evidence techniques are all aimed at proving ideas through demonstrable facts. *Crime Scene Decisions* recognizes two fundamental areas of evidence skills:

1. *Who* identifies persons and things. These are skills such as by DNA, fingerprints, and patterns.

2. *Did what* reproduces facts of the case, by explaining the overall case, and courses of action to obtain the evidence. These are skills such as critical thinking, information, photography, artifacts, and report writing.

Overview of the *Crime Scene Decisions* Process

There are two areas of investigations covered so far in this introduction, crime scenes, and evidence. Those two components come together in in the investigation process through the investigator decisions.

There are four main decisions for each scene; two for scenes, and two for evidence. The method emphasizes the scene in the beginning, with decisions about why it is a scene, and how it works. The concluding half emphasizes evidence, how it might be in a scene, and how to get it. Each of the four main decisions is made of many decisions, and there are few binary decisions in the method.

1. Designate the scene.
Scene Decision **Why is this a scene?**

There are four decisions that help an investigator understand why a scene is a relevant crime scene:

1. *Scene type*

2. *Discovery*
3. *Scene Group*
4. *Search*

2. Analyze the scene.
***Scene Decision* How does the scene work?**

There are four decisions that help an investigation understand how the crime scene works within the action:

1. *Restrictiveness*
2. *Volatility*
3. *Function*
4. *Capacity and Interaction Points*

3. Evaluate the evidence potential.
***Evidence Decision* How would the evidence work in this scene?**

There are six decisions that help an investigator understand how the evidence works within the particular crime scene:

1. *Production*
2. *Proof Ability*
3. *Quality*
4. *Timeline*
5. *Resilience*
6. *Collection*

4. Work the evidence.
***Evidence Decision* How to obtain the evidence from this scene?**

There are eight decisions that help an investigator understand how to obtain the evidence from the crime scene.

1. *Critical Thinking*
2. *Information*
3. *Photography*
4. *DNA*
5. *Fingerprints*
6. *Patterns*
7. *Artifacts*
8. *Report Production*

How To Read This Book

Crime Scene Decisions is designed to be a practical book to get to the goal of proving who did what. Reading the book from start to finish may provide an investigator with new ideas while reinforcing others. Sometimes the reader knows what to seek, and this book is also designed to allow for navigation.

The book follows the four part format. The Introduction covers the background of the process, and parts. Section I is four chapters, each one covering on of the major decision steps. Sections II through VI are the scenarios, one section covering each of the five scene types by using various example cases. The Conclusion wraps up the book, and looks to the future. The Glossary follows. The book is about investigating cases to prove presence and action. Those two ideas are covered as independent and collaborative topics. The book does not cover issues of policy or administration. The discussion of the decisions does not cover how the evidence is stored or routed for further processing.

Every scenario is presented as a report first, and then broken down by the method to show how the case works. The book is designed to also start with the scenes having the broadest situation, and move toward more specific situations. The public scenes could encompass every subscene covered afterward, and every subscene could fit into a larger scene. This is also a useful reminder to seek tools when working on public, private, or car scenes.

Sometimes a specific point in scenarios exemplifies general ideas. The book is designed to capitalize on those examples, and provide cross applicable details about them. This book provides examples and concepts but there few absolutes in the world of the investigator. Many of the issues are presented with the words, can, may, might, should, could, and sometimes. This is by design and a reminder there are no guarantees in investigations. The issues are not always covered evenly in term of word count. Some areas of the scenarios get detailed coverage, while others get one word.

Some ideas are covered by concept with sentences to transfer the meanings, while other ideas are covered with numbered lists. The four decisions present material in several different ways and perspectives. For example, scene functions cannot be detailed without overlap into critical thinking, and interaction points foreshadow collection.

The book is not a checklist because the goal is for the investigator to think about cases, and make decisions, not just perform a procedure. Checklists are a valid tool to perform tasks. Many parts of the evidence skills trained by checklists due to its completeness. The book does not cover the details of how to perform these tasks beyond what is necessary to show the method. The book also does not cover how to package, transfer, and store the evidence. Those details are often covered by evidence skill centered instruction.

The term *case* is interchangeable with investigation. Titles such as suspect or victim are not set in stone, and are preliminary titles used by most people within investigations. Sometimes persons are described by their actions rather than assumptions about case roles. The term *investigator* describes function rather than title, and could mean officer, detective, community service officer, crime scene investigator, or any other term for someone investigating cases.

Genders are not often relevant to the work, but using the pronoun *they* is too generic and implies multiple persons. Some persons in this book are male and female some female. Anyone can commit or investigate crimes.

Distance measurements are in English, but weights for drugs are in metric, as the amounts are often in the gram range rather than fractions of ounces.

Time is a challenging convention for a process driven investigation book. Times are either in 24 hours or 12 hours. Circumstances were in the past, but can exist into the present, and extend into the future. Most of the material is covered in the past tense because crime events happen in the past, and were investigated in the past. Often the non-changing details can be covered in the present tense, such as directions on the map, or functional designations, such as object. The historical aspect of investigations can include plans for the future, which becomes complicated when there is talk about the future that already happened years ago.

I. Crime Scene Decisions

An investigator should approach a case with a decision method designed to obtain the evidence to prove who did what through evidence of presence and action.

The decision making method for investigating crime is the operating system to control the overall process. This first section is the universal approach to investigate all cases based on scenes. The decisions are general enough to apply to all scenes; from large outdoor areas, as well as small tools.

The decisions are presented as questions any investigator should ask about a scene he works. Many of the points to consider appear to be more like questions than decisions, but the investigator will decide what things mean, and what should be done about it. There will be some variety in approaches, but the goal of proving who did what will always loom in the background, and every decision in the process contributes to deciding the fundamental decisions.

The Decision Steps

1. First Step, Designate the scene.
2. Second Step, Analyze the scene.
3. Third Step, Evaluate the evidence potential.
4. Fourth Step, Work the evidence.

1. First Step, Designate the Scene

Start by declaring a scene, looking at how it could interact with other scenes, and what is in the scene.

Scene Decision Why is this a scene?

Crime Scene Identification

The first step of any investigation should be to assess why a particular scene is the scene to work, and how it fits among the other related scenes. The initial phase of the investigation involves looking at four areas to define the crime scenes:

1. *Discovery*
2. *Scene type*
3. *Scene Group*
4. *Search*

Defining Crime Scenes

1. *Discovery* How did this scene came into the investigation? An investigator may respond to a scene, or the scene may come to him. An investigator can declare a scene with a low threshold of information. The investigator could declare anything a scene by the following supports:

a. Someone stated the entity was involved. This could be suspect, victim, or witness.

b. The investigator saw evidence indicating there was a connection between the entities and the crimes.

c. The entity has a proximity to the crime.

d. The entity is or was possessed, or controlled by an involved party, whether identified by name or role.

e. The entity is indicated as being involved by other evidence.

f. The entity is indicated by critical thinking, including things like MO, which must be supported by facts.

2. *Scene type* What is the scene type? The book organizes scenes into five groups based on common attributes. A scene is any entity connected with a crime amid other scenes, and because of the connection, it has interacted with other scenes, and may have evidence. An investigator decides what scenes to work and in what order. Each scene type has different features to influence the associated evidence.

While the traditional idea of a scene is a place, *Crime Scene Decisions* proposes interaction between two entities makes them scenes. Scenes can range from microscopic cells to globe spanning networks. Investigations begin with scenes because scene interaction produces evidence. All scenes lead to persons eventually.

The scenes fall into five identifiable categories before the investigator knows any details about the case. This is a summary of their categorizations, a detailed treatment of each scene type is the backbone of the book, and they all will be covered in detailed by section.

a. *Public* scenes are outdoor and indoor host scenes where the public has free access.

b. *Private* scenes are host scenes with restricted access.

c. *Car* scenes are mobile host scenes within other scenes (subscenes) and serve as locations, as well as objects of and tools for crime.

d. *Person* scenes are the bodies of a person involved in the event who is thinking, active, mobile, and has committed a crime or may possess information about a crime.

e. *Tool* scenes are devices and artifacts used by persons to commit and document crimes.

In every case, the main crime scene decision is always a form of how to prove who did what by proving presence and action. Every case has a starting scene, or opening scene. Cases may start at geographical scenes, like public or private areas, and may be the result of an incident getting out of hand, but while the first scene an investigator encounters impacts the case, it may not be the center of gravity.

3. *Scene Group* What are other related scenes? Scenes have relative importance among related scenes. How does this scene connect to the other scenes like a web, and within each organization there are different hierarchies and varying significance? Some ways to look at groups of scenes include, order of discovery, greater scenes with subscenes, and evidence richness or centers of gravity. Scenes are not equal, and have different emphasis seen from different perspectives. An investigator can and should look at the scenes in many different ways in order to work on the case.

A scene analysis compartmentalizes the scene to isolate the relevant evidence. Scenes contain smaller scenes, and have satellite scenes outside. The function of the scene, and who controlled it indicate the better potential evidence locations to establish presence and action.

Given every case has multiple scenes involved through actions there will always be a complement of scenes for cases, even if several of them are unable to be found or defined. Every crime has different scene types included in the group of involved scenes due to function. Person scenes are involved throughout as they use tools, drive cars, live places, and spend time in other places. A typical case breakdown will include:

a. A group of scenes related to at least one suspect person scene, with the suspect's tools, car, and private scene such as a residence.

b. A group of victim scenes should have the same accompaniment, but sometimes the victim is the state, such as for drug possession.

c. Neutral scenes, such as those belonging to other persons, or public scenes.

The parties interact with transit scenes both to and from the interaction scene (s) hosting the actual crime event. The interaction scene hosts the crime, and may be public, private, or a car. After the crime the parties interact with other scenes, creating evidence, and also reducing the evidence created.

The ideal combination of scenes includes a history of no interaction between the person scenes. A documented history of benign interaction including evidence exchange, and lack of evidence proving specific action between the scenes challenges the investigator to find other ways to prove presence and action.

Not every scene listed in a scene group is workable, and some scenes are theoretical rather than confirmed.

4. *Search* What search technique would work for this scene type? Every scene has a center of gravity where the action happened and where evidence exists. There are several different approaches to systematic scene searches, based on the specific scene and conditions. Systematic scene analysis includes walk-throughs with a knowledgeable person to explain the fundamentals of the scene before, during, and after the crime. Nonobvious evidence requires an explanation of how a person found it and determined it had evidentiary value. Investigators perform a scene search in almost case. The search function is often covered in greater detail when it is connected to a legal issue, such as whose scene is being searched. Search consent forms may be required, depending on who controlled the scene. Obtaining a person's permission to work the scene prevents misunderstanding.

a. *Lane search* A line of people walk shoulder-to-shoulder looking for evidence, often outdoors. Everyone travels on the same axis. An investigator can use this technique in large, open areas.

b. *Spiral search* One or two searchers start at one point, perhaps the geographic center of the crime, and spiral out. This method has the potential of destroying evidence on the way to the center point. An investigator can use this technique with fewer searchers.

c. *Grid search* Searchers have designated paths and make turns to travel along both the x- and y-axes, checking other searchers' work for larger geographical areas. An investigator can use this technique in large open areas.

d. *Zone search* An investigator divides the overall area into parts for each person. An investigator can use this technique in divisible areas, such as buildings with rooms.

e. *Point search* An investigator may have to use magnification, but scene is not searched in a conventional way such as a room or yard.

Securing the scene as soon as possible restricts contamination and provides safety. The investigator will often need to estimate the crime scene's physical dimensions to isolate the scene. Preexisting barriers help, but yellow crime scene tape is useful to keep people out who could contaminate the scene and derail the investigation.

2. Second Step, Analyze the Scene

Continue by looking at a scene for its specific attributes.

Scene Decision How does the scene work?

Defining Attributes of Crime Scenes

Every crime scene can be viewed by its eight attributes defining it among other scenes. The four attributes of any crime scene are:

1. *Restrictiveness*
2. *Volatility*
3. *Function*
4. *Capacity and Interaction Points*

The Analysis

1. *Restrictiveness* What is the level of restrictiveness and how is it significant to the case? Some scenes have specific parts with varying levels. This means a more restrictive scene with evidence of a person's presence may include a crime of presence alone, but accessible scenes may have little significance for a person's presence. This is the first attribute because it is obvious, and provides indications as to the possibilities.

2. *Volatility* How volatile is the scene? This is the term for how changeable and mobile scenes are. Every scene changes as the result of interaction with other scenes and from the environment. Each scene has its own pace contributing to its primacy in the evidence work. The fragility of the scene and evidence impacts investigator decisions and prioritizations.

This is an early stage where an investigator can shift priorities if it appears necessary, such as to prevent the destruction of evidence.

3. *Function* What is the scene's role and function? Is the scene either the object or subject in the sense of evidence flow from one scene to another? Both scenes are present, and evidence can flow both ways, but it is important to know how evidence moves. Subject scenes do the action. Object scenes receive the action. The evidence can travel either or both ways. This also relates to who controlled the various scenes during the crime process. As subject scenes are the active part of the pair, they are more apt to enact countermeasures after the crime. They may not carry the evidence of the object scene, but it is worth looking. Knowing these roles aids the investigator by pointing him where to look, as they are indicators.

In some cases the scenes function as they did when not a crime, and in other cases the scenes function very in new ways during a crime. Scenes can host crimes, perform actions, think, and move. Many of the functions in crime were there before, but while some scenes have common uses in routine use, their crime use is unique. Transit scenes are paths around the central scenes, and are object scenes, as the subject scenes travel through. Every scene has attributes making it advantageous and disadvantageous for crime use, and investigation. Positive features are always balanced against drawbacks, and features make scenes harder to use in crime, and in investigating crime.

4. *Capacity and Interaction Points* What is the scene's a capacity to host evidence? Evidence comes from interaction points and the more capacity a scene has, the greater the odds are for locating evidence. In many cases, these are predictable. The interaction points cover two areas:

a. Presence points, the scene bears evidence of contact with other scenes.

b. Action points, the scene bears evidence of action with or by one of the involved scenes.

3. Third Step, Evaluate the Evidence Potential

Continue by looking at the evidence and judging what the evidence could prove by its attributes.

Evidence Decision How would the evidence work in this scene?

Defining Attributes of Evidence Skills

Every scene can have some evidence and it is often easier to look at a case by breaking it down. Knowing why something is a scene, and how it works as a scene paves the way to look for evidence, even if the exact nature of the crime is illusive. A scene can be viewed with the eight attributes of evidence in order to look for evidence. The concept is to seek the evidence by its properties. The attributes of evidence at a scene are:

1. *Production*
2. *Proof Ability*
3. *Quality*
4. *Timeline*
5. *Resilience*
6. *Collection*

The Evaluation

1. *Production* How is the evidence produced, and why is it important? This is a continuation of the end of the scene analysis where the decisions centered on how scenes interact to create evidence by looking at the situation from the evidence, after looking at it from the scene.

2. *Proof Ability* What can a particular piece of evidence prove? Starting with knowing what a type of evidence can and cannot prove clarifies what can come from decisions. Some evidence may prove peripheral facts, and little evidence can prove an entire case. Often multiple pieces of evidence must be presented to show a synergistic outcome.

3. *Quality* What is the quality of the evidence? How unique and specific is the evidence? The more unique and specific the evidence, the greater the value in proving a specific fact, pointing to specific scenes, including persons. How will the evidence relate to the case? Just showing a person was alive during the time of a crime is not relevant, but showing he was out of custody when a crime occurred is relevant, just as showing he was in custody during a crime is relevant.

4. *Timeline* What is the timeline, and can the evidence support a timeline? The timeline refers to the events in a case, in both the form of when things happen, and when evidence is created by scene interaction. There is the actual time of events, and relative time compared to other events.

5. *Resilience* How well can the evidence resist forces of time, nature and environment?

6. *Collection* What order will the investigator process the scene, where, and what equipment will be used? This also covers where the investigator sends evidence for further testing, and storage. No matter how good the evidence is in quality, and what it proves, if it is not legally obtained, and properly handled the evidence may be excluded from the court process, and impact legal conclusions.

Evidence does a lot of different things and comes in varying values. An investigator should consider the following concepts when choosing evidence to emphasize. While the order of evidence skills is consistent for most scenes, the order can differ between cases based on circumstances.

a. The most restrictive and intimate evidence tends to be more definitive in person identification, and indicate actions.

b. The technique with the most promise to provide evidence proving presence and action.

c. The technique that can provide the most specific evidence.

d. The evidence with the most fragile or fleeting evidence, making it valuable due to its potential to not be there in the future.

This results in a lot of different ways to work a case. For example, a sexual assault case centralizes the intimate body parts as they are more restrictive, and hold evidence of identification. A stolen car would not involve intimate body parts, but the interior is the restricted area, and evidence from inside is more valuable than outside. A crowbar belonging to a serial burglar suspected in a series connects with a lot of victim (object) scenes. An outdoor sexual assault scene receiving rain may require immediate attention, and the body scene may be able to be delayed.

Prioritizing evidence work processes to prove presence and action within each individual scene increases the chances of finding useful evidence while reducing the risk of unintentional destruction of evidence. The investigator decides whether to conduct an investigation in the standard order or alter the order to best handle the case.

Evidence changes with time; bodies heal and exposure degrades evidence, so the investigator must consider working the most vulnerable scene first. Variations in processing order often follow the fragility of evidence. An investigator can and should reprioritize evidence work and provide as much documentation as possible while working the scene.

A large or specialized investigation may require assistance from skilled outsiders at other agencies, who have their own policies and procedures. It is important to document the substance of meetings with these staff by recording the names of other agency personnel participating, the information received, and any actions taken. Death scenes often require additional coordination, as the county medical examiner's office may send its own investigators or even a physician to the scene.

When the scene is a public, private, or sometimes a car scene, a scene log may be created to indicate who worked in the location scene of the case. There is some flexibility in this, but person crimes require more restriction and documentation with the processing.

In an academic setting, the investigator gets to assess everything first, and then proceed. The variable of time comes into many investigations and so assessments may come early with limited information, rather than later with an abundance of information. The first cycle of evidence work ends with the investigator reviewing the results of his or her work. The cycle then restarts as needed.

Further investigation may uncover evidence along the way, or new information may provide additional context. A final walk-through at the conclusion of on-scene processing protects against missing evidence or equipment.

The investigator may prove presence and action from two separate scenes and will thus need to connect the two parts of the case. The emergence of specific evidence components in such a way may change the order in which topics are presented in the report.

Key evidence decisions come from the attributes of the evidence in two areas; what the evidence can proves (such as identification of actions and persons) and what the evidence means (such as supporting facts of actions and presence).

Rarely will one piece of evidence make a case, although there are often strong pieces of evidence used in concert. If a piece of evidence proves a person's presence, or shows action, then it is useful. The opposite is true, as evidence proving a person was not present, or some action was not taken is also useful.

Evidence technique prioritization decisions may not follow the order in which the evidences were discovered, or the order of significance of the events, but the processes to obtain the evidence often follows the order of techniques because of the alteration of the evidence during the processing.

Groupings help the investigator look for additional scenes and evidence based on what is already there. Given every case has multiple evidences involved through actions there will always be a complement of evidences for cases, even if several of them are unable to be found or defined. A typical case breakdown will include the following, even if all parts are not accounted for:

A suspect set of evidence showing identification and actions of the suspect. The scenes could include the person, residence, car, phone, and other tools.

A victim set of evidence showing identification and actions of the victim. The scenes could include the person, residence, car, phone, and other tools.

Neutral sets of evidence, found in hosting scene, and a few transition scenes used to access and leave the hosting scene.

Third party data sets, such as the internet, or phone data. The data relates to a person, but it is under the control of a third party who is the controller of the evidence.

Sometimes the scenes are not identified as being connected, and they may be expressed in more general terms like hosting scene evidence sets and tool scene evidence sets.

4. Fourth Step, Work the Evidence

Work the scene with evidence techniques, applying them to areas most apt to yield evidence because Evidence proves facts.

Evidence Decision How to obtain the evidence from this scene?

Evidence Work

The fourth step in working a case is to obtain the evidence. Three steps all led up to collecting the evidence. The eight basic evidence skills start and end with executive skills; critical thinking, and report production. They sandwich the precision skills as metaevidence since they are about the evidence, not the evidence. Those two skills control how the others are managed in the investigation.

1. *Critical Thinking*
2. *Information*
3. *Photography*
4. *DNA*
5. *Fingerprints*
6. *Patterns*
7. *Artifacts*
8. *Report Production*

Each of the evidence skills are characterized by their eight attributes as a way to explain them. The ideas about evidence covered in the third step are the breakdown for each of the eight skills.

The Skills

1. Critical Thinking

Critical thinking about scenes and evidence skills prepares the investigator to obtain the evidence.

Evidence Decision How does the scene indicate evidence and what skills should the investigator use to obtain evidence?

Attributes
a. *Production* Critical thinking is the ability to see the provable facts of presence and action, without drawing conclusions. Solid critical thinking comes from a firm grasp of logic. The cases start with the scenes, and move into the evidence processing. The investigator must recognize evidence for its value in proving something. The greatest component of this work is to recognize the difference between an observable fact, and a conclusion. Facts are strong, and useful for arguments. Conclusions are supported opinions, and vary in their usefulness for a case.

An investigator has three areas to contribute to the critical thinking:

1. Background knowledge of the job, scenes, evidence, laws, etc. Cognitive abilities aid the investigator to think about the case, and what things mean in context, along with finding evidence.

2. Experience with the scenes, evidence, laws, etc. This is most variable, and there will always be gaps, and then comes the debate about good experience versus bad experience.

b. *Proof Ability* Critical thinking prepares the investigator to seek evidence, find it, and present it. The thinking must come with supportable facts, without opinions and conclusions. Critical thinking empowers an investigator look at scenes, and apply the evidence skills to find the proof.

Critical thinking is the investigator's way to formulate a plan of action for obtaining the evidence. Critical thinking synthesizes scene generalities with specifics, and evidence generalities to obtain specific evidence capable of proving presence and action from the skills.

Critical thinking is dismissed as an evidence technique in itself, but something included with the investigation. When critical thinking is formalized it becomes a technique for evidence. Thinking about scenes and their evidence is *metaevidence* because it is not evidence in itself, but is about evidence.

No matter what part of the investigation a person works on, an element of critical thinking is involved. An investigator must decide on the most basic level what any evidence proves or disproves.

Science is a base for proving cases, but it cannot be absolute in the search for proof. An investigator must be able to use science to search for the unknown, which means an idea of evidence is not proven at the outset. The key is to be very clear about what is proven, and what is believed, so the quest for evidence is not confused with actual evidence.

It is more useful to consider critical thinking as a skill to produce questions than as one to produce answers. Answers can be conclusions, and it is too early to have conclusions. The questions frame investigations to find evidence. Critical thinking has attributes just as the other skills for evidence. Critical thinking is when the investigator looks at the attributes of the scenes, and the attributes of the evidence to build a case.

Skepticism prepares the investigation for depth of proof. The investigator must question the reliability and accuracy of every statement, piece of evidence, and idea. He or she should question everything and work to determine the relevance, quality, and weight of each piece of information. An investigator does not have absolute knowledge of information, and he or she learns about it at varying rates, from different sources. An investigation starts with limited information and moves forward into addressing the unknown.

Scenes include physical and abstract voids. Details and large sets of information escape an investigator's knowledge. Information develops at uneven rates over time. Creative thinking is a part of working cases. Divergent thought accompanied by healthy skepticism help the investigator to consider possibilities. An investigator must be able to move about the case with divergent thoughts to work it.

After all the open-ended investigative inquiries, the basic critical thinking exercise for the investigator considers whether a piece of evidence proves presence and action. This is different than if the evidence proves a person's things were present, or if he is capable of action.

c. *Quality* Faulty logic hurts a case. Sometimes emotions prevent clear thinking, and solid conclusions. Thinking about how the evidence connects to the case in a meaningful way is a main issue of proof. An investigator should also view investigations beyond moral qualities, and step back from good and evil, suspect and victim. Overall thoughts about evidence should consider what is possible.

Focus on proof of presence and action supersedes proving crime. Some cases will rely on evidence of the victim's actions and presence, and the investigator never gets to the suspect component. Individualized and specific evidence has higher value for proving specific and unique facts. Without drawing too many conclusions, an investigator should recognize unique logical combinations, and specific groups.

d. *Timeline* Critical thinking timelines are best served with the actual time of events, as they also be used for relative times, while the relative times cannot produce actual times.

e. *Resilience* Critical thinking is a process of constant updates, and must allow for modification while withstanding nonfactual pressure. While collected evidence always includes resilience concerns, the critical thinking part of investigations means details must be preserved in writing.

f. *Collection* Critical thinking is a part of every aspect of a case, and the ideas should be collected in report form. Report production accompanies critical thinking throughout to keep thoughts on track and make the investigator reflect on the case.

An investigator must consider the way investigative components interact. Some evidence work is destructive, and should come after the nondestructive. Some evidence work introduces new material to scenes. There is no required equipment for critical thinking. Critical thinking is a mental process, but sometimes paper and pen help to sketch ideas and review them for clarity.

Critical thinking is a thought process beginning with the observations in the field. Isolating the scenes and evidence parts of a case makes them workable. The scenes intersected to transfer evidence, but must be kept apart afterwards to prevent the argument that the interaction during the investigation.

Decisions about priorities may not follow the order in which the scenes were discovered, or the order of significance of the events.

Determining the most important scene is choosing the best scene to process at the time. This can change with new information. The investigator starts looking at scenes with the goal of proving who did what. This means proving presence and action. When naming the priority scene the investigator makes the following decisions:

1. The most restrictive and intimate scene. Often a person scene.

2. The scene with the most promise to provide evidence proving presence and action.

3. The scene with the most interaction of other scenes.

4. The scene with the most fragile or fleeting evidence.

5. The available scene.

The issues will vary, but the goal remains to prove who did what, by presence and action. Sometimes they only prove part of the two. In identified scene types the investigator must choose the best option to process in the preliminary investigation. Person scenes can be the priority, but there may be too many barriers to using them, such as a person undergoing medical treatment after a fight.

Investigators should practice evidence work with careful attention to ethical, legal, physical, and emotional issues. They need personal protective equipment (PPE) for health and safety. Gloves and masks protect the wearer while also trapping DNA. The chain of custody is an important part of the evidence agenda, and preserving the evidence is a part of the chain. Evidence must include a trackable history of location, collection, manner of processing, and storage. If the chain is damaged, the evidence may not be usable in court.

Critical thinking guides the other processes. It must account for new information developed from discovered evidence. An investigator decides what evidence will be processes at the lab, and what will need to be sent somewhere for processing. The investigator or first responding personnel find and collect the evidence, but in most cases regional criminologists in large laboratories analyze the evidence.

The thinking must follow a logical, repeatable concept, in particular the scientific method. The American Society of Crime Laboratory Directors (ASCLaD) certifies labs to verify they are using accepted procedure for evidence handling and processing.

2. Information

All evidence is information, but not all information is evidence. Information is written representations of facts.

Evidence Decision What can information do to corroborate or refute other evidence in the case?

Attributes

a. *Production* Information is everywhere and of varying quality. Every investigation includes scene descriptions to define the scene and to point out the significant circumstances. Technology saves a lot of time and photos provide extensive the descriptions of scenes, but words show how the investigator understands a scene. A few sentences may cover the information needs sometimes; on other occasions, several pages are needed.

Crime circumstances have value when an investigator compares the details from before, during, and after the crime. Crimes produce information evidence as a by-product throughout the events involved. Information is converted to evidence when it can be used to prove or disprove a fact.

Information has three possible production paths:

1. The information is a factual measurement of a scene, or representation of a scene produced and collected by an investigator.

2. The information originated as a neutral witness statement, or uninvolved third party source.

3. The information originated from a person with an interest statement.

The production sources go from reliable to requiring corroboration. Statements can be great directions to the evidence, but are not evidence in their own rights.

Information covers all three time phases of crime; history, the crime action itself, and the subsequent investigation. In the *Crime Scene Decisions* method persons are considered scenes just as locations. Crime action information evidence details documentable facts about what happened and how it impacted the scene during the crime. Factual information evidence covers what the investigator did to work on the case. The phases may be intermingled in reports.

Information forms can be:

1. Historical information covers how things existed at the scenes prior to the crime.

2. Action information about what happened during the crime.

3. Outcome information about the results of the crime.

4. Graphical representations of the scenes, or processes.

b. *Proof Ability* Factual information proves things, and all evidence is information at the end state. Factual information encompasses documentable circumstances, including observations, measurements, background details, and statements. Even inaccurate and false statements have value in investigations as they provide details for comparison and contrast, helping prove reliability of involved persons.

Information also brings more specific details as to who, what, how, why, where, and when. Information corroborates the events by facts of before, during, and after the crime. Information supports context. It may be background information or specific measurements dealing with the crime scene.

Factual information defines the scenes, their functions, and their characteristics. All scenes have information including statements, observations, measurements, and other documentation, along with analysis and writing. The information covers the scene's appearance before, during, and after the crime. Sketches communicate more and different information compared to words. Mobile computing allows investigators to research information while at scene, giving immediate and applicable details.

c. *Quality* An investigator wants true and accurate information, but often information varies in reliability. It often requires corroborating information and evidence. So much factual information exists in any case and there is often a collection of facts for the investigator to look at. Some may be supportive facts showing a situation connected to the case.

The more specific information is, the more useful it is toward proving something. Information evidence ranges from vague and general to specific. Useful information clarifies, specifies, and differentiates the facts surrounding the case from general facts.

d. *Timeline* Much of the information in cases can be attached to a specific actual time. Factual information evidence can be divided into three parts: history before the crime, impact during the crime, and post-crime developments. Information decisions center on finding evidence and documenting the scene by presence and action. Factual information is often the circumstantial evidence heard about in court, facts used to prove something.

e. *Resilience* Information evidence may be very enduring as the facts remain, but information exists in environments, and an investigator must reach the factual information evidence. Also, the more information travels from scene to scene, the more apt it is to change, and degrade.

f. *Collection* Information collection and documentation do not damage evidence. The information, expressed in words, gives the locations of DNA, fingerprints, and evidence, as well as explaining the photographs. An investigator makes observations before collecting evidence, and pre-collection measurements ensure accurate information.

Observations continue throughout an investigation, as each new evidence find opens a new path to previously invisible evidence. Photographs alone may lack sufficient clarity or emphasis without the investigator's explanation of their significance.

A notepad is best for information collection and documentation. Smartphones have memo features, and digital recorders work well to transcribe notes later. An easier measuring device allows for quick measurements by one person, where a tape might take two.

The Internet has extensive information sources, and mobile computers and smartphones make information available to the investigator anywhere to provide contextual clues about the case. The Internet may be a good source of pre-crime photos.

Information fieldwork decisions center on how an investigator documents the interaction between two scenes to create evidence. Evidence work bridges the phases of production during the crime to discovery and collection during the investigation. The investigator also explains some details of the processing in reports to explain how he or she classified the evidence. Involved persons' statements provide information to aid in finding evidence.

Every scene has background historical factual information. This information includes people connected to the scene, functions of the scene, and details such as prior crimes. There are four ways to find information, and they are ranked in a basic order of implied reliability.

1. Observations by the investigator. Scene descriptions offer contextual clues about evidence at scenes. Sketches made during fieldwork are work aids, not finished products. The sketches reflect the beginning phase of evidence work. Often, multiple scenes are present at the same moment, and the investigator has limited time and resources. A quick and accurate sketch establishes scene understanding and prepares for the development of polished finished products.

Sketching techniques communicate facts in a different way from textual documentation. Scenes may not require sketches to be understood, or to enable prosecution, but they show the configuration and explain details. Overhead photographic opportunities are limited. Factual diagrams help with reconstructing the case later, as they document the exact locations of the physical scene and the components within it.

An investigator may create multiple sketches of the same scene. Initial sketches have simple features such as basic administrative information to explain the scene, a rudimentary scale, and orientation showing permanent landmark features. Significant scene features are not always crime-centered. Many objects can exist and influence the crime without enabling the crime. Evidence locations and obstacles preventing movement contribute to a person's choices and outcomes.

Voids also impact actions. Scenes evolve and change, creating voids, and the presence or absence of the smallest items means a substantial difference in the crime and its investigation. Time of day and lighting alter appearances with shadows and darkness. People add things to and remove things from scenes. Absent items impacted the crime when they were present, so the investigator may have to reverse-engineer the scene to understand voids.

People clean scenes before police arrive out of the desire to continue business with minimal interruption; employees may not care about how their business was victimized. A brief statement by the investigator explaining what happened can save unnecessary work.

2. Measurements and details are the practical side of information. Most measurements remain constant during all phases of an investigation. Scenes have multiple dimensions, including not only the depth, width, and height measurements and locations, but also the dimension of time. The precision or degree of measurement varies within case facts. Hit-and-run drivers put distance between themselves and the location of incident. On the other hand, a photographer should capture fingerprint locations on a windowsill with a scale

and ruler for measurement to fractions of an inch. Scenes contain objects impacting people's actions such as obstacles, or physical bottlenecks channeling travel and may yield more evidence.

3. Research into databases can show ownership, or activity data. Abstract crime scenes emphasize information. Financial crimes often have robust information sections. Investigation information includes paper trails, with document artifacts, and evidence information. Suspects need information too, and often a third-party information system has recorded their actions.

Financial crimes may require extensive follow-up, and even after vast resource expenditures, a case may be unresolved. Eventually, the investigation is forwarded to a detective, who relies on the report as his or her sole source of information.

4. Statements help investigators to find evidence and contextualize it. This is also the least reliable information product as it is influenced by the opinions of the statement giver. Testimonial evidence may bolster the case later, but the first responding investigators should work the scenes looking for evidence to find the best possible evidence to prove the case by presence and action.

5. A report preserves information, including digital file storage. If the information includes pages collected from the Internet, a screenshot of the page saves it. Some departments use a software program to save images of pages. The investigator may also print the page and preserve the paper copy. The Internet changes all the time, so a time stamped copy of information prevents someone else from revising your evidence.

An investigator works the scenes in the field but researches and writes the reports in the lab. This may be the reflection point where the investigator has a chance to corroborate the information with the other evidence. Factual information has its own history, and must be obtained from a reliable and legal source. It must be reproducible.

3. Photography

Investigative photographs are visual representations of facts at a particular moment.

Evidence Decision What can the camera show about the scene parts and evidence before, during, and after the crime with clear photos and comprehensive coverage?

Attributes

a. *Production* Photographable evidence is the visible and recordable product of how things look at a specific time and place. The reproduction image is what is collected. Photographic evidence has three possible production paths:

1. The things being photographed as they were before the events. Sometimes photographic evidence shows the scenes as they were before the event. These often come from involved parties.

2. The things begin photographed show the interaction of scenes during an event. Photographic evidence items showing the interaction of scenes during the event are the rarest, and can be very powerful. They are also often from involved parties.

3. The things being photographed are the results of events. This is the most common form of investigative photography. It can be the results of when two scenes come together. For example, a person leaves fingerprints on a windowsill. The evidence combines presence and action to be shown by photographable evidence.

Sometimes the only photographs available show the scenes with a lack of evidence. The evidence may have undergone noticeable changes, or it may remain as it looked during the crime.

b. *Proof Ability* Photographic evidence shows things in great detail. Photographs are also good at showing the results of an event, and relationships. Any case can be helped by photography, and provides reference points for people who think about the case. Visuals help investigators, juries, and everyone who sees a case understand what it looked like, even if the photographs are not sharing a central point.

Sometimes images show the results of what happened and provide context to the details. Photography presents decisions about locating and documenting scenes with their facts and evidence to show presence and action. All scenes have the potential to produce evidence worthy of photographic documentation. While information may require interpretation, photographs document the scene as viewed at a moment in time.

c. *Quality* Well composed photographs of high quality provide evidence. People are visual learners. Photographs are two dimensional visual reproductions of what is seen. They can show great detail and specificity from single vantage points. The greater the impacts on the scene, the more photographs show, the higher their relevance. No single image tells the whole story.

The photographer should seek thorough image collections of factual subjects. Every photo preserves the components from different perspectives. Techniques allow the photographer to show the evidence from different angles or distances, with various lighting, and in various contexts. Useful photographic treatment of evidence provides depth by showing the same subject in different ways. The more specific the photos are, the more useful they are toward proving something.

d. *Timeline* Photographs have a specific actual time.

e. *Resilience* Photographs offer a snapshot of scenes and evidence as they look at a specific moment in time. This documentary capability allows an investigator to overcome the fragility and change inherent to all evidence. As photography has moved to electronic storage, it is very resilient, but could be impacted by software changes.

f. *Collection* Photographs provide nondestructive support to the other evidence areas. Photographers collect images at the beginning (prior to moving anything in the scene), during the work, and after its completion. Descriptive writing supports photography. Photographs save time in the collection evidence by showing measurements in the scene, such as a ruler showing distances, or stickers showing placement. A photo shows an item at a particular location and provides the context for DNA, fingerprints, and evidence items.

Photography shows the evidence throughout the investigation, but the investigator may place the written section about it at the end of a report when the technical details do not provide critical information about the evidence.

Crime scene photography includes a digital camera, flash, tripod, rulers for scale, and a secure storage system. Photographic technology allows anyone to take photographs without focusing or having to choose flash strength. Digital photos provide immediate feedback permitting the operator to make adjustments. Sophisticated technology makes technical aspects of photography easier for the photographer. High-capacity memory encourages taking more photos. Metadata capacity stores all the settings for each shot, and many newer cameras also include GPS data.

Flashes fill the space with light while not washing out the details. People can turn the lights on or off to show different details. Most modern cameras capture the metadata, including the strength of the flash, and other settings. The lighting situation has greater relevance if the photographs document injuries or other uncollectible evidence items. Injury photo reports should mention the lighting situation, such as natural light, artificial light (bulbs), and flash.

An alternate light source (ALS) can make some otherwise invisible evidence visible expanding the field of visible evidence. The light does not damage the evidence and causes no chemical change. Light waves come in different wavelengths. Specific wavelengths make certain substances stand out, such as semen and fingerprints. The investigator uses colored glasses or photographs with colored filters to make the materials visible. For example, 450 nm light makes bruises and bite marks visible and works well on people with darker skin tones; 485 nm light makes fingerprints visible; 570 nm light illuminates a variety of material, making it a starting light for the process.

An investigator should refrain from using personal smartphones for crime scene photos. The device may become evidence. A judge can order the phone be searched, resulting in the disclosure of personal communications and pictures. District attorneys may prosecute investigators for unauthorized sharing of crime scene photographs.

Camera technology makes taking photographs easier, but photography still requires composition technique. An investigator should integrate photography throughout the process and then, at the end, document how the investigation left the scene. Photographic evidence should contain enough pictures to explain the scene to anyone. Stable, cold crimes are easier to photograph. An active scene, with people being interviewed and evaluated, presents a higher probability of missed evidence and requires the photographer to go out of order in his work.

Injuries change over time, and taking photographs a few days later often reveals new injuries. The alternate light source may show more bruising than unaided photography. Uncooperative subjects require people skills and yield poorer quality images. The investigator should consider a subject's reasons for not wanting to be photographed, and should document the subject's statements.

Perpendicular shots are best. Angle shots do not capture the subject well overall, but may show a particular detail or pattern. Sometimes the subject of the images may have features revealed by oblique lighting. This technique involves shining a light from an angle or from the side to create shadows. This is useful in exposing shoe prints.

The photographer should base each subject set on the concept of three; specifically, the photographs should include:

1. Overall photographs set the scene, capturing the possible ways of ingress and egress and observation points. They show layouts, rather than evidence in detail, and depict the approach to the scene.

2. Intermediate photographs show context. A ruler helps to show the sizes of items. Intermediates show evidence, their surrounding locations, and orientation.

3. Detailed photographs show evidence up close. Orientation arrows contextualize fingerprint photos. Pictures depict tool marks and damage to locks better any other medium save a reproductive cast. The two dimensional reproduction is transportable. Rulers as scales or even ruler stickers show exact sizes when one is photographing fingerprints and most other evidence.

Video photographic evidence shows the scene while one moves through it. Videographers start outside the scene and move inward, tour the scene, and then move outward. If there are multiple travel paths, several segments of video may be needed to show the pathways from outside the scene to inside. Audio commentary on the scene does not aid the investigation, since there is so much outstanding information. A plug in the sound jack protects against inadvertent recording of offhand comments.

A server or disc preserves digital photography evidence, including video. The previous generation preserved images on film negatives, limiting their usability.

Digital photography does not require a darkroom. A technician can save the images on the server and can use software to enhance or reduce features with working copies in the laboratory. Technicians can also email photo files to distant locations.

4. DNA

Deoxyribonucleic acid (DNA) offers proof of presence through a unique code in most cells throughout a lifeform's body.

Evidence Decision What should an investigator sample to identify and associate a person with presence and particular actions?

Attributes

a. *Production* DNA evidence comes from the person as a scene when he or she deposits cells with DNA at another scene. Only body scenes produce DNA evidence, but DNA can be present in any of the other scene types. It can be found on areas of direct contact, and cast off. Every living thing has DNA serving as instructions for building the life-form.

DNA is expressed in alpha numeric codes, and so every living thing is put together with the same basic parts in unique combination. A dog and a human have the same basic parts on the simplest level, but the DNA specifies how they are put together to be a dog versus a human.

People produce and deposit DNA evidence as cellular material, as do all animals. Material is transferred from one's body to another scene. Cells carry DNA as the specific code in biomaterial from an animal or plant. The identification of the specific type of biological material carrying the DNA helps to indicate action; for instance, semen cells have a different context from hair.

DNA identifies pets or even trafficked animals. Since DNA exists in all of an organism's cells, the type of cell left at a scene does not hamper an investigation. The material converts to evidence when it proves the presence or action of a subject. DNA travels from suspect to victim but can also go from victim to suspect.

The constant production and shedding of DNA at a scene by persons means a scene can include many DNA profiles. Portable items of evidence do not guarantee guilt or presence. A person's DNA may arrive at a scene without the person even having been present there. Corroborating evidence helps overcome a SODDI defense (*some other dude did it*) claiming the evidence was brought in by another party.

DNA evidence has possible production paths, starting with the more useful situations:

1. The DNA originated from a suspect, victim, or other lifeform and was left at the victim person as a hosting scene. Victims tend to stay around for investigations, and there is great value in showing how the victim was impacted by receiving suspect evidence.

2. The DNA originated from a suspect, victim, or other lifeform and was left at the suspect person as a hosting scene. Suspects may not be present, and this is harder to find.

3. The DNA originated from a suspect, victim, or other lifeform and was left at a hosting scene.

b. *Proof Ability* DNA is identifying evidence used to identify a lifeform connected to another scene, and by extension actions. DNA is used for identifying persons, but is not limited to that, since it can be used to identify other animals, and plants. DNA matching has greater expense than most other evidence, but offers an investigator options to identify persons based on almost any piece of their cellular material. The databases continue to grow. DNA identifies specific life forms through a combination of components unique to each living thing, except identical twins. The lifeforms include pets, and even plants.

c. *Quality* DNA is biological material and subject to forces of nature. DNA breaks down over time, and some things degrade DNA. As there is a mathematical component to identifying persons by DNA lower quality DNA sample, the larger potential group of persons connected with it. Even miniscule contamination of DNA samples creates doubt, rendering the evidence irrelevant. Tainted or cross-contaminated evidence is ineffective and may damage the overall investigation.

Buccal (oral cheek cells) come from a mouth, open to the environment. Blood cells are internal to the body and contain DNA. A blood transfusion brings new DNA into the body system, with the result of multiple DNA samples can be come from one person for a time after if the sampler collects the foreign blood cells.

DNA can prove presence and indicate action, but it has to be relevant to the case. Sometimes presence and action are nothing more than being in the wrong place at the wrong time. Most of the time there is no way to know if the DNA will be relevant until there is either a match to a person, or there is enough corroborating information to indicate the DNA was from an involved person. Supporting evidence tends to clarify the presence or absence of their DNA.

The more specific the DNA is, either by what the cells do, or where they are found, the more useful they are toward proving something.

Fraternal twins will have different specific information encoded in their DNA, but identical twins should have the same DNA. This reduces the pool of possible identification, but may not prove a case.

Most labs rule out blind DNA swab testing since they do not support confirmation of suspect DNA presence. A sample of the suspect's blood or identifiable body fluid has a high probability for identification, and DNA processing has a greater chance of paying off. Having the sample might help resolve the case even without sequencing it

d. *Timeline* On its own, DNA does not have a time, but can be narrowed to the lifetime of a person.

e. *Resilience* DNA evidence is very hardy on its own. However, it degrades based on its environment.

f. *Collection* DNA works best when supported by other evidence. As equipment evolves in its sensitivity, it solves both old problems and creates new ones. Microscopic samples provide enough material to match and identify persons. Lesser DNA presence still registers the likely presence of a subject, but there is not a defined legal threshold for how much DNA constitutes presence. More sensitive equipment may find multiple DNA profiles, including uninvolved persons, and several investigative persons.

DNA's potential for contamination means it should be collected prior to the start of fingerprinting, to negate claims the suspect's DNA was introduced via fingerprint powder.

DNA survives for centuries, complicating efforts to prove recency if a person claims to have visited a scene, no matter how long ago. The person's DNA could well have remained there intact. The quantity of DNA, a matter addressed by biostatisticians, may become an issue at trial.

An investigator collects samples with sterile swabs, sterile water, and envelopes. DNA evidence has assistive equipment to aid in decision making about the evidence before committing to testing samples. Inexpensive pretesting equipment clears appropriate material for expensive DNA sequencing and weeds out the inappropriate material. Use of an ALS may illuminate possible biomaterial including fluids, fingerprints, or patterns. Phenolphthalein is a chemical testing tool that turns pink when it comes into contact with even a small amount of blood. Semen tests indicate sexual activity. Biomaterial identification contextualizes action. Investigators have various options to determine the kind of biomaterial present.

DNA evidence collection should begin before an investigator spends too much time in the crime scene, depositing his or her own (contaminating) DNA. Investigators collect DNA by seizing the item carrying the DNA, or they can collect a sample of the suspected DNA material by using a sterile swab. Sterile water aids collection of dry samples.

Most scenes contain DNA, but locating the suspect's DNA is a challenge for the investigator. The suspect and victim's actions determine how obvious the microscopic DNA evidence will be. An investigator may notice body fluids or receive information from victims as to what happened and where to look.

People deposit DNA on anything. The ideal DNA-carrying evidence items have suspect interaction, along with absorbency to hold the material. For instance, a hat retains DNA better than a plate of glass with wind blowing over it. ALS can make the biological fluids visible. Photos of the sample locations clarify the scene.

Touch DNA is a way to describe DNA, but is an unnecessary distinction because the issue is the DNA. Streaks on a clean, smooth surface such as a window often have DNA included in biological matter. A person's sweaty forehead can make contact with a window, depositing cells on it.

DNA packaging material must seal the items to protect against contamination from outside. Evidence technicians store DNA and biological evidence in the freezer, but it can withstand dry storage at room temperature. Crime laboratories publish procedural guidance.

DNA as instructions is a massive set of data with combinations of options. This necessitates the statistical part of DNA research to show how unique the match is. Nuclear DNA sequencing accounts for the majority of DNA testing; the code is in the nucleus of the cell. Normal DNA has 23 pairs of chromosomes, represented as a twisting ladder, with half of each rung coming from the mother and half from the father. Each person has 23 ladders comprised of 46 chromosomes. The 23 ladders have 20,000 to 25,000 genes distributed among them. The person's gender resides in the sex chromosomes.

Modern crime labs look at 14 pairs of genes (of the 20,000 to 25,000) present in people. Thirteen pairs of genes do not correlate with obvious features, and people sometimes call them junk DNA. The sex gene is also included, which is visible, but gender can be obscured. As the population of persons identifying as transgender grows this could become a new challenge for identification of suspects and victims.

Mitochondrial DNA (mtDNA) resides outside the nucleus of a cell and has more than 16,000 base pairs, distributed among 37 genes. A person inherits his or her mtDNA from the maternal side.

Large-number statistics power DNA identification, with less than 1% variance between humans. The field of biostatistics studies the uniqueness of specific genes among populations. The combination of specific genes makes a string unique, like a ten-digit phone number. The genes remain the same throughout a person's entire inventory of cells. Matches are based on the mathematical probability that a person could have been the source of the

DNA found in cells. This reliance on statistics and math differentiates DNA from fingerprints.

The Combined DNA Index System or CODIS compares the sample to others in the system and also engages in familial DNA comparisons.

The investigation should identify the type of cell carrying the DNA as well. DNA does not indicate sexual activity, but semen does, and sequencing the DNA present in a semen sample identifies the person and hints at the context. Current practice identifies the cellular origin by specific test. Semen tests for chemicals rather than by using the genetic code. Future DNA testing may become less expensive and may use massive data systems to produce detailed descriptions of where the cells came from on a person's body, leading to knowledge of function and contact.

No lab technician wants to spend time working on a DNA long shot. Information in the report allows criminologists to make decisions based on the merits of each swab and the odds of success. Expensive DNA testing uses scarce resources. Quality control up to the point when a sample is submitted ensures a return on investment through high-quality evidence.

DNA, its collection, and processing are technical procedures. Any deviance from best practices could negate the value of the evidence.

5. Fingerprints

Fingerprint decisions offer the possibility of proving presence and sometimes action by showing hand contact with a scene.

Evidence Decision How can fingerprints on a scene identify a person and indicate his or her actions?

Attributes
a. *Production* Fingerprints indicate who made the most recent mark on a particular location with the scene. Fingerprints are impressions or copies of the scene in question. Everyone has unique fingerprints, although fingerprint technicians have misidentified people at times by making classification errors. Fingerprints are one type of biometric evidence among many; others include ear prints, dental records, and footprints (from birth records). The individual ridges on a person's fingertips and hands (and feet) result from a baby's movement within the womb. Most people secrete oils and water in the sweat through the pores in their skin. The ridges transfer the prints to anything a person touches. Smooth items collect the oil in the pattern of the raised

ridges on the person's skin. A small number of people do not secrete oils from their hands and do not leave their prints in oil. The ridge detail remains, so they can still leave prints in other substances, but they do not provide their own marking material.

Fingerprint evidence production is limited to transfer by hand touch, and the evidence travels in one direction:

1. The fingerprint originated from a suspect, and was left at a scene.

2. The fingerprint originated from a victim, and was left at a scene.

3. The fingerprint originated from a third party, and was left at a scene.

b. *Proof Ability* Fingerprints are identifying evidence used to connect a person to a scene. Fingerprints identify a person by patterns on the hands and fingers unique to each person. They can be found on areas of direct contact with a person's fingers, and depend on the contact scene to be able to received and maintain the patterns from a person's hands and fingers.

Fingerprint matching occupies the largest subset of pattern matching and remains the core of identification activity after a century of use. Fingerprints rely on features to reduce the field of options, comparing features between images or representations of the patterns on a person's skin. Fingerprints have robust data systems to match cases nationwide.

Fingerprints present many of the same challenges as DNA. Fingerprints require a known sample to match to the crime scene print. Fingerprints provide more unique identification without DNA's identical twin duplication. Fingerprints cannot be easily imported into a scene like a blood transfusion bringing foreign DNA.

Fingerprints provide unique signatures and imply intentional touch, as opposed to brushing up against something and thus depositing DNA there.

Fingerprints and DNA support each other as the fingerprints indicate recent contact by their fragility and have a low likelihood of portability. Fingerprints transfer from person to item, as opposed to the problem of DNA passing by secondary transfer from person to item to person, to item, and so on. Five DNA samples present on a blade solve nothing, but fingerprints indicate more recent handlers.

The lack of fingerprints does not mean a person never contacted a scene; rather, it means there are no collected matching prints. No expert can determine a print's age or time of deposit.

c. *Quality* The fingerprinting process alters the evidence and introduces foreign powder into the scene. Single-use fingerprint kits are available to ensure no foreign DNA is introduced to the scene. If a fingerprint is smeared, or unidentifiable an investigator may collect usable DNA from it instead of making failed fingerprint attempts. The decision should be made prior to deployment of fingerprint dust resulting in scene contamination.

Fingerprints can prove presence and indicate action, although they are limited to a person's hands were doing during an event. Most of the time there is no way to know if the prints will be relevant until there is either a match to a person, or there is enough corroborating information to indicate the print was made by an unidentified but involved person.

The more specific the print is, either by clarity and identifiability of the person who made the print, or where they are found, the more useful they are toward proving something. Restrictive scenes give prints higher value. Portable evidence items carrying fingerprints have less value than prints on immovable objects. Fingerprint evidence from unrestricted scenes still has value but needs other evidence to bolster the case.

The fingerprint databases have great coverage to take advantage of the uniqueness of fingerprints. Most people in the DNA database have their fingerprints on file, but most people in the fingerprint database do not have their DNA on file. Automated fingerprint processing costs little as it determines a numeric identifier for each print and then compares the prints.

d. *Timeline* Fingerprints cannot be attached to a specific actual time on their own, but they have a great value in relative time, such as belonging to the most recent person to touch an item.

e. *Resilience* Fingerprints are delicate and easily prevented, damaged, or destroyed. Photographs preserve fingerprints well, but must be collected properly. Fingerprint evidence is often based on a person's oils and sweat from his hands making a pattern mark in liquid on a surface. The liquids can evaporate, based on a person's chemistry, and the environment of the print.

f. *Collection* Dusting for fingerprints alters evidence, requiring photos before, during, and after this activity. Even collection by image requires a scale, which alters the scene. Fingerprinting results in a cross-contaminated DNA environment after the dust is applied. The dust may damage sensitive items in the scene, and the owner may not want the processing.

Fingerprinting equipment makes the print visible and storable. There are several means of fingerprinting:

1. The future of fingerprinting is digital; in cameras and computers. Photography equipment helps to identify, collect, and preserve fingerprints. The technology aids an investigator in finding a print, collecting it, forwarding it to a lab, and matching it to a suspect before an investigator even leaves the scene. Lighting may make the print visible without dust, and speed the process. At some point in the future, instant identification will eliminate the need to return to the scene and interview the victim about whether the person connected to the print had authorization to enter.

People leave fingerprints in blood and other substances. An ALS helps to reveal prints so photographs can preserve visual copies.

2. Technicians have used powder, tape, and mounting cards for over a century. Powders come in a variety of styles for different applications: basic black powder, colored powders for different backgrounds, and magnetic powder. Powder makes the prints visible by adhering to the oils, and upon collection with tape, the examiner compares them to other prints. Magnetic powder works well on shiny plastic materials when applied with a magnetic brush. Technicians photograph prints with a scale and upload them as images.

3. Cyanoacrylate processing uses heated cyanoacrylate glue in a humid chamber with the items being processed. The glue particles fix to the ridge details on fingerprints and preserve the print by hardening it into a permanent pattern. An investigator photographs the print with an alternate light source and enhances visibility using fingerprint powder.

4. Heptane ninhydrin develops fingerprints by reacting with the chemicals in the oils a person deposits on an item in the form of fingerprints. Checks and other questioned documents may need fingerprints to prove contact, and the chemical reaction gives the invisible prints a purple tinge for photographing and comparison. Humid air helps the reaction.

5. Polyvinylsiloxane gel can collect fingerprints from rougher surfaces and expands the capacity for fingerprint collection. This technique resembles a tool mark collection. A painted windowsill has uneven surfaces holding prints standard dust and tape might not collect. The fingerprinting technician applies powder and gel to overcome the irregularities. The investigator

collects the hardened gel and sends it to the lab for potential identification. The lab staff may have instructions about how they want the evidence to be provided.

Fingerprint evidence work is limited to hand-touched items. The evidence can be collected by powder, tape and card, or it can be collected with prescribed photography including a scale.

Fingerprint processing finds the print, makes it visible, and preserves it. Transportation of evidence items requires logistics and increases the risk of damage to fingerprint evidence. Collecting the print in the field provides access to the most pristine scene. The investigator should mention unsuccessful attempts along with the successful ones. Investigators should document each print location on the item. The absence of fingerprints does not guarantee the suspect wore gloves.

An investigator uses tape to save traditional dusted fingerprints onto a card. Digital photography transfers print storage from film and paper to a server. Using digital photography, the field investigator collects, preserves, and prepares a print for comparison at the scene. Eliminating steps compresses the process by reducing the fingerprint examiner's time commitment and efforts.

The Federal Bureau of Investigation (FBI) bases its fingerprinting on the Automated Fingerprint Identification System (AFIS).

Criminalists are technicians who match the pattern on an item to the pattern on a person's hand. Examiners break the fingerprint down to recognizable features, including arches, whorls, and loops, as well as defects in the skin. Categorization by features reduces the pool of potential matches to review when searching for a match. Dividing the prints by features was necessary before computers catalogued and compared the prints. The prints are reviewed side by side with others to seek a match. The more matching features, the more certain a match is. Technological processes identify a potential match, but a live person still looks at the images of prints to determine if they indeed match, and a second person reviews the results to validate them.

Fingerprint examiners prefer comparing fingerprint evidence to known fingerprints to a blind search. Suspected match searches reduce the time required, since a technician can assess a set of prints against another set much faster than against millions. In-custody cases take priority.

There are few procedural problems with the actual collection of fingerprints. The discipline requires practice, and documentation along the way. Laws still limit collection.

6. Patterns

Anything can leave a pattern, and impressions transfer to and from scenes.

Evidence Decision How can a pattern mark connect scenes and help identify a specific person's actions?

Attributes
a. *Production* The pattern of one item often imprints onto another when they make contact. Pattern mark production comes from the subject which is the mark maker scene, and goes to the object which is the mark receiving scenes. Matching patterns is science independent of the roles of suspect and victim. Pattern evidence has possible production paths:

1. A suspect controlled item left a pattern on a victim or other entity controlled scene.

2. A victim controlled item left a pattern on a suspect or other entity controlled scene.

3. Another entity controlled scene left a pattern on a suspect or victim controlled scene.

This is complicated by which components are still available to process, and sometimes the marking may not identify what made the mark.

b. *Proof Ability* Patterns link a pattern-making item or scene to a pattern left on another scene, physical, chemical, visual, or informational. Subject scenes leave a mark on object scenes. The two are linked by the pattern one made, and the other received. Pattern matching describes the process, but the reports emphasize the actual things used in the matching *tool marks*. They could be impressions, or even unique pieces of identifying information left on another scene. The investigator decides how to preserve and analyze the evidence, often while only having one of the items in his or her possession. There are different ways pattern matching comes to be, and each proves different things:

1. Physical patterns, or imprints prove force was used via the tool to mark the substrate or receiving scene.

2. Visual patterns are identification of two dimensional representations, such a looking at a photo of a person.

3. Chemical patterns prove a specific combination of ingredients comprise something. On a molecular means matching a pattern of a known substance, such as identifying drugs, or blood typing.

4. Information patterns prove specific transfers of information indicating actions and identification by combinations of data, such as logins, a web address, or phone call records.

c. *Quality* Casts and photographs preserve marks well. Pattern matching can prove presence and action, which is often central to the case. The marks are often obvious given their location, and context of scenes including tools. Pattern-matching evidence decisions can yield firm evidence in the absence of the immediate prospect of identification through DNA or fingerprints.

The more specific the pattern is, the more useful it is toward proving something. Pattern-producing items have two sets of characteristics: class characteristics and individual characteristics. Class covers the features of all common items, such as a specific shoe tread pattern sold on a specific brand of shoes. Individual characteristics differentiate the particular item from all others in its class, such as a gouge from the sole of the aforementioned shoe. Individual characteristics make an item unique among all similar items, offering proof of identity. These variables may lead an expert not to match two items, but to rule in or out a possible match. This triggers the need for corroborating evidence to build the case.

Scene restrictiveness supports identification, but the goal remains to connect a person to a scene, and a greater number of matching details makes the evidence stronger.

Pattern matching may only be able to answer *what did it*, and not answer the question of *who did it*, since proving contact between scenes does not always prove who controlled the contact.

d. *Timeline* Physical patterns cannot be attached to a specific actual time on their own, but they have a great value in relative time, such as belonging to the most recent person to touch an item. Data patterns often do have an actual time attached to them when information handling machines interact.

e. *Resilience* Pattern matching evidence is often very enduring when it does not involve living things. Metal tools endure. Softer the materials take impressions well, but if they are not cohesive, or can melt they are less enduring evidence.

f. *Collection* Pattern matching's attractiveness ranks below a DNA or fingerprint match. Pattern-matching one scene to another can constitute powerful evidence when combined with evidence such as fingerprints or DNA that connect a specific person as a scene.

Pattern matching relates to other evidence processes as a later process and tends not to disrupt the earlier efforts. It comes later in the evidence cycle unless an irregularity compels the reordering of processing. Electronic matching for Internet addresses relies on contact records instead of physical impressions, and an investigator can research the history during other processes.

Pattern-matching equipment overlaps much of the fingerprint collection equipment discussed previously. Cameras, lighting, and ALS help to discover and document patterns. Magnification shows the details to match the pattern. Fingerprint powder aids pattern visibility. Silicone gel or plaster casting captures the pattern marks. Packaging material, as covered below under evidence artifacts, preserves the items and keeps them free from damage. Computers assist in magnification and matching with enhanced images.

The investigator may document an object scene bearing a pattern mark, and must plan to collect the subject or marking item. Often one half of the pair remains at a particular scene, and this evidence work bets on the future. Fragile shoe prints in dust may necessitate processing them first on a high-use area of the floor.

Pattern matching sometimes can be collected with photography; sometimes one or both scenes must be collected. Informational pattern matching requires the data be collected.

Patterns are preserved by booking the item into evidence. Photographs make pattern-matching evidence portable and comparable with scales.

Pattern-based evidence matching takes place in a laboratory or on a computer when both of the potentially matching patterns can be compared. Pattern marks are not always distinctive to the naked eye. Greater magnification means differentiation in practical terms, and lab work can provide the magnification process to distinguish whether an object carries the mark of a subject.

Odontologists use bite marks to match particular persons to a scene by connecting a bite mark to a person's dental pattern. There are fewer problems with the actual collection of marks since the evidence is often retained as an item.

7. Artifacts

Evidence artifacts are the most traditional evidence used to prove guilt or innocence.

Evidence Decision How can artifacts or items, be used to prove facts?

Attributes

a. *Production* Evidence artifacts can include devices used, items moved, or contraband created. Artifacts can be familiar items, but can also be microscopic particles, hairs, fibers, and even gases. An item transitions to evidence status when it can prove something. Evidence is a tangible fact. The category of evidence artifacts thus overlaps with tools like DNA. Typical artifacts include weapons, documents, drawings, jewelry, and computer software.

Artifacts have possible production paths differing from DNA, fingerprints, or pattern marks because those three are created at the same time as the crime event, and most evidence artifacts exist before and after the crimes. Artifacts offer several possible origins:

1. The item originated elsewhere, and was left at the hosting scene.

2. The item originated at the hosting scene, and was left at the hosting scene.

3. The item originated at the hosting scene, and was removed from the hosting scene to elsewhere.

4. The item originated elsewhere, was brought to the scene, and was removed from hosting scene to elsewhere.

The first two are easier for the investigator's job. The last two rely on evidence from the item as a scene, in the style of working a tool scene.

Evidence artifacts also differ because they can play different roles, as:

1. The object of crime, or target.

2. The tool of crime.

3. The result of a crime, or a fruit of a crime.

b. *Proof Ability* An evidence artifact may prove a fact of the case which is a broad category. The item could be a tool, or connected to another scene by pattern. The item could belong to one person in the possession of another, or just be illegal to possess. This requires logic-based skills to recognize what a particular thing means to a case. Scientific skills obtain evidence proving presence, actions, and outcomes.

Artifacts reflect the interaction of multiple scenes, including person scenes. Evidence artifacts are scenes connected to the case because they were used as tools, or objects of the crime. They can be evidence, help create evidence, and hold evidence such as material, DNA, fingerprints, or pattern marks. Someone controlled the evidence artifact at some point in the crime, and it functioned as either a cause or effect. Evidence artifacts can overlap other categories and include tools as their own scenes, but they can also be physical items or even traces of material transferred among scenes. Evidence artifact decisions lead to using items to prove ideas.

Artifacts are often portable, which complicates what they prove. If an investigator finds a possession of a person in a crime scene it may not prove anything more than that person's item was in the scene. Corroborating evidence is always helpful to prove facts.

Sometimes evidence items are not present to be processed. Stolen items, or tools used to break in are carried away. Those items will become evidence if they are recovered.

c. *Quality* Evidence artifacts have higher quality when they are unique and identifiable, such as by serial number or personalized modifications. The artifact should be connected to at least one scene, but also bridge scenes such as showing how valued items from one person's control to another. The relevance of evidence artifacts is obvious given the statements of involved persons.

The more specific the artifact is, the more useful it is toward proving something. This relates to identifying by presence, and action. Scene restrictiveness supports identification. Identifying evidence with the item increases its value. A person-connected evidence artifact in a restricted-access scene or evidence artifacts tied to multiple scenes can move the case closer to being solved.

d. Artifacts often cannot be attached to a specific actual time on their own, but they may have great value in relative time, such as belonging to the most recent person to touch an item.

e. *Resilience* Evidence artifacts can be very enduring, but could be subject to environmental forces.

f. *Collection* The evidence artifact can serve as a vehicle for other evidence, such as DNA or fingerprints, prompting interoperability decisions. They can be their own scenes. An investigator collects more fragile evidence early, like DNA and fingerprints. Artifact collection begins after these other forms of evidence have been obtained. The investigator may opt to collect evidence proving the contact or action rather than the artifact itself. Collection decisions center on size, value, and importance to the owner or possessor.

Investigators may discover the evidence of specific artifacts at multiple scenes. Documenting the evidence history answers many of the questions about the case. Evidence capabilities relate to ruling possibilities in or out. Available biological material can bring contextual relevance to a case, since each item indicates a body part interaction.

Private citizens may collect and provide photos or video footage as evidence items. They may add to a case, but they do not substitute for investigative photography work which can corroborate details.

The investigator discovers evidence in many ways, but discovery should damage the item as little as possible. Fresh gloves reduce cross-contamination. Evidence collection and storage material should protect evidence artifacts thoroughly, using high-technology evidence location devices and suitable packaging to preserve the items. Electronics may need special equipment to extract their information. Chemical detection kits collect material to be processed in a lab.

Evidence artifacts are collectible scenes. An investigator identifies and isolates evidence of various priorities for testing. Sometimes items become more important over the course of the investigation and need further testing, so the items should be sealed as soon as possible, near their discovery location. Immediate isolation prevents cross-contamination and reduces the effectiveness of claims of contaminated evidence.

Evidence must stay available in the same condition as collected for court proceedings and for potential retesting. Photographs aid in this process. Secure property facilities preserve evidence for court cases. It should follow prescribed procedures in accordance with best practices.

Labs collect photographs, DNA, patterns, and fingerprints from evidence artifacts. Some processing requires shipping the items to other labs.

The actual collection of the artifact must limit damage, and change to the item. Laws still limit collection of items and the seizure of items. The state or county audits property rooms for adherence to procedures and laws.

8. Report Production

A well written report expresses all the elements available about the case, including the proof as to who did what.

Evidence Decision How should the all of the case facts be presented in writing?

Attributes
a. *Production* A report should stand alone, allowing any reader to grasp the case. Reports include everything. The next person to receive the case will want an analysis of where the case stands, including its strengths and weaknesses.

The report should be organized according to scenes rather than focusing on the crime classification, since investigative work should precede classification. An investigation that overemphasizes the type of crime limits the investigator's actions to what he or she might expect with a particular type of crime. A legal classification mentality brings some cognitive bias by encouraging investigators to expect things based on crime classification rather than searching for evidence.

An investigator should produce a report structured to have several sections:

1. *Narrative.* The narrative covers everything in the overall body of the investigation and involves the most detailed writing. It starts with the administrative information and progresses into the scenes and evidence areas. This evidence, like the critical thinking, is produced by an investigator based on the situation.

Report organization varies with regard to how evidence is presented:

a. Chronologically, either by time of event or evidence discovery.

b. By location, of evidence.

c. By evidence function, in particular the context of the evidence and what it proves.

d. By connected person, such as the role of a person, and the evidence surrounding the person.

Ordering emphasizes locations, strength (or lack) of evidence, discovery order, and processing. Organizing each scene by the best evidence emphasizes the proof rather than chronological discovery and keeps the emphasis on the crime instead of on the investigation. A complex investigation spanning multiple scenes, times, and witnesses may be better suited for the chronological format, as an investigator may have applied information from one scene while working another scene around the same time. Appropriate headings organize large amounts of information and enhance readability.

2. *Summary.* An investigator should be able to distill the crime and investigation down to a few sentences and cover what level of crime is involved. Summaries boil down many pages and hours of work. The first part should provide a brief overview of the crime and people involved. Summaries also describe the outcomes for the people involved and their destinations—e.g., hospital, morgue, or jail.

Summaries can use fragmentary bulleted lists to cover key points. Whereas the narrative should employ active voice to cover who did what, the summary can express points using the passive voice to cover the basics with results, such as "fingerprints collected." Of course the narrative explains who collected the fingerprints, from where, and how, so the information exists in the report.

3. *To-do list.* An investigator at the beginning of a case may notice important aspects of evidence needing more work. To-do lists remind the next person receiving the report of remaining tasks needed to complete the case. An investigator can tailor lists to cover hypotheses, check alibis, and request research into things like ownership.

The narrative section may end with a paragraph titled "Disposition" to sum up the scene status at the time of report completion. Evidence items are sent to the lab, or the investigator may wait for items from victims. The disposition may also indicate the custody status of suspects. The to-do list can replace this paragraph, depending on the case's progress.

b. *Proof Ability* A report is an organized collection of facts showing the progress toward proving who did what, by showing presence and action.

Reports provide structure and content by describing investigative decisions and the crime situations, and details. This may indicate a suspect, or provide information toward identifying a list of characteristics. Often the report will mimic the type of search used by the investigator.

Report production is the other side of critical thinking and is the product of how the thinking guided all the actions in the investigation. Report production is also a *metaevidence* skill as it is thinking and writing about evidence in a formalized way to present the findings in a case, after all the work based on critical thinking. There investigator puts structure and content into a report.

At the outset of cases there may be few conclusionary facts, and no identifications, which is acceptable since the report is a collection of facts, and the lack of conclusions and identifications are facts.

c. *Quality* A report must be well-written to be understood. Organizing the information in a direct format with a navigable series of facts contributes to a strong investigation.

Fundamental writing with concise words and sentences increases report usability. Sentence fragments are fine when information is provided in list form. The report should reflect a neutral, systematic approach to presenting relevant details about the case. Using the active voice expresses facts and observations by explaining how a subject performed an act with or to an object. The active voice answers the question, "Who did what?" Writing "pictures were taken" makes the reader wonder who took the photos and how. A direct style of writing, such as "I took pictures with the department-issued camera," makes the information flow better and communicates a stronger sense of accuracy and credibility to the reader. Attorneys appreciate active language for trials, since active language identifies the people whom they will call as witnesses.

Active language provides more clarity than passive language, but sometimes passive language covers a state of being in the most direct and appropriate manner or reflects an ill-defined situation better. Writing "the window was broken" indicates the action was connected to a burglary without overcommitting to the specifics of the action since it was not witnessed. The broken window is a state of being, and could warrant passive voice. Other options are to indicate what the investigator saw ("I observed the broken bathroom window"). The investigator can ask the victim, and he can conclude or theorize based on information ("The thief broke the bathroom window during the break-in"), but grammatically correct English may clog the information flow of the report. The use of the verb *to be* also implies a conclusion, which works well for things like measurements and documented facts, but the investigator should stick to confirmed details rather than making leaps of judgment.

An investigator should use the same verb tense throughout the report. Usually, an investigator writes reports in the past tense. Contractions should be used only when quoting someone's speech.

Opinions and conclusions indicate leaps provided by the writer for the people who will look at the investigation later. An evidence-based investigation should present no opinions or conclusions at the beginning. Using the words "in this investigator's opinion" signals the report writer lacks the evidence to prove a case. Opinions should be expressed only with regard to what drew an investigator's attention to particular evidence or activity.

Connections unsupportable by their own facts, as signaled by phrases like "consistent with," do not aid the investigation. An investigator emphasizes a point by dedicating a paragraph to it. The phrase, "it should be noted," is one way to inject an opinion into the report by emphasizing the particular detail.

Factual reports with information to show the situation keep the case on track for the next people to address it. Reports should be all relevant to proving or disproving facts. The more specific the report is, the more useful it is toward proving something. Factual details strengthen report writing. Every fact is a discrete and specific piece of information to be connected to others.

d. *Timeline* Reports document specific times, and relative times.

e. *Resilience* Report production serves the investigator and everyone to preserve the record. The facts and details of a case are not always recallable, and so the record overcomes that.

f. *Collection* The report must address the issues to interoperability to answer the questions any reviewer would have about how the evidence work

Report production requires standard office equipment. Some organizations have report writing software.

The investigator puts the case together in a written report. The documents are formatted to show the scenes as they were after a crime, documenting results and proof.

Every investigation must provide the basic clerical information organizations use to organize cases in their database. The report software captures this documentation, such as locations, suspects, property involved, etc.

The work of an investigation is in the field, but the case is often written in the office.

The investigator writing the report must convey knowledge of the technical subjects, as well as what is legal and proper.

Report writing is the presentation of the scenes, situations, and investigative actions. It is the distillation of the case designed to be understandable to all. Report readers want to know if the case can prove who did it, and they look for the evidence to prove it. An investigator makes a case description deeper by considering the perspectives of the other involved people. A detective reviews an investigation for its completeness and readiness for court. He or she may identify evidence to be tested or ask follow-up questions of people about the evidence. The prosecutor receives the case and looks for adherence to the law and any holes in the case. He or she wants to make certain there is sufficient admissible evidence to charge the person accused of the crimes. The defense attorney also receives the case and wants to ensure the same things, probing the evidence for its applicability. The judge ensures the evidence and all proceedings adhere to the rules of court. The judge gives the jury instructions on how to consider the case. The jury wants a thorough investigation to make its decisions supportable.

II. Public Scenes

Public scenes are accessible, larger hosting scenes not often controlled by a person beyond the crime event.

Step 1. Designate the Scene

Scene Decision Why is this a scene?

1. *Discovery* The public scene often comes to the investigator's attention by a call from a witness or involved party.

2. *Scene type* Public scenes are identifiable as large, messy, and unsecured crime scenes presenting many options.

Some examples of public scenes are open space, parking lots, and roads.

3. *Scene Group* The public scene is often loosely defined at first, and hosts other subscenes. Public scenes are often the largest scene in a case, and host subscenes including private scenes, cars, persons, and tools. They may be defined within a larger area, such as a neighborhood. All crimes are within a public scene, such as a body in a car in a parking lot, in a county park.

4. *Search* Public scenes may not have natural borders and require the investigator to define and secure them. Crime scene perimeters may need modification. An investigator may determine the theoretical crime scene borders, and double the area for safe measure. Investigators should tape off the scene, and photograph the tape as well as the scene.

An open area public scene might warrant a lane search, or grid search. A spiral search may fit rougher terrain, and limited personnel. Limited personnel work well with the zone search and a walk through providing basic scene information.

Zone searches with multiple investigators allow an investigator to work the entire scene, thus avoiding possible miscommunication about the scene and evidence.

Step 2. Analyze the Scene

Scene Decision How does the scene work?

1. *Restrictiveness* Public scenes provide high accessibility with little or no privacy. Soft scene borders mean geographically undefined scenes. Many unrelated scenes interact with and within the public scene, and often presence alone is not a crime.

2. *Volatility* Public scenes may change with higher volumes of scene interactions. They are often exposed to the elements. The scenes generally do not move, but there are exceptions, such as public transit.

3. *Function* Public scenes are usually the object of a case, or host the object of the crime. Public scenes are often not the target, but receive the evidence when they interact with subject scenes. While there is legal ownership, anyone can control public scenes in contrast to ownership.

Public scenes function as accessible host locations for crimes, and sometimes travel routes. Public scenes are very common crime scenes because there is much shared space in the world. This allows for anonymity of involved persons.

Easy access means more possible routes, and interactions along with reduced scene control mean more anonymity. However, this also means less control of potential witnesses, and public scenes may require travel to and from, exposing a car scene to identification.

An investigator may underestimate the value of evidence in public scenes because processing the scenes requires work, with minimal potential payoff. Minor car crashes turn fatal with fragile people, leaving the investigation without reproducible measurements. The investigator may derail a public scene case by failing to secure it from people who do not belong, and failure to collect the evidence in the scene.

The ways public scenes function creates challenges for the investigator:

a. Larger, looser defined crime scenes make the center of gravity more difficult to find and process.

b. Accessibility means many people could impact the scenes, regardless of involvement.

c. Proving a person's presence in a public place might not make the case. The suspect may admit presence in an accessible place without admitting involvement. False statements denying presence rely on evidence to prove facts.

4. *Capacity and Interaction Points* Public scenes may be natural or man-made with evidence collection and carrying capacities. Some have easily locatable interaction points. A higher volume of scenes interacting causes the odds of relevant evidence to go down, thus a busy public scene could have a high capacity for evidence, with constant renewal of evidence.

Public scenes have many potential interaction points for an investigator to consider when looking at a case. The interaction points have less structure and architecture contributing to fewer predictable evidence transfer points and often show the following:

a. The entry point to the scene may be unrecognizable and may be as simple as parking a car in a lot, or walking in. The exit point also has the same obscurity.

b. Any public scene requires transit to, from, and often within, but the scenes may be unrecognizable.

c. Any waiting zone, as sometimes people arrive at different times, and loitering can mean the production of evidence, but many people do this in public scenes without committing crimes.

d. The center of gravity of the case and the zone around it may still not be identifiable, and may have no surfaces to collect evidence from even if the persons in the scene interacted with the scene.

e. Sometimes the only interaction points are incidental to the scene, and not connected with the action of the crime. Railings, and water fountains are metal, and may yield evidence. Public restrooms have many surfaces to collect evidence also.

The lack of restrictions on movement makes possible to have multiple scenes over distances, leading to multiple locations, and subscenes. Easy scene access means anyone could have done the crime, and proof of presence holds less value as proof than in a secured home. Some common subscenes within public scenes are related to interacting with the scene, including masks and disguises, along with equipment to reduce leaving fingerprints and DNA.

Step 3. Evaluate the Evidence Potential

Evidence Decision How would the evidence work in this scene?

1. *Production* Evidence can be produced by interaction of the public scene with another subscene such as a person, or car, but it can also host evidence created between through the interaction of subscenes.

2. *Proof Ability* Proving presence and action in public scenes can have two distinct requirements because a person can be there without involvement.

3. *Quality* Public scene evidence varies in quality since it is exposed to more interaction. The most relevant evidence may be unrecognized, gone, or destroyed. The public scene evidence may not be very unique since there can be a number of persons interacting with the scene for legitimate reasons.

4. *Timeline* Public scene timelines may have pinpoint accurate actual times, but often they are relative given the reporting can be delayed. The time of the call is a good marker, which can be used as an anchor for relative times.

5. *Resilience* Public scene evidence may be resilient as any other evidence, but varies in how well it can resist forces of time, nature and environment since it is often exposed.

6. *Collection* Public scene evidence may require express collection given the higher interaction within the scene. Public scenes often have element or people exposure. Weather might cause a reordering of the evidence work steps. A storm washes away evidence, or hinders processing, requiring immediate evidence collection. Spray paint marks collection locations. Information about the type of case eases the evidence identification process. Public scenes have a higher likelihood of tainting of the scene, but they also have a lower likelihood of violating a person's rights and violation of the law.

Step 4. Work the Evidence

Evidence Decision How to obtain the evidence from this scene?

1. *Critical Thinking* The first three decisions indicate public scenes present the investigator with many more decisions. They act as umbrella scenes to host other scenes with unrestricted access, and varying levels of predictability. Evidence production may not be recognized, or found given the high potential for impact, and difficult to find evidence transfer points. Public scenes may require outside agency coordination given their visibility and greater impact on members of the public.

Public scenes are often larger scenes with many subscenes, because people travel into public scenes, building movement into the crime. Their lack of structure increases choices for determining routes in and out. It also means there may not be evidence associated with a point of entry or exit. Public crime scenes function as gathering places and transit locations. An unknown number of people move through them. Public spaces can have specific uses like streets, parking lots, or businesses, but they also host multiple uses for several different groups, People use public parks for sports, a hang out, homeless encampments, meeting places for illicit affairs, prostitution, and drugs sales. Commercial buildings with retail businesses are private property open to the public. Most of the involved persons are allowed in public scenes. Their presence signifies a connection to the case, even if accidental or uninvolved.

2. *Information* The high volume of low value information can overwhelm any public scene investigation providing little return on investment toward the goals of proving presence and action. The investigative process eliminates and includes persons with a lengthy public scene suspect list.

Measuring scenes builds knowledge by defining the dimensions. Include immovable objects as monuments or landmarks if such exist. A factual diagram, sketch, or annotated overhead image makes the spatial relationships much clearer to a viewer.

An automatic license plate reader can record the cars in the vicinity of a public scene. Automation appeals to a desire for no-work evidence, but has limits since it does not always recognize a suspicious situation as a person does. Systems fail, and people have dirty or unreadable license plates. A foot canvasser makes notes about cars, and their visible features, such as obscured plates, or weapons in the passenger area.

3. *Photographs* Public scenes also tend to have more space, leading to more photographs. Even with greater distances, the images can show what people in the scene could see. The images can serve as maps showing the relationship between different scenes, and evidence components.

A search of the internet may yield photos of the scene before the crime, or even show the crime being committed. Some members of the public enjoy the entertainment value of police work. Photographing spectators may yield leads of suspects observing the scene after the crime. Facial recognition software may help identify people in a public area.

4. *DNA* Finding the right DNA challenges the investigator given the cost and concerns about finding the correct sample to sequence. DNA testing

loses its effectiveness when dealing with a lot of different DNA donors. A public restroom faucet has DNA, but often too many profiles. Supporting the DNA evidence with information provides context and clarity. The stabbing scene blood may belong to anyone including the suspect or victim.

5. *Fingerprints* Presence through fingerprints in a public scene presents a lot of the same challenges as DNA in public places by overwhelming the investigation. Large numbers of people means larger numbers of fingerprints. An investigator capitalizes on knowing fingerprints' low tolerance of touching, so the fingerprints belong to the last person to touch the bathroom faucet, or at least the last person to leave fingerprints.

6. *Patterns* Matching patterns in public scenes presents the scene as the recipient of another scene's action. The investigator may not be able to collect the receiving area of the scene, and must settle for a facsimile of the marks. This often means tire tracks, or shoe prints, as well as a tool mark.

7. *Artifacts* The volume of persons traversing public scenes complicates defining relevant public scene evidence artifacts. As anything within any scene could be evidence, the greater size of public scenes increases the potential field of evidence. Evidence is often brought into public scenes, although it can be made there. An investigator requires information to determine an item's classification as evidence. Spectators might take their own photos and upload them on to the Internet. A canvasser may find private security video for the main scene, and adjacent locations. Sometimes the soil is distinctive, and can provide a link to the public scene.

8. *Report Production* An investigator can structure public scene reports to cover larger areas by locational evidence, or fact supporting evidence. The larger scenes require coordination between different workers, and may cover logistics. The investigator may cover the content by moving inward or outward, or may cover multiple areas in a clockwise manner. Sometimes starting with the key scene will not present as the obvious way, but can emphasize the evidence.

A crime scene log shows who entered the scene, and when.

Public Scene Scenarios

5. Public Park Stabbing Scene
6. Public Outdoors Sexual Assault Multi Scene
7. Retailer Armed Robbery Scene

5. Public Park Stabbing Scene

An anonymous caller reported a knifing at a picnic area. The injured person ran through the park, and stopped when he arrived to an ambulance at another picnic area. He stated he had been drinking with friends in the picnic area, drinking an unidentified male stabbed him.

Summary
Knifing, one injured person taken to the hospital, non-life threatening injuries. Photos taken. Bottles collected, fingerprinted, DNA swabbed. Weapon not recovered.

To Do
Follow up with victim at hospital and photos.
Fingerprints to Central ID.

Investigation
At 00:20 HRS on 6/17/15 I arrived to the north end of the park. Officer Ward briefed me.

Scene Integrity
Officer Fong taped off the main assault scene and maintained an entry log.

Victim Images
Upon arrival I photographed the victim in the ambulance as he was treated for his wound.

Scene Description (See sketch)
The scene is an unsecured public park. It was closed during the time of the assault. The park is in the middle of a residential neighborhood, and has a baseball diamond, picnic areas, and a pond. It is approximately 1000 feet on the east west axis, and 900 feet on the north south axis. There are no security cameras in the park. There are three main subscenes as depicted on the sketch.

a. The picnic area, where the assault occurred. This area is south central, approximately 800 feet of the east edge of the park, and 100 feet north of the south edge. The area has four concrete picnic tables.

I saw the remains of a meal including take-out chicken, and beer bottles on the table. I also saw what I thought was blood on the ground near the tables. I saw a shoe print in blood at the picnic scene. The blood trail led north toward the pond.

b. The blood trail led north to the scene on the west edge of the pond. This area is central, approximately 800 feet of the east edge of the park, and 450 feet north of the south edge. This is a clearing, and had no furniture. The victim and appears to have stopped there as the blood drops appear more plentiful here than in the southern parts. The blood trail continued north for 150 feet and terminated at scene C, near Garfield Park Rd.

c. This area is north east, near the east edge of the park, and 600 feet north of the south edge.

I saw many blood drops in the vicinity of scene C where the ambulance driver saw the victim and stopped for him. Officer Sneed found the victim here being treated for injuries there.

Evidence
I photographed the blood trail traveling northward from picnic area scene A. I photographed every ten feet. I also searched for possible evidence, such as discarded weapons. I used a rolling tape measure. The path travelled northward and eastward until I arrived at scene C, the parking lot.

I collected the bottles and cans from the picnic area in the event new information surfaces placing the suspect, victim, or other persons of interest in the area.

Biological Evidence
I photographed the scene from multiple angles, and levels of magnification. I placed numbers showing the evidence numbers near the items and photographed them. I collected potential biological evidence with swabs. I titled the swabs in the Property Section as S (for Swab). See Property Section for details on swabbing. I swabbed each area with a separate sterile swab with sterile water on it. I placed each swab in its own envelope and sealed as evidence. Prior to swabbing each area I changed gloves so no areas would have cross contamination. I sealed the items and placed them in the Crime Lab Freezer.

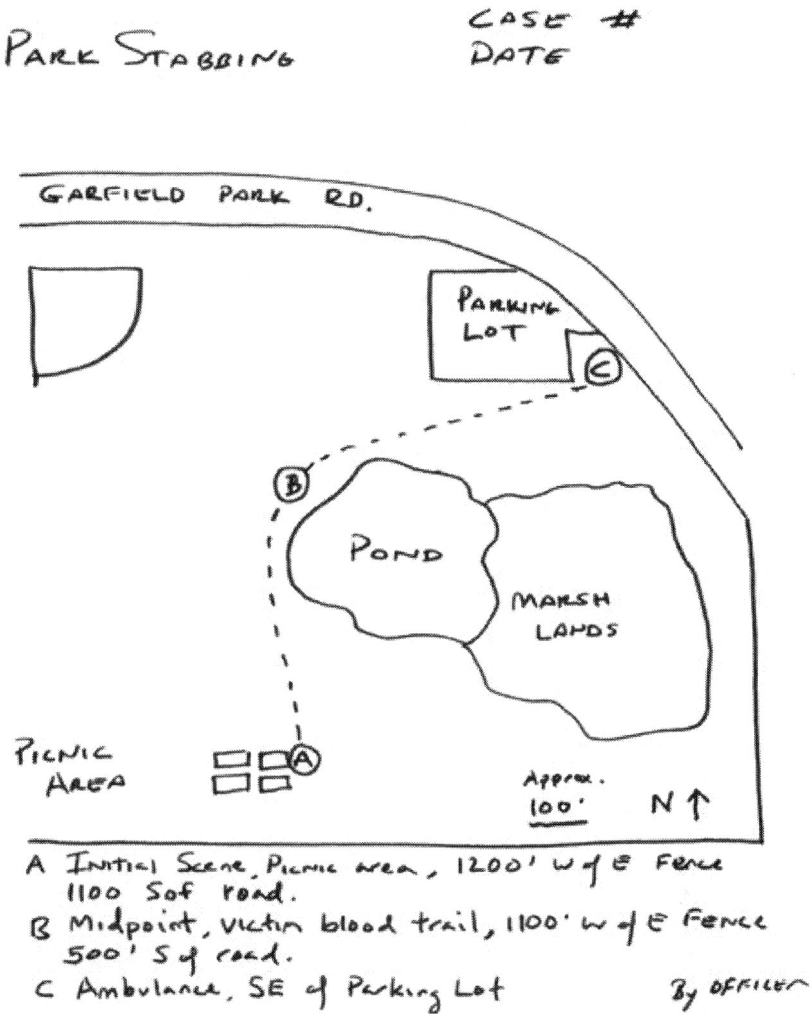

Swab Collection by Locations:

S0. Swab with sterile water.

S1. Swab of rim of beer bottle, Scene A.

S2. Bite mark in fried chicken sandwich, Scene A.

S3. Swab, unused, sealed.

S4. Swab, blood, midpoint. Scene B.

S5. Swab, blood, endpoint. Scene C.

S6. I collected a partially eaten chicken drumstick from the picnic area. I swabbed the bite marks

S7. Swab with sterile water.

Fingerprints
The picnic table is concrete and did not yield fingerprints. I will fume the beer bottles with cyanoacrylate to develop fingerprints after DNA swabbing.

Shoe Print Pattern
I saw a shoe print in blood near the southwest picnic table in the primary scene. The print was located 12 feet east of the west edge of the concrete pad holding the picnic table, and 18 feet north of the south edge of the pad. I photographed the print with a scale and noted the orientation. I was unable to collect the print by tape. The print appears to be a size 10, lug boot sole. It does not match any of the officers' soles, nor the victim's shoe.

Evidence Items
I collected 6 six beer bottles from the initial crime scene at the picnic area. I will swab them for DNA, and fingerprint them.

Suspect
Investigators do not know the suspect's identity, and nobody has provided a description or photograph. No one has provided information about the suspect's injuries.

Victim
Charles Durning stands 5 feet 8 inches tall, and weighs 170 pounds. He received a facial cut. See physician's report for details. The victim provided his fingerprints and DNA for comparison

Step 1. Designate the Scene

Scene Decision Why is this a scene?

1. *Discovery* The investigator determined the scene by responding to a 911 call. The victim indicated the hosting scene in a public park.

2. *Scene type* This public scene is identifiable as an overall scene where the victim travelled from the attack site to the medical intervention site where the ambulance began treating him.

3. *Scene Group*
a. Park.
b. Assault scene, picnic area.
c. Stop places along transit route.
d. Transit scene.
e. Medical intervention scene.
f. There could be a car parked in the area, or even a bike.
g. Injured person scene.
h. Suspect person scene.
i. The tool / weapon.
j. Bottles in the assault scene.

4. *Search* The large area complicated securing the path of travel, but investigators canvassed the area to look for evidence. A non-evidence work investigator might interview the victim during the activity to find information about evidence. An open area public park scene might warrant a lane search to cover the larger areas when looking for discarded items. A grid or spiral search may fit rougher terrain, and limited personnel, or may be useful when the centers of gravity are located. A zone search would be best when the area is contained to a smaller section of the total scene.

Step 2. Analyze the Scene

Scene Decision How does the scene work?

1. *Restrictiveness* The scene is an accessible hosting scene anyone can enter or leave. There are many possible paths the suspect could have travelled.

2. *Volatility* The scene is stationary, but as it is outdoors it is subject weather, and potential change.

3. *Function* The scene is an object scene receiving evidence. The scene functions as a meeting place, and hosts people. There is nothing about the attack scene to make it an appealing place to ambush someone. This could indicate less evidence discipline for the involved persons. There were no items of value there.

The park offers no restrictions to entry for occupants. This means more potential witnesses, but they will often be anonymous. The area has a high population over time, meaning an admission of presence may not be time verified, and forensics could indicate a large group of people. Large space-crime scenes make finding evidence difficult sometimes, in this case the weapon. The impromptu assault may indicate less evidence discipline, and more opportunity for the investigators.

4. *Capacity and Interaction Points* The scene has the hosting capacity for DNA, fingerprints, and patterns, such as shoe marks. The investigator may be able to find identifying evidence on items left in the scene. In this case, the bottles, and leftover food may provide identifying evidence. So far there are no components such as railings that might hold a print.

The main interaction area is the picnic table, where several persons placed evidence items. The table itself yields no prints. The blood trail indicates a path of travel which may yield discarded evidence.

Step 3. Evaluate the Evidence Potential

Evidence Decision How would the evidence work in this scene?

1. *Production* Person scenes had contact with the bottles, depositing DNA and fingerprints on them. The slicing of the person caused a loss of blood. Eating the chicken also caused a transfer of biological evidence to the uneaten food.

2. *Proof Ability* The fingerprints and DNA on the bottles could prove presence at scene preceding the assault. If located, the knife or slicing tool could connect the suspect and victim to the location were it to hold evidence of both the suspect and victim scenes.

3. *Quality* The investigator arrived to the scene when the victim was still on scene. It was a fresh scene with plenty of evidence. Among the bottles, there should be enough quality material to obtain identification information of some persons present.

The bottles and food remains evidence may yield evidence to prove presence. The blood on the ground is relevant, but the victim is already identified, so if it is from another person it can indicate presence, and action of a cut, even if it was a mistake by an assailant.

DNA and fingerprints provide unique identifiers. There are no unique evidence items, such as weapons.

4. *Timeline* Other than the 911 call, there is no actual time. The events in this public scene started several hundred feet away so an investigator can calculate the events relatively, with the travel path coming after the assault scene.

5. *Resilience* This evidence is somewhat delicate, but the investigator collected it soon after the crime.

6. *Collection* The investigator's initial decision is whether to process the victim or the park scene. The victim received life safety treatment preventing scene processing aside from a few initial photos. This moved the park into the role of primary evidence scene.

The investigator secured the scene, and performed some of the processes in the field, and saved some for the lab. There appears to be no problems with processing the scene in order with the standard CSI tools to avoid cross contamination. There is no indication of foul weather, but sprinklers are a common hazard to evidence in open land scenes. The water could necessitate either shutting off the systems, or finding and protecting the subscenes, or perhaps photographing, and collecting the evidence to be processed later at a lab.

Step 4. Work the Evidence

Evidence Decision How to obtain the evidence from this scene?

1. *Critical Thinking* The investigator thought about the public scene as an anonymous meeting place that hosted a disagreement between two persons within a larger group of people. The altercation escalated to the point where one person stabbed another. The only scene where both the persons were collocated was the picnic area. The person who did the stabbing is gone, and so is the weapon. The investigator sought to identify as many people as possible, hoping the stabber is among the group. He sought DNA and fingerprint evidence as a way to identify persons by their contact with the bottles and food at the picnic area. The investigator knew the blood drops likely came from the stabbed person, but took the longshot, since the information was not clear enough to rule out two injured persons.

The suspect might have followed the victim northward from the scene. Either person may have dumped evidence along the blood trail. The specific evidence obtained this scene is not processed yet, but it could prove presence of multiple persons.

2. *Information* The investigation highlights the scarcity of information at the outset of the case. Factual observations allow another person not at the scenes to have an idea about the start and finish points of the victim's movements. A sketch shows how it fits together, and allows all persons to show their positions on the map.

3. *Photographs* The scenario is about the park scene, but the victim's presence in the scene provides a fleeting opportunity to get a picture of the injuries before they are treated by medical personnel. The park scene also has fleeting

evidence photography opportunities as the blood trail could spoil, footprints disappear, and people move evidence items.

The unknown suspect remains unphotographed. An investigator should take photos upon contact, even with the passing of time.

4. *DNA* Swabs appear to be the best identifying evidence to place persons at the scene. Blood trails show the path of travel to aid in locating other evidence, even when they lack usefulness as they come from an identified bleeding person. The stabber may have bled, making sampling a prudent approach to identify the person.

The bottles and food could place persons at the scene. Detectives may defer sequencing decisions about the preserved swabs until they have more information. An investigator swabs for DNA to find the suspect, as a calculated risk, as at least one known person bled in the scene. There are often far more swabs to collect, and the investigator must determine the best candidate sample to yield a potential suspect. The investigator has limited time in the secured scene, and will analyze in greater detail later with more contextual information.

5. *Fingerprints* The bottles may yield fingerprints to place persons at the scene. Investigators will process the collected bottles for prints later. The table top offers no opportunity to prove direct person contact with the scene.

6. *Patterns* The shoeprint is a longshot for identifying a suspect compared to the DNA, and fingerprints. However, the case is still young, the DNA and fingerprints may not work out, and perhaps a lead will come through other channels making the shoeprint relevant.

7. *Artifacts* The cutting tool with both suspect and victim's DNA or fingerprints on it could connect the two, if someone finds it. The suspect operated in a large location, and had time to discard the tool. The next best option ties the people to the scenes with evidence to the scene. The collected bottles come with a list of tasks for a later time.

8. *Report Production* This report emphasizes the evidence by location. As presence is the main provable point, specific locations are essential to the evidence.

6. Public Outdoor Sexual Assault Multi Scene

At approximately 2:30 AM an anonymous passerby reported a woman screaming near a construction yard. Police responded and learned the woman was an active prostitute who met a man at 2:00 AM, and the two walked a few blocks to find a place to have sex. The man attacked the woman in the bushes of a business, and beat her in the process. Lucas Rd. Police cordoned off the area in the early morning and began a search when few people occupied the area. Just before 7:00 AM, a waitress at a restaurant noticed a suspicious man and called 911. Officers converged on the man in his booth, and took him outside where the victim's friends identified the suspect.

Summary
Sexual and physical assault, injured victim taken to the hospital, with no life threatening injuries. Victim SART kit. Photos taken. Evidence items at outdoor scene collected. Suspect arrested, SART kit collected in jail.

To Do
Follow up with victim at hospital and photos
SART kits to crime lab
Victim identification of the scene evidence.
Collect and photograph victim's shoe to explore connection the broken strap at porch scene.

Investigation
At 07:00 HRS on 4/11/13 I arrived and spoke with investigator Pfenton who briefed me on the situation. He found the victim in front of the business at 691 Lucas Rd. He provided first aid, and took initial photos of her in the ambulance.

Scene Integrity
Patrol officers taped off the assault scene at 691 Lucas Rd. at the sidewalk. A sentry limited entry to the named officers. Personnel secured the other scenes and released them after searching for evidence.

Crime Scene Administration
I am the Primary CSI responsible for the overall scene B, and the secondary scene search. CSI Pfenton is the Secondary CSI responsible for scene preservation, primary scene search, scene evidence collection. He is also responsible for scene C. CSI Lautrec is the Tertiary CSI responsible for victim evidence collection, and scene A.

Main Crime Scene Description
The overall scene is an incorporated area of the city with hotels, restaurants, and light industry. Lucas Rd. is a six lane road running north and south with many controlled intersections. There are three main scenes, with travel routes between them. Their distances are in noted on the sketch.

Scene A. The Short Motel. 802 Lucas Rd.
This is a budget hotel where the two persons met around 2:00 AM. Officer Lautrec is seeking lobby video for possible evidence.

Scene B. Wade Construction Co. 691 Lucas Rd.
(See attached sketch showing locations and measurements for the porch.) The lot is on the west side of the divided roadway. No onsite lights illuminated the scene. Nearby street lamps in the median provided ambient light. The lot is divided between the equipment yard to the west, and the office yard to the east, with street access. The lot is 115 feet from the west fence to the west curb line of Lucas Rd., and 85 feet from north to south property line. The businesses to the north are biosciences. An animal kennel occupies the business to the south.

The business office sits on the north part of the front yard. The building is 63 feet along the west axis and 25 feet along the north axis. The building is 52 feet west of the west curb line of Hurd, and 10 feet south of the north property line.

The front porch is 10 feet west of the east wall of the building. It is built into the building and is obscured from the street by the building and landscaping. The porch is 12 feet wide and 6 feet deep (north).

An uninvolved truck belonging to the business was parked in the south side lot.

I collected the listed evidence at the locations from the front porch of 691 N. Lucas Rd.

Item A Victim's shoe, right, tan leather
3 feet west of south east corner of the porch
3 feet north of south east corner of the porch

Item B Matchbook, 5 Star Hotels
8 feet 6 inches west of south east corner of the porch
3 feet 9 inches north of south east corner of the porch

Item C Moist tissue
0 feet 1 inch west of south east corner of the porch
5 feet 11 inches north of south east corner of the porch
I placed Item C in the drying cabinet in the Coffeetown PD HQ to dry the moisture prior to storage.

Item D Suspect Cigarettes
11 feet 6 inches west of south east corner of the porch
5 feet 9 inches north of south east corner of the porch

The doormat location is shown on the map as both an evidence item and a reference point.

I booked all items into secure dry storage unless otherwise noted.

Photographs
I took 231 photographs at the scenes. See camera file for metadata on settings. I used a flash, natural light, and artificial lighting for images. I photographed all items prior to collection.

DNA
I requested the Crime Lab swab items B, C, and D for possible DNA samples.

Fingerprint Evidence
CSI Pfenton dusted the main scene without locating prints.

I requested the Crime Lab swab items B and D for possible DNA samples.

Scene C. The Sit Down Restaurant. 802 Lucas Rd.

The restaurant where the suspect was captured at 7:00 AM. This restaurant is on the north side of the hotel grounds.

CSI Pfenton photographed the scene.

Suspect Car

Officers performed a neighborhood canvass and did not find the suspect's car.

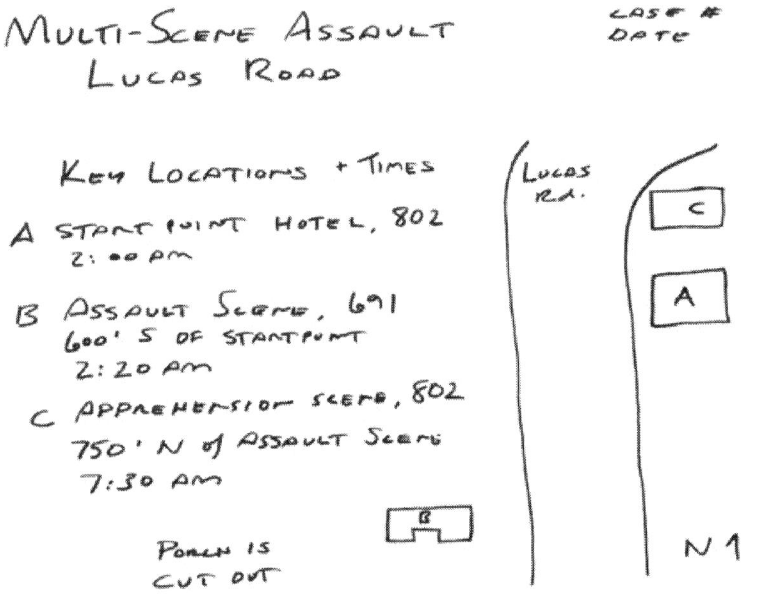

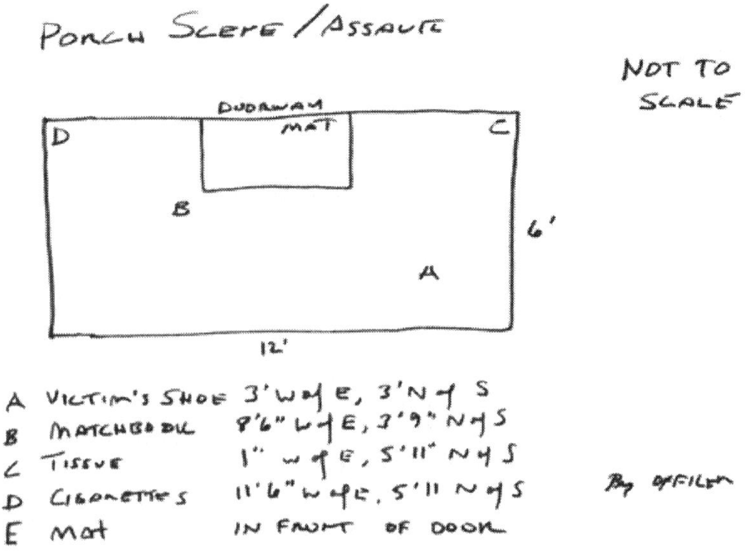

Step 1. Designate the Scene

Scene Decision Why is this a scene?

1. *Discovery* The investigator declared the scene by responding to a 911 call of a woman screaming, and her identifying the location.

2. *Scene type* This outdoor public scene has multiple subscenes. The outdoor public scenes tie the two parties to a location.

3. *Scene Group*
a. Overall neighborhood.
b. Porch assault scene.
c. Hotel meeting scene.
d. Restaurant apprehension scene.
e. Victim medical intervention site.
f. Transit scenes.
g. Victim body scene.
h. Suspect body scene.
i. Suspect's outstanding car is a potential scene.
j. The male person's possession such as a smartphone.

4. *Search* Zone for the porch. Public street scenes involving travel from scene to scene might be best searched by lane search since the paths of people tend to follow the sidewalk.

Step 2. Analyze the Scene

Scene Decision How does the scene work?

1. *Restrictiveness* The scene is an accessible hosting scene, with robust normal traffic. The porch scene has well defined borders and sparse furnishings. There is one way in an out for the scene.

2. *Volatility* The scene is stationary. It is outdoors, and semi-protected from the weather.

3. *Function* The scene is an object scene receiving evidence. The scene was designed to function as the protected entryway to a business, but was used by the involved persons as a secluded liaison spot. There were no items of value there.

Larger geographical scenes have more potential evidence searching. Both suspect and victim were anonymous in the scenes, and had no history there.

The scenes in this case are all open to the public. have the potential for evidence tainting.

4. *Capacity and Interaction Points* The scene has the hosting capacity for DNA, fingerprints, patterns, and items. The investigator may be able to find identifying evidence on items left in the scene. The scene may contain identifying evidence (DNA and fingerprints) of the suspect and victims contacting the hosting scene. There may also be evidence artifacts left behind in the scene. So far there are no components apt to hold a print.

There are several points in the scenes offering evidence of interaction. The initial meeting scene at the hotel may have interactions points such as a desk or even coming into a security camera view. The assault scene at the porch may have areas where either touched it, or left items. The apprehension scene had areas where the suspect interacted with the booth he was seated in, although there is no need to prove him there because he was contacted by police there. The travel scene when the two walked may have had cameras where the two contacted the view of video.

Step 3. Evaluate the Evidence Potential

Evidence Decision How would the evidence work in this scene?

1. *Production* Person scenes had contact with the scene. The investigators tried but could not locate any identifying evidence there. The matchbook from another location and the shoe strap are evidence items the two persons brought into the scene and show the outcome of scenes interacting in a fight..

2. *Proof Ability* The items on the porch should be able to provide some proof of presence, and the action of a struggle. Proving the action is much more difficult. The torn shoe strap indicates a struggle.

3. *Quality* The items could yield DNA and fingerprints. They could provide good evidence as those subscenes had limited contact. DNA and fingerprints provide unique identifiers. The matchbook, and shoe strap are pretty unique, and can be supported by the victim's information.

Presence proving evidence is more relevant to the scene. An assault may not provide much evidence at the public scene, as it would for person scenes.

4. *Timeline* The 911 call is the only actual time. The initial meeting site of the motel may be able to timestamp time and location by video or billing. Some security system may also have a timestamp in the travel path.

5. *Resilience* This evidence is pretty hardy. The moist towel could degrade, and may require DNA testing earlier.

6. *Collection* Violence and sexual assault places the emphasis on the person scenes, but at the opening of the investigation, the victim was unavailable for medical treatment, and the suspect fled. The standard CSI tools will support the investigator's efforts to get the evidence. The investigator performed some of the processes in the field in order to avoid cross contamination.

The public attack scene portion of the case takes immediate priority in the investigation because investigators outsource the victim person scene to SART, thus the attack scene is the best opportunity remaining. The person scene section covers suspect processing when he is found a few hours later.

Step 4. Work the Evidence

Evidence Decision How to obtain the evidence from this scene?

1. *Critical Thinking* The investigator thought about the public scene as an anonymous meeting place that started as a sexual encounter, and evolved into physical fight and sexual assault between two persons. The investigator knew the two persons met at the hotel, and travelled together to a second scene for the attack. The attack scene appeared to have the most evidence, as it hosted sexual activity as well as a physical fight. The person who attacked the woman spent several hours on the run, freeing up the investigator to process the assault scene. Then, after the scene was processed, the suspect was discovered near where he started.

Since the suspect was not at the hotel, nor the assault site, the investigator sought to connect him to the assault site, and a fallback for the hotel site where they met. He wanted identifying evidence such as DNA or fingerprints to prove his presence. The artifacts indicated a struggle, which could be connected to the victim's personal items, and some were attributed to him.

2. *Information* The majority of information comes from witness statements pointing to suspects, and evidence. No one seems to have any connection with the scene.

3. *Photographs* Images of the porch scene showed the remains of a fight. Lighting conditions show how it appeared during the assault.

4. *DNA* Biological material might tie the suspect and victim to the scene, in particular the porch scene. If the SART results do not connect the suspect and victim the investigation may require some other evidentiary way to

connect the two person scenes, even if by collocation. The victim is a sex worker. While the DNA from the SART may have findings, it may not be able to name a specific person scene from which the DNA came from.

The towel, matchbook or cigarette package may provide DNA to put both persons in the same place.

5. *Fingerprints* The porch had few smooth surfaces to retain fingerprints, and the scene required no barrier to entry. The investigator has limited evidence opportunities, but the cigarettes or matchbook could provide a fingerprint.

6. *Patterns* There is no indication of tool marks, or shoe prints at this stage.

7. *Artifacts* The broken shoe strap supports a struggle at the porch. The investigator should plan to collect the shoe and photograph it as a connection as soon as practical. The victim said the suspect smoked cigarettes establishing a potential evidence link for presence.

8. *Report Production* The report starts with a chronological account of arrival, and why the case was handled as it was. When the victim is stabilized, the emphasis shifts to the porch scene, and to the suspect. The evidence is organized within the geographical divisions, as there were multiple scenes divided among investigators.

7. Retailer Armed Robbery Scene

A clerk from a computer store called 911 on Christmas Eve, saying man entered the crowded store, approached the cashier and displayed a handgun to the clerk. He took some computers and left without paying for the merchandise.

Summary
Robbery achieved by presentation of firearm. No injured persons. Suspect still outstanding. Take was computers. Photos taken. DNA possible on receipt item. Fingerprints collected from cashier countertop.

To Do
DNA to Lab
Fingerprints to Central ID

Investigation
On 12/24/14, I responded to Hi-Technology Computers, 1255 West Chan Road to assist Officer Barajas with a robbery case. At 1801 I arrived and Officer Barajas provided me with the details of the case.

Evidence Administration
LT Brewer secured the front entrance with yellow crime tape as I arrived. I secured interior areas 1 and 3 when I arrived. Flynton Officers Jefferson and Payne arrived at 1845 HRS to view the security footage in the office.

I am the Primary CSI. I divided the store into subscenes based on the robber's path. I organized the investigation around subscenes to allow for multiple investigators to work simultaneously. I processed the interior of the store at the cash register, and the front door; subscenes A, B, and D.

Officer Levin is the Secondary CSI. He photographed the exterior, and processed the laptop displays scenes and the cables aisle. He also viewed the security video. See map.

Scene Security
Officer McMillan taped off the scene, and posted as a sentry before I arrived.

Security Video
I collected the security images from the manager and booked it as evidence. He used a brand new USB device for the images. I viewed the video on a computer. The footage shows the suspect entering the store, and touring the interior for about 10 minutes. He selected his items and went to the cashier. The cashier worked with the register, and turned back to the customer. After a brief interaction, the customer produced an object from his waistband in front. The camera image shows a blurry item, but the clerk backed away from the suspect, and he walked out. The video also shows the suspect not wearing gloves, and touching the glass counter top during the transaction.

Photographs
I photographed the victim at the scene in the clothes he wore during the robbery.

I collected 68 digital images.

Crime Scene Description (See sketch)
Hi-Technology Computers, 1255 W. Chan Road is on the north side of the Chan Road (westbound lanes), near the border with Flynton. The business is the sole tenant of the building, among a string of commercial business buildings. There is one retail entrance on the south side, 70 feet north of the street. There is no back entrance from the parking lots on the north side. The north side of the parking area opens into a residential neighborhood. The front wall is glass, but holiday promotional displays reduced visibility.

The store is 75 feet on the west axis by 60 feet on the north axis. Aisles fill the north section of the store, while aisles and other displays fill the south section. The repair section and restrooms are in the northeast corner. The sketch notes camera locations and their approximate fields of view. The floor tiles are 1 foot by 1 foot for reference.

There are four subscenes: A / B are the cash register counter, C is the displays, D is the doorway, and there is the exterior. The scene description integrates evidence.

Subscenes A / B are the cash register counter where the clerk was helping the suspect when he presented the gun. This subscene is 40 feet east of the west wall, 25 feet north of south wall. The area is south central in the store. The victim helped the suspect and the suspect showed him his handgun at the east cash counter. The two east side glass counters have a 4 feet north axis, by 2 feet east axis, and 3 feet elevation. The cash register rests atop a wooden case 2 feet north axis, by 2 feet east axis, and 3 feet elevation. The clerks stand on the west side of the counter, the customers on the east side. The cash register is at the south end.

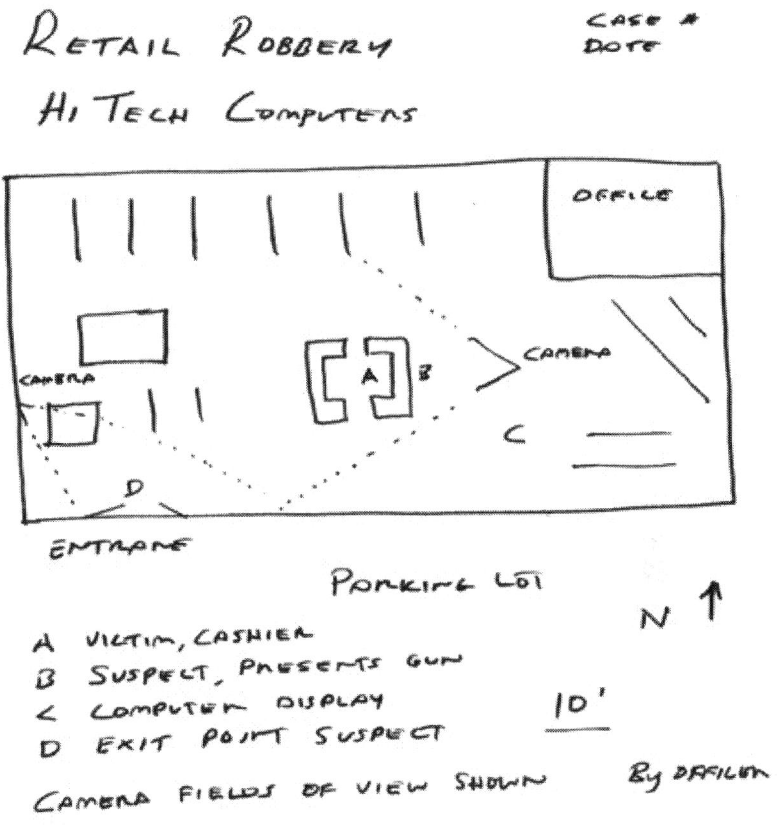

Evidence

When I arrived, I saw a sales receipt (G3) on the counter, at the south end of the glass case, 6 inches north of the cash register. The receipt showed a time stamp of 5:48 PM. The video showed the suspect taking the receipt from the victim and holding it for a few seconds.

Possible Biological Evidence
The video showed the suspect and victim handling the transaction receipt (G3). The victim provided a sample of his DNA for elimination.

Victim Carney consented to his DNA being searched. I filed his signed form. I designated the swab in the Property Section as G5. Prior to swabbing I donned fresh gloves to avoid cross contamination. I used a sterile swab without sterile water. I placed the swab in its own envelope and sealed the evidence after collection. I placed the items in the Crime Lab Freezer.

Latent Fingerprints
I dusted areas within the two the interior scenes to develop fingerprints. I used black powder applied with a fiberglass brush. I collected 9 samples from locations inside the business. I photographed the prints with ruler labels prior to collection for orientation.

I also collected elimination prints from the manager and the victim.

Subscenes A and B
Card #2. Large. Fingerprints at the cash counter. North counter top, east side, southeast corner. North of Card #3.

Card #3. Large. Fingerprints at the cash counter. Junction of north counter top and south countertop, east side. South of Card #2, north of Card #4.

Card #4. Large. Fingerprints at the cash counter. South countertop, north east corner. South of Card #3, north of Card #5.

Card #5. Large. Fingerprints at the cash counter. South countertop, north east corner. South of Card #4, north of Card #6.

Card #6. Large. Fingerprints at the cash counter. South countertop, east metal lip. South of Card #5, east of Card #8.

Card #7. Large. Fingerprints at the cash counter. South counter face, east glass, below metal lip. Below Card #4 and Card #5.

Card #8. Large. Fingerprints at the cash counter. South countertop, south of Card #5, west of Card #6.

Card #9. Large. Fingerprints on the cash tray. Back side, top.

See cards for orientation.

I forwarded the cards to the Regional Fingerprint Identification Unit.

Subscene C. Laptop displays. 20 feet west of the east wall, 12 feet north of south wall. investigator Levin processed this area. See his report for details.

Subscene D. Front double swinging glass doors with metal frames. Entry and exit point, 45 feet east of the west wall, south wall.

Latent Fingerprints
Same process as documented.
Card #1. Large. Fingerprints at the exit point. Point of Exit, east door, interior, glass. Right palm on the left door (east) as one exits. 65 feet west of east wall, 5 feet 6 inches elevation.

Exterior
Officers canvassed the area and found no signs of any additional evidence.

Step 1. Designate the Scene

Scene Decision Why is this a scene?

1. *Discovery* The investigator declared the scene by responding to the 911 of a crime at the store location. The business manager wanted the case investigated, thus opening the store to the investigators.

2. *Scene type* The investigator has only the retailer scene, and the best subscene is the cashier's counter.

3. *Scene Group*
a. Neighborhood.
b. Store.
c. Cashier stand.
d. Exit scene.
e. Displays.
f. Victim person.
g. Suspect person.
h. Receipt.
i. Suspect's gun.
j. Stolen merchandise.

4. *Search* Zone for the interior. An investigator searched the exterior neighborhood in a spiral pattern starting at the store and found no related scenes.

Step 2. Analyze the Scene

Scene Decision How does the scene work?

1. *Restrictiveness* The scene is an accessible hosting scene anyone can enter or leave during business hours, but the furnishings channel occupant paths, and activities.

2. *Volatility* The scene is stationary, and as it has solid borders it can be secured, and preserved from potential change.

3. *Function* The scene is an object scene, receiving evidence. The scene functions as a place for people to meet, and exchange money for goods. The scene contains items of value.

This public scene had items of value, but with high access during a crowded time there were many witnesses. Witnesses played little role in the case, but the idea can influence actions. The suspect in this case did not appear concerned about cameras, nor wearing gloves to protect his identity, and the camera showed this lack of concern. The main complication of scene tainting was avoided when the business shut, and isolated the crime scene.

4. *Capacity and Interaction Points* The scene has the hosting capacity for DNA, fingerprints, and patterns. The video may not be enough to match a suspect, but it can provide a pattern to help identify him. The scene also hosted the evidence artifacts taken by the suspect.

The glass counter top is the center of gravity, and appeared to be untouched after the crime. Security images show the suspect contact locations to help the investigator decide which subscene presents the best chance for evidence. The door handles are unlikely to produce a match because of the high number of people who touched it. The displays may offer similarly low returns on investment.

Step 3. Evaluate the Evidence Potential

Evidence Decision How would the evidence work in this scene?

1. *Production* Person scenes had contact with the counter tops, depositing fingerprints on them.

2. *Proof Ability* The fingerprints on the glass could prove presence at scene and identification. The video proves the actions, even if poor quality.

3. *Quality* DNA and fingerprints provide unique identifiers, but the DNA is from a high-traffic area which may retain prior DNA deposits. The fingerprints should provide high quality evidence, as the store was secured after the crime, and the glass itself is an excellent collector of prints. The gun has relevance, but an image of the gun is captured on video. The suspect left with the stolen items. Identifying evidence could place the suspect there.

4. *Timeline* The store's security video provides great actual times for the investigation, and the investigator can match it with the 911 call. This also shows relative time.

5. *Resilience* This evidence is somewhat delicate, but the investigator secured and collected evidence soon after the crime.

6. *Collection* The standard CSI tools will support the investigator's efforts to get the evidence. The investigator performed most of the processes in the field. The investigator will place the evidence in dry storage, and the freezer for biological evidence. The fingerprints will be forwarded to laboratories.

Step 4. Work the Evidence

Evidence Decision How to obtain the evidence from this scene?

1. *Critical Thinking* The investigator thought about the public scene as a place where items of value are sold for money, making it a target. The facts of the case indicate the man produced the gun to steal the computers at the cashier area, and touched the countertop in the process. Much of the preliminary work is done by watching the video to determine how and where the suspect interacted with the scene. The investigator decided fingerprints offered the best prospect to identify the suspect.

The public scene took immediate priority in the investigation because the suspect left, and the only physical contact he had with any entities was the public scene, at the counter.

2. *Information* Victim and witness statements, as well as watching the video covered the information about the case. The employees shut the store after the robbery, protecting the scene. The scene description is limited to the interior since there is no report of action outside the store. A sketch showed minimal evidence information, but addressed presence, choices, and actions.

3. *Photographs* Images from the surveillance video and those of evidence assist in documenting the crime as it happened, and the investigation efforts.

4. *DNA* The receipt may yield identifying evidence, but exhaustion of DNA evidence options brings forth fingerprint decisions.

5. *Fingerprints* Prints on the glass counter top present the best chance of identifying a suspect. The cashier station glass yielded plentiful fingerprint evidence, but a glass countertop would yield many prints any random day, providing no guarantee of identifying a suspect.

6. *Patterns* There is no pattern matching in the investigation for the public scene, such as shoe marks, or tool marks. The security video might be considered a pattern to match the suspect to if he is located. Research into the stolen computers could provide identifying information to seek activity by those particular machines on the internet.

7. *Artifacts* Evidence fragility surrounding preserving the potential DNA evidence on the cash receipt warrants its collection soon after discovery. Information makes the receipt priority evidence for collection and preservation.

8. *Report Production* The report starts with key evidence, because the video provides insights. The report moved into geographical based evidence because although there were subscenes, the main scene is the casher area, and all key evidence comes from there.

III. Private Scenes

Private scenes are restricted, smaller hosting scenes controlled by a person.

Step 1. Designate the Scene

Scene Decision Why is this a scene?

1. *Discovery* The private scene most often comes to the investigator's attention by a call from a victim, whether the victim controls the scene or not, or through investigation.

2. *Scene type* A private scene offers predictability through structure, as humans built or occupy most private scenes. The private scene is often well defined by man-made borders. It is usually closed, with fewer options, but can host as much evidence as public scenes.

Some examples of private space are houses, motor homes, and offices.

3. *Scene Group* Private scenes fit into larger public scenes in an absolute sense, but in a practical sense they are often the largest scene in a case, and host subscenes. There may be evidence outside what is considered the private crime scene. Often there can be a barrier to entry, making for an additional subscene.

4. *Search* Zone searches work best for most private scene searches, given the scenes' natural divisions. An open area private scene might warrant a lane search, or grid search. An investigator who fails to conduct a private scene walk through with a knowledgeable person may miss evidence, or spend resources on non-evidence. The tour will not always include all evidence and may have some bias included on the part of the guide.

Step 2. Analyze the Scene

Scene Decision How does the scene work?

1. *Restrictiveness* Private scenes provide restricted accessibility with privacy and tend to be smaller. Hard scene borders mean geographically defined scenes with limits. There are potentially fewer scenes to interact with a private scene.

2. *Volatility* Private scenes may change with higher volumes of scene interactions, but often the restrictiveness reduces the changeability. They are often protected from the elements. The scenes typically do not move, but there are exceptions, such as mobile homes. Private scenes may not have frequent occupants and this may delay reporting the crime, and reduce the evidence.

3. *Function* Private scenes are mostly the object scenes of a crime, even if they are controlled by the suspect. They host the subject and object scenes of the crime. Like public scenes, while there is legal ownership, anyone can control private scenes in contrast to ownership. Private scenes function as host locations for crimes, and sometimes travel routes, just as public scenes do. They can be targets, or bases of operation. The persons and other subscenes in them can have an anonymous connection to the hosting scene. This contrasts with car scenes, where the owner / occupants do not have an anonymous association with the hosting scene.

The ways private scenes function creates challenges for the investigator:

a. Some scenes can be restricted from the investigator, either by uncooperative suspects, victims, or third parties.

b. There may be no way to distinguish criminal activity evidence presence in the scene from benign activity evidence presence in the scene.

4. *Capacity and Interaction Points* Private scenes are usually man-made with greater evidence collection and carrying capacities, and easily locatable interaction points. Architecture contributes to more predictable evidence transfer points. With a lower volume of scenes interacting, the odds of relevant evidence go up, thus an isolated private scene could have a high capacity for evidence.

Private scenes have many potential interaction points for an investigator to consider when looking at a case:

a. Entry into a restricted scene can require effort and contact with the entry point. The entry and exit points may offer another evidence opportunities to prove presence and action via showing whether force or no force was used in entering the scene.

b. The path of travel within the scene, which is often a hallway, stairway, or elevator.

c. Any waiting zone, as sometimes people arrive at different times, and loitering can mean the production of evidence.

d. The center of gravity of the case, and the zone around it. This is often well defined within private scenes given the organized space.

e. Multiple people can control private places, and provide direct evidence of presence, and circumstantial evidence of action.

Barriers to entry often mean a protected suspect controlled scene during his time in it. Outsiders lack legitimate reasons for presence in the private scene, so someone may have difficulties explaining this evidentiary presence. Many people feel more comfortable committing crimes in their own space, so the suspect controlled private space may have evidence from outside scenes being brought in. Private scenes allow a suspect protected time to work and reduce evidence.

Step 3. Evaluate the Evidence Potential

Evidence Decision How would the evidence work in this scene?

1. *Production* Evidence can be produced by interaction of the private hosting scene with another subscene such as a person, or car, but it can also host evidence created between through the interaction of subscenes.

2. *Proof Ability* Private scene evidence should prove presence and action of a person in the hosting scene. Action and presence may be related, but not interchangeable, as presence is an action, and action is presence, but the presence may not prove a particular action.

3. *Quality* Private scene evidence is often protected, providing fewer persons legitimate access and interaction with it. The restrictiveness of the scene also increases the evidence's relevance since its presence in the scene is the result of deliberate decisions.

4. *Timeline* Private scene timelines may have pinpoint accurate actual times, since the scenes are structures, and can have monitoring systems. Often the times are relative with delayed reporting. The time of the 911 call may not be a good marker since the time past might be significant. On a relative scale the times can be accurate.

5. *Resilience* Private scene evidence may be resilient as any other evidence, but varies in how well it can resist forces of time, nature, environment, and

actions of persons in the scene. Evidence is often protected, but in a suspect controlled scene, it is vulnerable to destruction.

6. *Collection* An investigator may find coordinating evidence work for private scenes easier than public scenes due to smaller size, ease in securing and stabilization. The case may also require crime scene tape, and establishing an entry log.

Step 4. Work the Evidence

Evidence Decision How to obtain the evidence from this scene?

1. *Critical Thinking* The first three decisions indicate private scenes present the investigator with fewer decisions than public scenes. They exist within larger, often public scenes, and host other scenes with restricted access, and higher levels of predictability. Evidence production is often recognizable, given the high potential for an outsider in the scene who interacted with evidence transfer points.

An investigator must confirm the borders and entry points.

Determining how a person entered the scene indicates the actions taken to obtain presence. An investigator also looks at specific actions shown in the subscenes within the private scene. Private scene suspect activity includes efforts to prevent his evidence from transferring to the scene, whether it is his evidence in a victim controlled scene, or a victim's evidence in his controlled scene.

An involved person may provide a guided tour of the scene providing insight into evidence available to prove presence and action. Knowledge gain outweighs risks hindering evidence work. A person's habits tend to reflect in his private place as he believes the permanence of his privacy. Lifestyle indicators point to case evidence, baseline evidence, and clarifying departures from the norm.

Suspect entry to a private place can include aborted attempts before success. A thief may attempt to slide open windows before breaking a window or kicking a door.

2. *Information* Evidence work can support or refute a denial of presence by the suspect. Predefined scenes limit the volume of information for private scenes. A room has measurements established long before the crime. Available floor plans reduce an investigator's workload as he can just add commentary. Private scenes have history such as previous crimes. The

Internet provides usable scene information as do insurance companies and real estate businesses.

Private place accessibility helps define a suspect list. Private scenes have unwritten attendance lists of allowed people. Someone has authority over the scene. Considering the controlling person helps establish the relationships to the other persons. The investigators should document the person who granted consent to search and processing.

Sketches and diagrams explain private crime scene configurations and the spatial relationships between subscenes, and evidence.

3. *Photographs* Private scene photography with well-defined spaces may yield fewer images than public scenes, but space limitations create challenges. The photos can show configurations and relationships when supported by information.

4. *DNA* Restricted access makes biological material high yield evidence for private scenes. Finding DNA still challenges the investigator, but evidence collects in the contact and action points, such as blood on a broken window. Finding the useful and relevant DNA among the unrelated DNA poses a greater challenge. An investigator must support the DNA evidence with information. A person who declared his presence in the scene reduces the value of DNA evidence, but the victim may add to the information. DNA endurance reduces its efficacy as a private place may contain several profiles

5. *Fingerprints* Persons touch things inside a private scene, but finding the evidence challenges an investigator. Suspects may wear gloves in public and private scenes. Entry points often provide excellent material to collect fingerprints, as they are made out of glass, metal, and painted wood. As most private scenes are built, there are often hard materials near or at the center of gravity of the crime.

6. *Patterns* Matching patterns in private scenes presents as the scene as the recipient of another scene's action to execute the crime, like a tool mark on a doorframe. The private scene may be the marking half, and leave a mark on the outsider scene.

7. *Artifacts* An investigator often finds evidence artifacts either brought in, or made there. Sometimes the artifacts were already present in the scene, and became the tools of opportunity and thus artifacts. The items can have many different purposes, from entry, to action inside. Private scenes can present evidence in layers, requiring regular re-photographing, and attention to documenting the positioning.

8. *Report Production* Private scene reports are structured around showing presence and action like other scenes, but also include coverage of the barriers to entry. The descriptions often start outside the scene, and move inward. The content is may show how a person entered through the barriers to the scene. The report is often geographical or locational, with key evidence points by area.

Private Scene Scenarios

8. Office Burglary Scene
9. Hotel Room Gun Scene
10. Residential Burglary Scene

8. Office Burglary Scene

The facilities manager from a large technology company called 911 to report someone broke into their company overnight.

Summary
Commercial burglary including data system breach. Suspect outstanding. Photos taken. Fingerprints collected. Evidence items recovered.

To Do
Fingerprints to Central ID
Evidence items to lab.

Investigation
On May 3, 2015 at 7:30 AM I arrived to the scene and found the impacted areas unsecured by the company, but closed off from the public. I conducted a walk-though with the facilities manager, Jason Tweed. He indicated the impacted areas, and showed me potential evidence items. Tweed provided me with an annotated building map.

Scene Description
The building, 2219 E Magnet Rd. is occupied by High Speed Database Corporation. They sell computer software pertaining to the management of databases. The building has both office space and an IT room. The building is on the south side of Magnet Road west of the McKeever Expressway. The building is bordered in all directions by a parking lot in an industrial neighborhood.

The building has three stories totaling 74,000 square feet; 200 feet on the west axis, and 120 feet on the north axis. Personnel doors provide access on the north, west, south and east sides. Any of the ground floor personnel doors are the possible point of entrance. The lobby security video was inoperative at the time. The same lock model secured all doors in the building. It has a lever handled lock, with a key cylinder made of brushed steel or aluminum. There are glass windows on all sides.

The majority of the first floor had construction equipment and materials, and bore no evidence of suspect activity. The second floor showed no indication of suspect activity either.

The third floor is an open office with has cubicles in the northwest, northeast, and southwest quadrants.

The IT room is in the center of the floor, with has limited card key access entry logging. The suspect entered the IT room, and corporate technicians are working on determining the actions with the data systems. Technicians have confirmed a data system breech, but there is no physical damage, and their technicians are working on determining what the suspect did with the computers. Tweed did not want processing of the room due to potential damage of the equipment.

There were three areas along the north side of the floor burglarized. A is a cube in the northeast corner, numbered 1.3.033. B is an unnumbered printer station northcentral. C is an unnumbered desk area in the northwest.

Subscenes and Evidence
I documented the collected items on a property report.

Subscene A. Cubicle 1.3.033 is in the northeast quadrant. It belongs to Bill Reed, IT manager. His cube housed a safe guarding the most guarded company passwords. I saw a 3/8 inch hole bored into the lock. Papers atop the safe concealed the drilling.

I collected the papers left on top of the secret safe. (Item 4).

Subscene B is the printer station, north central. The printer is linked to the company's system, and prints for anyone on the network. Tweed showed me a map he found left on the printer.

I collected the paper building map left on the printer. (Item 1). The tool used to access the map, and print it is still unknown.

Subscene C. is Blaine Gerd's desk. Tweed showed me the papers that were moved when the suspect took the computer from the desk. He also specified the clock that was moved.

I collected the following.
Clock moved by the suspects to take a computer (Item 2).
Paper moved by the suspects when they took the computer (Item 3).

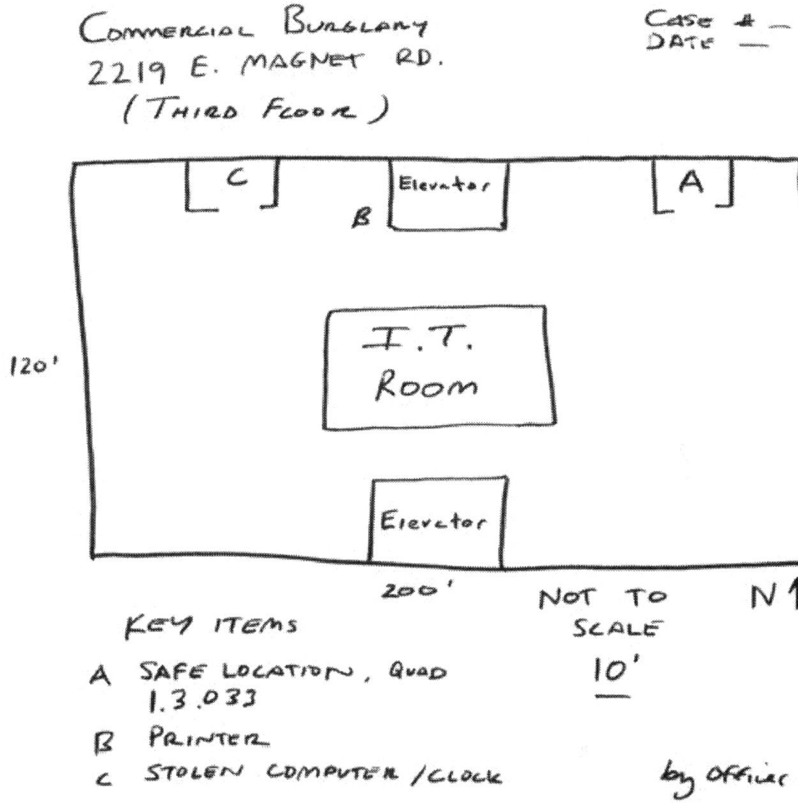

Photographic evidence
I photographed the scenes and documented my investigation using my department issued camera. See digital files for metadata recorded settings. I used a flash, natural and artificial light. The photos document evidence in their locations.

Fingerprint Evidence and Processing
I found no viable area at the scene, and collected no fingerprints from the scene.

Cyanoacrylate Print Development
I attempted to develop fingerprints on the moved clock. I processed them in the cyanoacrylate chamber to develop finger prints. I dusted them using black powder. I collected 3 fingerprint cards. See cards for details.

Card #1 (Large) top and sides of white metal clock.
Card #2 (Large) front of white metal clock.
Card #3 (Large) sides of canned snacks.

Chemical Print Development
I used heptane ninhydrin to develop fingerprints on the papers. I bathed the papers in the solution for 20 seconds and hung them to dry in the fuming chamber with humid air.

The map from the printer had several crisp fingerprints on it. I photographed the prints with a scale to preserve the evidence, and sent the disc of photos with the fingerprint cards.

I forwarded the cards and CD to the Regional Police Department Identification Unit.

Step 1. Designate the Scene

Scene Decision Why is this a scene?

1. *Discovery* The investigator declared the scene by responding it after the business requested an investigation. The business limited the investigation.

2. *Scene type* The private office scene contains multiple the subscenes impacted by the suspect.

3. *Scene Group*
a. Neighborhood.
b. Building.
c. Third floor.
d. IT room.
e. Cubicle with the clock.
f. Cubicle with the safe.
g. Transit scenes.
h. Suspect.
i. Office occupants / victim persons.
j. Printer, which had the map.
k. Map.
l. Computer tool the suspect used to print the map remains unknown.

4. *Search* The multitude of scenes in different areas indicates a zone search. The possible travel paths appear to offer little in the way of related scenes.

Step 2. Analyze the Scene

Scene Decision How does the scene work?

1. *Restrictiveness* The scene is a restricted access hosting scene with control points, even if the point of entry is not determined. The space is structured, but not to the point where the order of events is clear.

2. *Volatility* The scene is stationary, and indoors meaning it can be controlled and preserved; however employees have high potential to taint the scene.

3. *Function* The scene is an object scene receiving evidence. The scene functions as an office, meaning limited people use it, but a large group over time. There were items of value in the scene, but given the IT room breach, the focus appears to be information more than taking a laptop.

This private scene offered the suspect privacy as once he gained entry, there was no burglar alarm set off. He was able to work for several hours. The suspect had to navigate a large scene himself. He printed off a map, which would turn out to be key evidence. The office building is a restricted area, but people could have tainted the crime scenes.

4. *Capacity and Interaction Points* The scene has the hosting capacity for DNA, fingerprints, and pattern matching for hand tools, and information machines.

The investigator may be able to find identifying evidence (DNA and fingerprints) of the suspect and victims contacting the hosting scene given the clear indications of what the suspect made contact with. The center of gravity is the map on the printer, as it will provide the identifying prints of the suspect, but it is within the private office scene. There may also be evidence artifacts left behind in the scene.

The office building scene has elements of a public scene since it hosts person traffic during business hours. The crime happened during a non-public time making it private and proving the suspect forced his way in. The thief travelled from the public part of the business, to the most secure and private part, the server room, meaning there may be less evidence confusion in higher restrictive locations. The possible points of entry showed no damage, but those subscenes were not secured. The walk-though helped identify the centers of gravity. The investigator would not have recognized the map in its context without the manager's input, and might have focused on a much lower payoff scene like the doors.

The IT room will be handled by the company's internal investigation; their technicians had already contaminated the scene prior to police arrival.

Step 3. Evaluate the Evidence Potential

Evidence Decision How would the evidence work in this scene?

1. *Production* Person scenes had contact with the evidence items such as the map, depositing fingerprints on them.

2. *Proof Ability* The fingerprints on the map could prove presence at scene, but also prove action, as the map is used to navigate the crime scene.

3. *Quality* The suspect printed map is the most relevant evidence artifact within the scenes. It shows his presence and his actions as well as potentially holding evidence. The fingerprints on the map have high quality since the map was recently printed, and protected in the scene. Fingerprints provide unique identifiers, and the map is unique to that building.

The drilled out safe presents minimal evidence compared to the map, but given the contents of the safe, it indicates action. The clock and other papers have similar quality. The clock also uniqueness, as few people would touch someone else's clock at work.

4. *Timeline* The timeframe is large at the start of the case, and the forensics for the computers have not been reported yet, so there is no actual timeline. The printer may have data about when the map was printed. Until there is more detailed information the timeline is relative. The keys events were the suspect making entry, printing a map, and finding the safe to drill for the key, entering the IT room, and leaving. The thefts from the cubicles happened between entry and exit.

5. *Resilience* This evidence is somewhat delicate, but the investigator collected pretty soon after the crime. Photographs will preserve the scene showing the fingerprints.

6. *Collection* The standard CSI tools will support the investigator's efforts to get the evidence. The private scene offers security from the elements, but there are still employees who come and go, damaging the evidence. Collecting the map after photographing it in place was a priority action for the investigator.

Commercial burglary scenes are often cleaned by a well-meaning employee before police arrive. Scene alteration documentation should come towards the beginning of the report. The employee may see an investigation as of small significance compared to the image of a stable and strong business. Supervisors want to continue business with minimal interruption. Small personal losses impact some employees more than major employer losses. Victims jeopardize collection, which made safeguarding the map even more important.

The investigator performed some of the processes in the field. The ninhydrin and other chemicals used to reveal the prints are in the lab, and are not brought to the field. Photos collect the fingerprints in this case. The DNA and fingerprints will be forwarded to laboratories.

Step 4. Work the Evidence

Evidence Decision How to obtain the evidence from this scene?

1. *Critical Thinking* The investigator thought about the private scene as a meeting place where a limited group of persons spent time doing work in their personal spaces, and travelled in between personal spaces in public places. A large population of persons regularly interacted with the same points.

The manager provided guidance for evidence and identified a map which was not something a routine person who belonged there would have printed. The investigator understood fingerprints on the map could prove presence, and action. The map was still just a bet until the prints could be matched to a person, and the person was deemed to have no legitimate reason for being in the scene.

2. *Information* Statements provide good context about the potential evidence in the scene. In this case the facilities manager provided contextual information to identify evidence.

3. *Photographs* Photos support the evidence and the prints developed with heptane ninhydrin are temporary, and will not remain clear. Photos are necessary for preservation, transfer to other agencies, and analysis.

4. *DNA* The investigator found no potential DNA evidence in the assessment analysis. Only a viable sample earns an identified suspect through DNA sequencing, which could have been through the oils left on the fingerprints.

5. *Fingerprints* Locating and collecting the fingerprints on the paper maps proved presence and action to solve the case. The suspect printed the maps during the crime, defining the fingerprints' recency.

The investigator used multiple processes with different applications helped obtain the fingerprints. The investigator found no usable prints on the host scene. The investigator evaluated evidence items with the potential to yield usable prints when processed with additional lab based processes. The prints developed with heptane ninhydrin offer a great evidence opportunity as the origin of the evidence is established, and there are few prints on the paper.

6. *Patterns* The drilled safe provides a potential pattern matching opportunity, but the investigator cannot find the drill bit to match it. There were no identifiable marks anywhere else.

7. *Artifacts* The maps show intent, and they hold can a fingerprint for a technician to develop with chemicals later. The fingerprints on the printed maps present the best form of identification evidence.

8. *Report Production* This is a geographical report with emphasis on particular evidence.

9. Hotel Room Gun Scene

An officer discovered a stolen firearm within a hotel room while investigating suspicious activity, and requested an investigator.

Summary
Firearm possession case, three suspects in custody. Photos taken. Fingerprints. Firearm and drugs recovered.

To Do
DNA collection from suspects.
Fingerprints to Central ID.
Evidence items to lab.

Investigation
At 15:35 HRS on 12/12/12 I arrived to the scene. Officer Gillman briefed me on the details of the case when he conducted a walk-though with me to explain the locations and evidence.

He detailed in his report how he obtained permission from the residents to search their room.

Crime Scene Description
The Nomad Inn at 2232 W. Richland Ave. is a hotel, with over 60 rooms. The hotel is L shaped, with the convergence in the northeast corner. Room 113 is on the ground floor, of the east wing, near the south end. The front door faces west. I found the suspects' car (WA 1234567) parked 65 feet to the northwest of the front door of room 124.

The room is 25 feet on the west axis, and 12 feet on the north axis. The entry door is in the southwest corner. The bathroom is in the northeast corner. The room has two double beds with their heads against the north wall. The bureau sits along the south wall, with a TV on top. The sink area is against the east wall in the southeast corner. Officer Gilman told me he discovered the weapon, and after rendering it safe, he placed it on the sink. I saw 3 bullets of 9mm hollow point ammunition in the magazine.

A. The built-in wall tissue dispenser was installed in the wall, to the north of the sink, 4 feet elevation, 2 feet west of the east wall. I saw the lid was on the counter. The box of tissues also rested on the counter.

B. Officer Gilman found the green leafy substance on top of the refrigerator and the baggie was filled with 4 small baggies. Total weight was 28 grams.

C. The luggage for the three suspects sat on the floor between the refrigerator and the gun.

Crime Scene Sketch
I created a crime scene sketch to show the layout of the room, and property locations in relation to the gun.

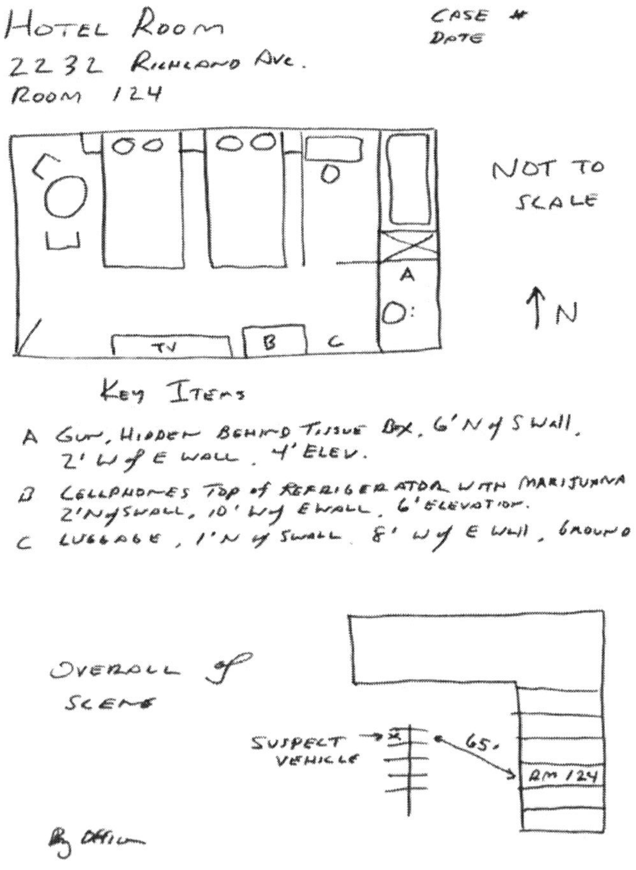

Evidence Items
I removed tissue box from the wall using a hammer to pry the nails. I wore gloves.

I collected the firearm, its magazine, and ammunition from the sink area.

I collected suspect Clifton's $487 for safekeeping / evidence.

I booked a copy of the rental agreement for the room showing Kegan paying for two days.

Officer Gillman handed me five smartphones he collected from the scene. See his report for details about the phones' locations and attribution information.

Officer Gillman booked the marijuana. See his report.

DNA Evidence
I spoke with each of the three suspects in the jail and requested their consent to collect DNA. Each refused to provide a sample.

I forwarded the gun to the regional lab for DNA evidence and fingerprints. See the Tools section on guns.

Tissue Box Prints
I attempted to develop fingerprints on item 3, the face plate for the tissue dispenser. I processed the item using black powder. I processed 5 print cards.

Card #1 (large) Exterior, Side of face plate.
Card #2 (large) Exterior, Side of face plate.
Card #3 (large) Exterior, Side of face plate.
Card #4 (large) Interior, Side of face plate.
Card #5 (large) Interior, Side of face plate.

I forwarded the cards to Big City Police Department Identification Unit.

I attempted to develop fingerprints on the tissue box. I processed the item in the Cosmopolitan Police Department's cyanoacrylate chamber to develop finger prints. I dusted the item using black powder. I processed 1 print card.

Card #6 (large) Tissue box (Item 4) Bottom of the box.

I forwarded the card to Big City Police Department Identification Unit.

Fingerprint Known Suspects
I copied the booking sheets for the three suspects and attached them to the fingerprint cards I sent to the Central Identification Unit, for comparison.

Step 1. Designate the Scene

Scene Decision Why is this a scene?

1. *Discovery* The suspects established their presence by being there when the officer arrived. There is not an outsider in this scene, but the weapon, is the outsider artifact, or scene. The investigator declared the scene by responding to the scene after his colleague declared it a crime scene.

There is some privacy in a private scene as this hotel room is like a rented residence to the people staying there. The business supported the investigation, and at some point the room will revert back to their control.

2. *Scene type* A hotel room presents the unique challenge of being a private place, with a lot of unknown people. Scene control changes often with new residents, creating an environment with a lot of possibilities.

3. *Scene Group*
a. Neighborhood.
b. Hotel.
c. Hotel room.
d. Tissue box.
e. Suspect car.
f. Suspect persons.
g. Gun from the tissue box.
h. Drugs.
i. Cellphones.
j. Luggage.
k. Money.

4. *Search* Zone.

Step 2. Analyze the Scene

Scene Decision How does the scene work?

1. *Restrictiveness* The scene is a limited accessible hosting scene; a few people have access per day, but over time, there can be many people with history in the scene, thus, recency is tied to accessibility. The restrictiveness of the scene created a situation for the suspects to explain their denial of a connection to the gun.

2. *Volatility* The scene is stationary, but has the high potential to change, as maid service is scheduled every day, and new potential residents rent the room.

3. *Function* The scene is an object scene, receiving the action of hiding a gun. Any hotel room scene can function as a residence, and meeting place, which often means unguarded actions by occupants. A hotel room can serve as a person's home, but hotel rooms have many functions as locations for crimes; from murders to financial crimes and the setting for many an extramarital affair. The suspect(s) chose the scene. It presented temporary privacy and security with the vulnerability of records, and non-permanence.

The gun stash location was intended to be a place to store paper handkerchiefs. The suspect used the spot as a place for hiding something, and is hidden, and restrictive. Any identifying evidence on it presents a presumption of knowledge by the person whose evidence is attached to it.

4. *Capacity and Interaction Points* Hotel rooms have a lot of occupants over time, and their evidence is not cleared out with each new occupant. The scene has the hosting capacity for information, DNA, fingerprints, and patterns. There is not a lot of challenge to connecting the residents to the room they rented; luggage and the billing information show presence. The challenge lies in connecting persons to the contraband items in the room, and eliminating all other possibilities.

The area around the tissue box is the center of gravity, as it will provide the identifying prints of the suspect, at the stash location of the weapon. The cellphones, drugs, and luggage may also provide evidence, however the further removed from the gun, the less value they have in the case.

The interaction points in a hotel room are like those in a home, and presence by the suspects is easy to prove. There are the entry way points, including door areas, and windows. There is a bathroom where a person uses the toilet, shower, and sink. Another interaction point for a hotel room is the billing to pay for it.

The suspects controlled the scene, so it is more challenging to prove presence and interaction at the points of the crime in a way that shows them to be only for crime. In this case the facial tissue holder was an area of interaction for the suspects.

Step 3. Evaluate the Evidence Potential

Evidence Decision How would the evidence work in this scene?

1. *Production* The majority of evidence in this case is produced by persons touching things like the tissue dispenser.

2. *Proof Ability* Fingerprints on the paper box, and the metal container could prove presence at scene at the very point where the firearm was hidden. Identifying evidence may also prove the action of possessing a firearm. The drugs, cash, and number of cellphones may indicate a lifestyle of drug sales, but information could also be used as a way to seek evidence.

3. *Quality* The evidence located at the stash location has the most relevant evidence as it indicates presence and action. The fingerprints were located on a restricted scene a hotel guest would not normally touch. Persons had contact with the stash location, depositing fingerprints on the scene. Fingerprints provide unique identifiers, and coupled with an unlikely place to touch they provide strong evidence

4. *Timeline* The hotel room timeframe may start with check-in as an actual time, and include police action, which is also an actual time. The other times are relative, such as when the gun was hidden. An external source may provide a timestamp, such as a cellphone photo.

5. *Resilience* The evidence is hardy, but the scene will be modified by removing the tissue box holder. Photographs will preserve the scene before processing, and show the fingerprints.

6. *Collection* The standard CSI tools will support the investigator's efforts to get the evidence. The investigator performed some of the processes in the field. Photos are critical for the fingerprints. The investigator processed the items for prints at HQ. Sometimes it is better to address all evidence needs at once.

The private scene offers protection from the elements. There are no exigencies or concerns to modify the order of processing. The scene work for this case is limited to the hotel room. The gun, drugs, and cellphone are separate subscenes, addressed elsewhere.

Step 4. Work the Evidence

Evidence Decision How to obtain the evidence from this scene?

1. *Critical Thinking* The investigator first saw the suspects in the parking lot, a very public area near the private areas of hotel rooms. The investigator thought about the private scene of the hotel room as a temporary home, and as a potential meeting place where a person could do anything he might in a home, office, or other place.

The investigator theorized while there would be not any outsiders in the scene, there would be many outsiders' identifying material still in the scene. The private scene hosted different persons with different reasons for being there, and different actions in the scene.

In this case, the scene was under the domain and control of the already identified suspect person. This allowed the investigator to more on to the more relevant quest to decide how to obtain evidence to prove who touched the inside of the tissue box.

The stash location is a supporting scene for actual weapon scene, but if the evidence on the weapon turned out to be inconclusive, the surrounding scene could make the case work. The hidden gun presented its own subscenes of the gun, and the hiding spot. The investigator outsourced for processing, but the hiding spot presented a scene to connect to a person's presence by touch, and actions of hiding the weapon.

2. *Information* The investigating officer oriented the investigator to the scene during the walk-through assessment. A sketch would not strengthen scene understanding, as the photos cover the items and their locations. The rental agreement establishes presence.

3. *Photographs* The photographs of the hiding spot can explain it better than words by showing how it works.

4. *DNA* While the fingerprints are evidence to show access to the gun hiding spot, the DNA on the gun may present evidence to take the investigation in another direction to show a more historical connection to a crime weapon. There is no question about the presence of the suspects in the room, only with the weapon.

The request for suspect DNA may later result in a search warrant to collect samples from each.

5. *Fingerprints* Proof of contact by fingerprints confirmed activity within the scene, and presence at the hiding spot. A person could deny knowing about a hidden gun in a high-traffic hotel room, requiring the investigator prove presence on the gun. The investigator used black powder for printing the tissue box, but processing it with cyanoacrylate increases the chances of enhancing the prints. The cardboard box may absorb the fingerprint oils, and the glue maximizes the prints for collection.

6. *Patterns* There is no pattern evidence at this point in the investigation.

7. *Artifacts* The hotel room scene evidence around the gun supports the possession allegation. An officer discovered the gun in a hidden location within a high population location, providing a defense in a hotel room case (or any other case involving shared space). The *Tools* section covers the firearm, drugs, and phones as scenes.

8. Report Production The report starts with the other officer's discoveries, and goes into the geographical discovery of evidence.

10. Residential Burglary Scene

A woman called 911 after she returned home from a long weekend to find her home burglarized. A thief ransacked her bedroom, and stole her jewelry.

Summary
Residential burglary, suspect outstanding. Photos taken. Swabs collected. Fingerprints taken. Evidence items recovered.

To Do
Fingerprints to Central ID
Evidence items to lab.
DNA swabs to lab.

Crime Scene Investigation
On Sunday 1/1/16 at 7:30 PM I arrived to the scene and spoke with the resident. She invited me in and requested I investigate the scene. She provided me with full access permission to the home. She said she locked her residence and left town for the weekend on Friday at 6:00 PM. She came home at 7:00 PM on Sunday evening to find her back door kicked in and her home ransacked. She provided a list of stolen items. She did not know of any suspect in the case. The victim walked me through the scene, and she indicated evidence.

Security of Scene
The home has no burglar alarm, no cameras, and no dogs.

The victim told me her boyfriend Karl Van Loren was the only authorized recent visitor in her home. She provided his contact information. The private residence scene hosted no external guests.

Neighborhood Canvass
Officer Ponder contacted the following residences.
565 Willow Ave. Home all weekend, nothing seen or heard.
569 Willow Ave. Out of town.
568 Willow Ave. Noticed a magazine sales person Sunday morning. 25 year old white female. 5'6" tall brown hair. Dressed in gray sweatshirt and blue jeans. Rhonda Farnsworth, available for contact 555–555-5555.

Crime Scene Description
The single family home at 567 Willow Avenue is a single-story, 3 bedroom residence. The house sits on the north side of the street, with residential neighbors. The front door faces south to the street, and is visible to passersby. The front door has a clear glass window and windows adjacent to it. Two undamaged locks secure the front door. I saw no tool marks. The kitchen window is to the east of the front door, and obscured by curtains.

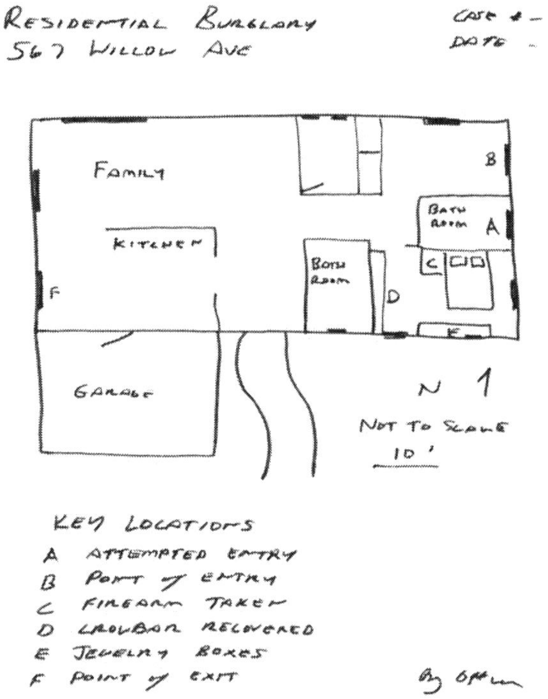

Unlocked gates provide backyard access on the east and west sides of the home. A 6 foot fence surrounds the back yard. The home has no video cameras, burglar alarms, or dogs. The owners converted the garage to a family room not for car storage. Two undamaged locks secured the rear door. I saw no tool marks.

The undamaged sliding patio door on the west wall of the home, 20 feet north of the west gate was open when I arrived.

Attempted Point of Entry, east bathroom
The suspect attempted to gain entry by the east bathroom window. The burglar removed the window screen, and left it on the ground. The window is on the east wall, 12 feet south of the north wall. The window measures 2 feet 10 inches wide, by 3 feet 10 inches tall, with an elevation of 5 feet 8 inches. A safety pin allows the window to open a maximum of 2 inches.

Point of Entry
The suspect gained entry by the northeast bedroom window. The window is on the east wall, 3 feet south of the north wall. The window was not broken. I saw no tool marks on the window. The lock on the window was undamaged, and in the lock position, the window was ajar. The screen was on the ground. The window measured 1 foot 2 inches wide, by 3 feet 10 inches tall, with an elevation of 3 feet 10 inches. The window was 2 feet south of the north wall of the home.

Locational Evidence Notes:

Family room, northwest. Not ransacked.

Kitchen and dining area, west central. Not ransacked. Sliding patio door, point of exit.

Garage, northeast corner. Not ransacked. Nothing reported stolen.

Bathroom, east central, small window ajar. Not ransacked.

Master bedroom, south east. Ransacked. The bed head was against the east wall. The bureau was against the north wall. The victim stored the firearm in the northwest night stand.

The jewelry box from the bureau was left on the bed. I collected swab S1 from the heart shaped box on the bed.

I found a foot long crowbar on the floor of the bedroom in front of the closet door.

I collected swabs S2 and S3 from jewelry boxes on the bureau. See photos.

North central and north east bedrooms ransacked.

I saw no indication of a staging scene.

Possible Biological Evidence
I collected possible DNA evidence. I designated the swabs in the Property Section as ES. (Evidence Swab). I collected some swabs with sterile water, and designated them with +SW. I donned fresh gloves for each collection to avoid cross contamination. I used a sterile swab for each. I placed each swab in its own envelope and sealed as evidence. I placed the items in the Crime Lab Freezer. I took photographs of each swab during collection.

Swab S0, and S4 are plain swabs to start and finish the process with controls.

The victim consented to her DNA being searched.

Latent Fingerprints
I dusted areas on the exterior and interior of the residence to develop fingerprints. I used black powder applied with a fiberglass brush. I developed two collectible samples from the residence. I discarded the three unsuccessful attempts.

Card #1. Large. Crowbar.
Card #2. Large. Top of bureau
Discard, window sill bottom, point of entry, family room window. No prints
Discard, master bedroom nightstand top, no prints
Discard, sliding patio door, smudges, no prints.

See cards for orientation.

Physical Evidence
I collected the crowbar from the scene.

Step 1. Designate the Scene

Scene Decision Why is this a scene?

1. *Discovery* The investigator declared the scene by responding to the victim's residence at her request.

2. *Scene type* The victim's residence is a private scene, enclosed in a structure.

3. *Scene Group*
a. Neighborhood.
b. Residence.
c. Point of entry window.
d. Rooms.
e. Transit routes in home.

f. Bedroom.
g. Jewelry boxes.
h. Bureau that held the firearm.
i. Suspect person.
j. Victim person.
k. Victim's boyfriend.
l. Crowbar.

4. *Search* The multitude of scenes in different areas indicates a zone search.

Step 2. Analyze the Scene

Scene Decision How does the scene work?

1. *Restrictiveness* This is a restricted access hosting scene controlled by the victim. Any evidence indicating a person's presence would require an explanation.

2. *Volatility* The scene is stationary, and has low potential to change, as it is protected, and the victim chose to allow the investigator to work the scene.

3. *Function* The scene is an object scene, receiving evidence. The scene functions as a private residence, with occasional guests.

The suspect chose a residential scene to burgle. The victim was out of town for a prolonged period. The obscured bathroom window provided a place to gain entry out of sight of potential witnesses. There is no indication of a security system. The main complication is the addition of the victim's boyfriend's potential evidence in the home. This is mitigated by his cooperation, and the knowledge of his potential impact on the crime scene.

4. *Capacity and Interaction Points* The scene has the hosting capacity for DNA, fingerprints, and patterns. The information about the stolen artifacts is hosted there too, and may be useful if the items are found.

The suspect interacted with several points in the home starting with the point of entry, which were the window and surrounding areas. There may be prints by the point of entry. The suspect's path inside the home is not obvious. The center of gravity is in the bedroom at the bureau where the suspect interacted with the jewelry box. The area around the jewelry box will potentially provide the identifying prints of the suspect.

Step 3. Evaluate the Evidence Potential

Evidence Decision How would the evidence work in this scene?

1. *Production* Persons had contact with the scene, possibly leaving fingerprints. Leaving the crowbar in the scene created evidence.

2. *Proof Ability* The crowbar shows the intentional break-in. The fingerprints on the jewelry box and bureau could prove presence at scene, and action.

3. *Quality* The restrictive scene means any evidence connected with a suspect inside is relevant to the crime. The fingerprints on the residence scene could provide excellent evidence as unique identifiers. The crowbar could be a unique piece of evidence if a tool mark connects it with other scenes. Tools to break in are easier to connect. The crowbar is good evidence, but it is portable, and could have been brought into the scene by someone other than the person identified. A person could borrow a crowbar from a friend to commit a crime.

4. *Timeline* The timeframe is pretty large at the start of the case, and there is nothing to indicate an actual timeline. The suspect broke in, and took the items from the bureau, leaving his tool. Then he left. This is all relative.

5. *Resilience* The evidence is hardy, and secured. Photographs will preserve the scene showing the fingerprints.

6. *Collection* The standard CSI tools will support the investigator's efforts to get the evidence. The private residence scene offers protection from the elements. There are no exigencies or concerns to modify the order of processing. Photos are critical for the fingerprints. The DNA and fingerprints will be forwarded to laboratories.

Step 4. Work the Evidence

Evidence Decision How to obtain the evidence from this scene?

1. *Critical Thinking* The investigator thought about the private scene of the home where a person lived with limited, authorized guests sometimes in the scene. The investigator knew the thief was not a regular presence in the home, and his actions of breaking in, and ransacking may hold the identifying evidence of his presence. The bedroom is the center of gravity for evidence of interaction, and where the suspect left a tool.

2. *Information* Victims provide pre-crime insight as they know their own homes. The information covered how the scene was before and after the

crime. The abbreviated sketch identifies source item locations and not DNA and fingerprints.

The victim disclosed a potential tainting of the crime scene. If the fingerprint database has Mr. Van Loren's fingerprints, eliminating him as a suspect early saves time. He said he spent time in the home, and touched parts of the scene. An investigator should obtain his prints to rule him out. The potential exists for investigators going after the wrong person, and wasting resources while other investigative avenues may lead to the real suspect's evidence.

Officer often canvass the area, and while seeking witnesses find evidence dropped by the suspects, as well as statements pointing to evidence. The 50 hour timeframe dilutes potential leads.

3. *Photographs* Photos show the results of the crime, and evidence locations.

4. *DNA* The scene description has DNA swab samples integrated into it, and photos show the exact sampling locations.

5. *Fingerprints* The fingerprints in the case are present at the center of gravity, but could belong to the victim. They could identify the suspect several months into the future.

6. *Patterns* The suspect did not use the tool to break in, however the evidence item of the bar could be retained for comparison to similar crimes with tool marks.

7. *Artifacts* The crowbar may yield a DNA sample connected to a suspect, but a fingerprint on the victim's property is another goal to connect a suspect by actions, not just his property within the victim's home. The crowbar may connect the suspect to other similar crimes by action and presence. The window was unlocked prior to the crime, reducing odds of a tool mark. The suspect could have misplaced the tool during the crime.

8. *Report Production* The investigation emphasizes evidence by location. An abbreviated writing style often best communicates points in large reports.

IV. Car Scenes

Car scenes are limited access, smaller, well defined hosting scenes and tools.

Step 1. Designate the Scene

Scene Decision Why is this a scene?

1. *Discovery* The car scene can come to an investigator's attention by a report from an involved party, or when the investigator on-views the car (and driver) involved in suspicious activity.

2. *Scene type* A car scene offers high predictability through structure, as humans built all car scenes. The car is a well-defined, restrictive hosting scene, capable of moving from scene to scene, and capable of many roles and options.

Some examples of car scenes are sedans, and vans, but also motorhomes, and bicycles.

3. *Scene Group* Car scenes fit into larger public scenes such as driving on a road, or parking in a lot. They also fit into private scenes, such as in garages. They host subscenes inside including person, and tools. There may be evidence outside what is considered the car crime scene. Often there is a barrier to entry, making for an additional subscene. Car scenes also include subscenes of value including record keeping on-board computers, pattern-making tools like tires, and component subscenes such as trace evidence to be collected.

4. *Search* Predefined divisions in a car lend themselves to zone searches, and work well when lacking a guide for an assessment.

Step 2. Analyze the Scene

Scene Decision How does the scene work?

1. *Restrictiveness* Hard scene borders mean a strong layer of security to entry, and they are defined scenes with limits. They tend to be smaller and fewer scenes interact with and within the interior car scene, but the exterior is accessible.

2. *Volatility* Car scenes may change with higher volumes of scene interactions, but often the restrictiveness reduces the changeability. A suspect may get a car detailed and change the evidence potential inside. Car interiors are often protected from the elements, but the outsides are not. The scenes are highly mobile, making finding the car scenes themselves a challenge in some cases.

3. *Function* Car scene interiors are object scenes receiving evidence, but they may be extensions of a person scene, and can act like subject scenes. The exteriors can be object scenes to receive, but they can also be the subject scenes when the car was controlled by a person as a tool to perform a function. There is legal ownership but anyone can control car scenes in contrast to ownership.

The function of a car can change based on who controls it during a crime. Car scenes function as transportation, host locations, targets, and tools for crimes. They may support crimes by conveying people and things, or be at the center of gravity.

Mobile scenes offer private and public components while traversing public scenes. Car scenes offer mobility, security and anonymity with the vulnerability of identifiability and potential loss of the car as an object. An investigator may not notice parked cars at scenes. Cars also have to be stored, making them a potential liability to the owner.

Car scene cases have similar pitfalls to private and public scenes in conducting the walk-through, or assessment with a knowledgeable person who might give good information. A victim may explain a suspect controlled car scene. The ways car scenes function creates challenges for the investigator:

a. Victims or witnesses have brief glances at mobile scenes.

b. Cars move, challenging locating the scenes.

c. A suspect who stops using or discards a car reduces the odds of solving the case.

d. Several people may have legitimate history in the car. An investigator struggles to prove one person occupied the driver's seat.

e. Exposure and human action with the car can limit evidence collection opportunities.

4. *Capacity and Interaction Points* Car scenes are man-made with greater evidence collection and carrying capacities, and locatable interaction points. Cars have their own value, and contain value. Architecture contributes to more predictable evidence transfer points. With a lower volume of scenes interacting, the odds of finding relevant evidence go up, thus an isolated car scene could have a high capacity for evidence. Car scenes also can deposit evidence, in particular patterns, onto other scenes.

Car scenes have limited and formatted evidence locations. A car has control points requiring controller contact. Presence inside a car also requires contact. Cars have predictable components of high interaction reflecting their actions; steering wheel, radio, seatbelts, and stored items, all of which simplify car scene analysis. As entry into a restricted scene can require effort and contact with the entry point, the entry and exit points may offer another evidence opportunity to prove presence and action. There may also be evidence in the car to indicate activity, such as drugs. There may also be on-board electronics systems to record details about what was happening with the car just prior to the collision.

Car scenes have many potential interaction points for an investigator to consider when looking at a case.
a. Entry point to the scene, as in doors.

b. Control points such as ignition, shift, brake, radio, even rear view mirrors.

c. Seatbelt buckles.

d. The center of gravity of the case, which is where the action happened, and the zone around it. This may be the back seat, trunk, or exterior of the car.

e. Newer cars have systems to record actions such as the *Black Box*. Some are also connected to the internet or satellite.

f. The path of travel within a larger scene where its presence is recorded.

The lack of restrictions on movement makes possible multiple scenes over distances, leading to multiple locations, and subscenes. Easy scene access means anyone could have done the crime, and proof of presence holds less value as proof than in a secured home.

Step 3. Evaluate the Evidence Potential

Evidence Decision How would the evidence work in this scene?

1. *Production* Evidence can be produced by interaction of the car hosting scene with another subscene such as a person either driving or present, or event tools. The car exterior interacts with the driving surfaces, and other car subscenes.

2. *Proof Ability* Car scene evidence can prove presence and action of a person in the hosting scene. This means, who was driving the car, and who was riding in it, as well as what else was present. The actions taken by the controller of the car are also provable, since the exterior of the car may interact with other scenes.

3. *Quality* The car scene evidence may be very unique when there can be a smaller number of persons interacting with the scene for legitimate reasons. Car scene evidence may be of lower quality when it is exposed to the elements and interacts with a number of occupants. Car scene evidence sometimes serves to prove who the scene hosted, and other times it proves how it was used as a tool scene, such as hit and run, or even as a weapon. Cars are mass produced, so the combination of multiple evidence pieces creates the uniqueness a single piece of evidence cannot.

4. *Timeline* Car scene timelines can have pinpoint accurate actual times, if there is a collision to set off the black box, or if the infotainment system is investigated. Sometimes there is no internal way to get an accurate time, but an investigator can rely on external systems, such as toll booth cameras to provide a time and location correlation. Also, cars can be more revealing by relative times, such as a thief breaks a window, and then steals items from the car.

5. *Resilience* Car scene evidence can be less resilient because of the movement, but cars are made to be durable, and some of the evidence is very enduring. In a suspect controlled scene, it is vulnerable to destruction.

6. *Collection* One of the greatest hurdles is finding the suspect car scene. Collection becomes more restrictive inside the car. Car scenes have a lower likelihood of unintentional tainting of the scene, but a higher likelihood of intentional tainting since a suspect can control the scene, and modify it as he wishes. Failure to secure the scene from people who do or do not belong in the scene may include a tow truck driver removing the car, or investigator searching without gloves.

An investigator may find coordinating evidence work for car scenes easier than public or private scenes due to smaller size, ease in securing and stabilization. The scene can be transported to a secure facility, allowing an investigator to look at other scenes.

Step 4. Work the Evidence

Evidence Decision How to obtain the evidence from this scene?

1. *Critical Thinking* The first three decisions indicate car scenes function as a host scene, transport, or tool. They fit into scenes, moving among them. Cars present the investigator with two sets of decisions within one type of crime scene. Exterior decisions address accessible scene parts, while interior decisions address restricted access parts. Both parts are predictable, with recognizable and collectible evidence with evidence transfer points. Mobility of the scene type challenges the investigator to find it. Another challenge is how to connect specific persons, and their tools to the car, as well as the car to the hosting public scenes, other cars and sometimes private scenes. The investigator may be able to prove presence and action simultaneously, but they may be separate evidence components.

Major collisions go to traffic investigators with specialized training, but beat cops investigate most cases at the beginning contributing to a collision investigation by fundamental scene work: making observations, taking photos, and collecting evidence. Each car within any crime scene has three basic subscenes; interior and exterior. The exterior of the cars indicate contact and the interiors indicate drivers and occupants. The evidence connects car to car, and car to person. As the black box technology becomes more widespread, the third scene for cars will be data.

People identify cars by the exterior, and sometimes the case begins with a car type identified. Cars carry signs of contact with other scenes. People and their items occupy the interior of car, showing occupation and use. Interior evidence work varies depending on whether the car belongs to the suspect or victim, how the car relates to the crime, and to establish presence and action. Cars have high populations of users over time, making them less exclusive. Taxis provide public accessibility and frequency of different occupants but may have interior video.

Car scene suspects often act to reduce their exposure through car scenes. Sometimes disposable car scenes support the crime. Suspects might wipe the car clean, or burn it. Suspects borrow cars for single crime use. A suspect who keeps the license plate secret using a different car each time for serial crimes has a better chance of eluding police. People change a license plate on a car just as they wear disguises. People use their own cars for crime, and steal a plate to hide their identity. People also put legitimate plates on stolen cars. A few people occupy the car at one time, but many different groups occupy the car over a period of time.

2. *Information* Car descriptions start outside and move inward, noting evidence and points along the away to reinforce thoroughness. Car scene information starts with a detailed history of ownership and features of the car. Each car has unique features, down to make, model, color, year, and serial number – referred to as the Vehicle Identification Number or VIN. The VIN never changes, while license plates can. The VIN should match the information on both the registration and the insurance paperwork, preventing confusion. The car's status as salvage might provide clues later.

Drivers and occupants personalize cars, even within a short time, making them unique for identification. The car's configuration and modifications reveal priorities and choices. The car may appear new, clean, cluttered, or run down. Owners decorate their car with stickers. Current car conditions show recent goings on in the vehicle. Thieves also consider variables during their activities such as the car's condition concerning open windows, unlocked doors, or damage.

Car scenes require using many details about the location of the car: its visibility, amount of traffic, conditions, appearance, upkeep, and any other relevant features. Parking location options include; street, driveway, commercial lot, apartment lot, carport, garage, park, or more functional specific, such as convenience stores or grocery stores. The parking configuration may reveal a larger scene conducive to crime. Visibility and lighting may factor into crime scene location attractiveness. Security cameras or guards provide potential witnesses. The car location's lack of witness visibility expressed by distance to the nearest structure may relate to its attractiveness.

Car ownership is connected to finance, and finances connect to crime. A simple statement, reinforced by a document about car finances early prepares to strengthen a case later. A false statement about the car being paid off provides useful context.

3. *Photographs* Car scene photographs become more challenging moving inward from reduced room. The rule of three still applies as does the requirement for perpendicular treatment of the subject. Photographing the measuring tape shows the evidence locations.

4. *DNA* The DNA on the car structure supersedes DNA on an artifact in the car indicating a different evidentiary presence. DNA evidence collects in the ignition area, gear shifter and handbrake. If a suspect assaulted a victim in a specific place within the car, there will be a DNA center of gravity independent of driving the car.

A car with one owner may still include multiple uninvolved DNA profiles, including mechanics, car wash personnel, and riders. Artifacts within the car often have DNA on them may offer a better chance to have one profile. The portability of the items creates the challenge of proving how they came to rest inside the car scene.

Car exteriors are exposed to the elements, and in most places the interiors heat up in the sun, degrading biological evidence.

5. *Fingerprints* Most persons leave fingerprints in cars they occupy, and fingerprints have a lot of the same challenges as DNA. Windows may have fingerprints on them. High use smooth surfaces provide greater opportunities, including the seatbelt buckles, rear view mirror, and seat adjustment lever. Colored powders work well with dark colored interiors. Silicone gel collects prints on rougher surfaces when tape would ruin the evidence. Photography synergizes fingerprint efforts. An investigator develops fingerprints on items within the car scene while fingerprints on the car structure establish facts of presence in the car, versus presence with the artifacts in the car. An investigator operates within the situation.

The elements degrade fingerprints like DNA. The sun can dry out fingerprints.

6. *Patterns* Car scenes have opportunities for pattern matching to tie scenes together. The tire treads may connect the car to a specific location by pattern. Hit and run collision damages on the different cars usually match up like two puzzle pieces. There is also paint transfer trace evidence, but the shape of the paint chips may fit a pattern. Seatbelts often leave marks on passengers, indicating their presence at a crash, and perhaps a specific location in the car.

7. *Artifacts* Car scenes hold artifact subscenes to indicate presence and action, connecting them person scenes. Car scenes exist within another scene. GPS history, black box, or external witness support including security footage bolsters the presence of the scene within another scene. Evidence artifacts help an investigator build a timeline of events, and may connect the car to different scenes as their locations change. Time stamped business receipts provide specific locations and maybe incrimination or alibis. People hide

evidence and tools in their cars. The car's black box houses information evidence in the form of data.

There are many predictable items present in a car including hats, masks, gloves, and tools. These can be processed for DNA or fingerprints. An investigator can swab drink cans first, and process them for fingerprints. The fewer people who contacted a scene, can increase the likelihood an investigation will confirm a specific presence through DNA. The large number of people with car contact complicates DNA evidence as three collocated profiles complicate DNA identification.

Transportation of a car scene exposes it to receiving new influences modifying the evidence. Fragile evidence may require collection before moving the car.

8. *Report Production* Car scene reports vary depending on the function of the car. The structure covers how the car was a part of the case, and the content gives the evidence. The description often starts outside, and moves in. Like private scenes, there may be a need to prove entry, and interior activity. Evidence centered reports may emphasize action, while location centered reports may emphasize presence.

Car Scene Scenarios

11. Hit and Run Scene
12. Car Burglary
13. Car Sex Crime Scene

11. Hit and Run Scene

A witness called 911 to report a hit and run collision. A driver approached a major intersection and when the light turned green he drove forward (northbound) into the intersection to turn left and head west. A westbound car struck the first driver's car on the passenger side. The westbound driver fled the scene. An ambulance transported the remaining driver to the local hospital for minor injuries.

Summary
Hit and run. Victim driver hospitalized with minor injuries. Suspect vehicle found, driver arrested. Photos taken. Paint chips from both vehicles collected as evidence.

To Do
Follow up with victim photos.

Investigation and Scene Description
At 1800 HRS on 6/14/14 I arrived to the intersection of Rio Vista Ave. (north and south) and Damonte Rd. (east/west). Four way traffic signals control this intersection, including left turn arrows. Two lanes of traffic go each direction, along with a single left turn pocket for each. A fast food restaurant occupies the northwest corner, with patio seating. The other corners are occupied by banks.

I did not see any fresh marks on the pavement and connected with this collision. The debris field began at 55 feet north of the south roadway edge, and 45 feet west of the east roadway edge. It continued at a west by northwestern arc for 45 feet, and included pieces of broken glass, plastic, and fluids.

When I arrived, I saw driver Smith' car (License CA ABCD123. green four door, 2014 Roadster) pointed northwest in the center of the intersection. I saw emergency ambulance and fire personnel attending to the sole occupant of the car seated in the driver's seat when I arrived. The car showed major damage to the passenger side, with the passenger front door bent into the interior of the car at least two feet. I saw no indications of alcohol or drug use in the interior of the car. The windows appeared undamaged, clean, and provided visibility. The driver's seat belt was still attached, with the belt fabric stretched.

Victim driver Smith's statement correlated with his starting in the left turn lane of northbound Rio Vista to go west onto Damonte Rd.

Sketch

I created a sketch of the scene. See sketch for locations of evidence items.

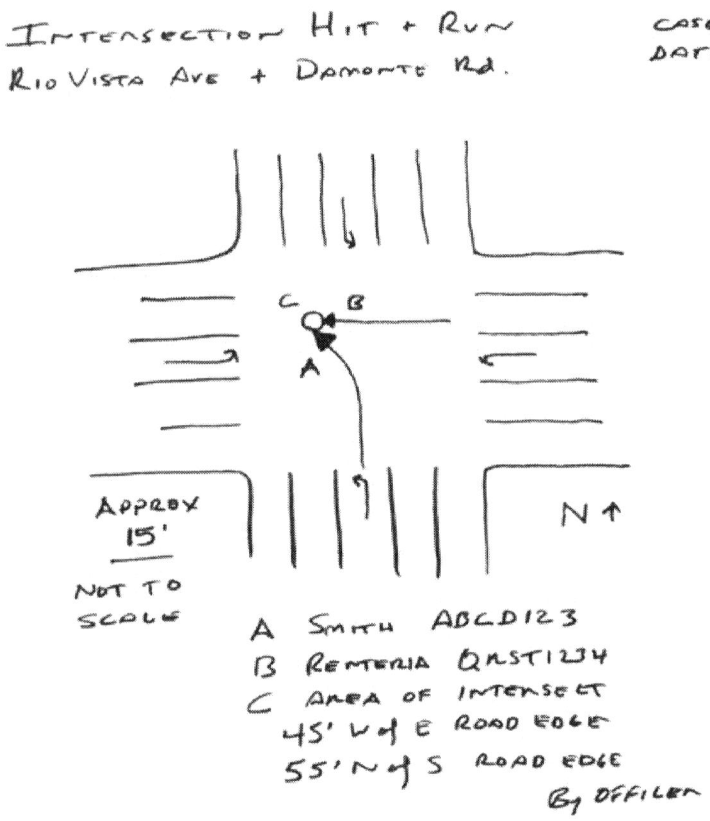

Photographs

I photographed the scene with my department issued camera. I used orange spray paint to mark the scene with fundamental areas: the resting point of the car and the debris field. I photographed the scene with the paint, and evidence, and again after evidence removal.

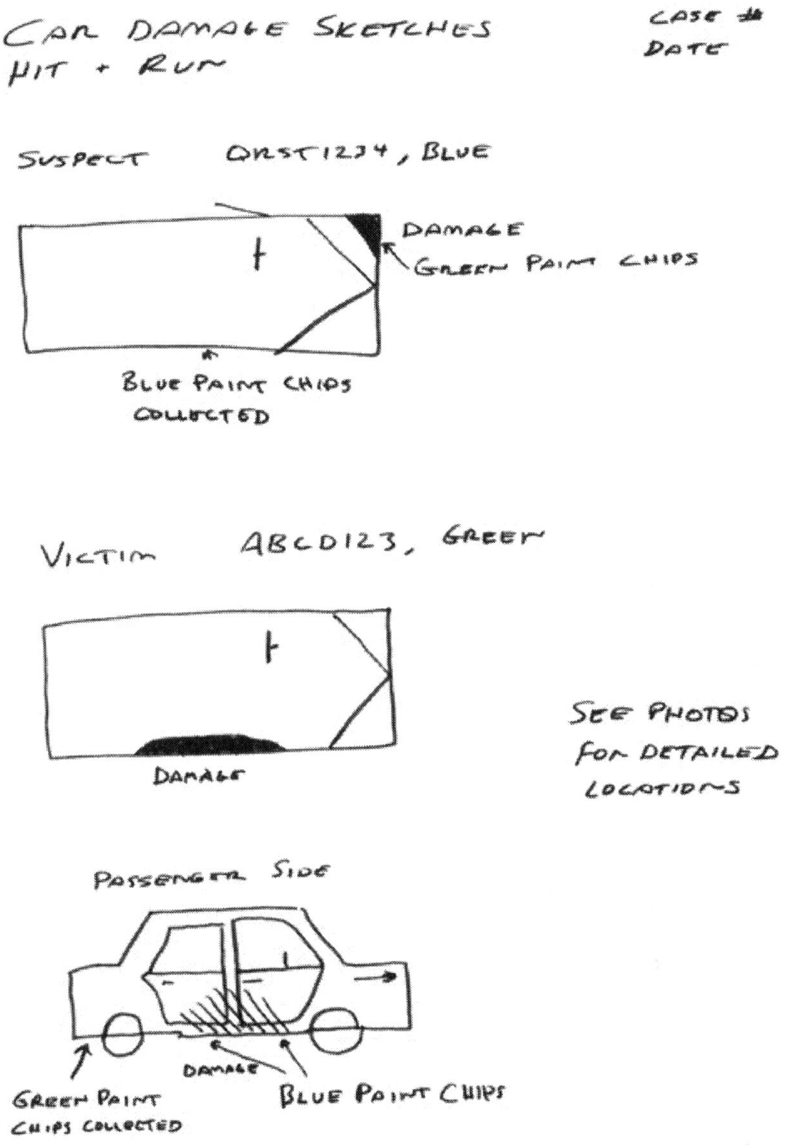

Victim Car Evidence

I collected two samples of green paint from the victim car; one from the damaged panel, and another from an uninvolved section. I collected two samples of blue paint left behind from the other car. Evidence items 1 and 2.

Suspect Vehicle Identification

I found no other involved cars at the scene. Officers Janting and Ubaldo spoke with several witnesses at the scene, including diners on the patio restaurant. See their reports for details. Several reported seeing a blue two door car, CA plate QRST1234 being involved in the collision, and leaving prior to police arrived. They described the suspect driver as a teenager.

Suspect Car Scene

The license plate to the car indicated Michael Renteria owned the car and lived four blocks away. I sent Officers Swerdlow and Neenby went to the address in search of the car. Registered owner Michael Renteria (66 years old) answered the door. His car was in his garage. Mr. Renteria told officers his son, David (20 years old) drove the car recently, and struck a pole in a parking lot. Michael and David both drive the car on a regular basis.

Suspect Car Evidence

I processed Renteria's car as evidence at the scene and released it. The car showed minor front end damage, and I saw green paint chips on the driver's side of the front bumper. I photographed and collected several green paint chips as well as blue chips from the damaged part of the car, and uninvolved parts. Evidence items 3 and 4.

The air bag deployed, and was visible. I swabbed the airbag to collect possible DNA evidence as it was sealed prior to activation it contacted the driver's chest and face at the time of the collision. The driver's seat belt was still attached, with the belt fabric stretched.

See property section for details.

I discovered a glass pipe for smoking methamphetamine under the driver's seat. Item 5.

Suspect Driver Evidence

David Renteria refused to provide a statement to officers. See their reports.

Officer Jones brought witnesses to the house for a field show up. Witness Boyer said David Renteria drove the suspect car. See his report for the protocol for show ups.

I placed Renteria under arrest for felony hit and run, (leaving the scene of an injury accident).

David Renteria's face was red with scrapes on his nose, and chin. I photographed Renteria at HQ with his shirt removed. I saw a 2 inch wide diagonal red mark from his left shoulder to his right hip, and another 2 inch wide red mark running from his right hip to his left hip. The injuries correlate to where the driver's seatbelt would mark a person in rapid deceleration. Renteria complained of a sore neck but refused medical attention at his house, the scene, and later at the jail. (See photos).

Step 1. Designate the Scene

Scene Decision Why is this a scene?

1. *Discovery* The investigator declared the scene after citizens reported the suspect car was involved.

2. *Scene type* The main scene of this case is the fleeing car.

3. *Scene Group*
a. Neighborhood and intersection.
b. Roadways between scenes.
c. Suspect garage.
d. Victim car exterior.
e. Suspect car exterior and interior.
f. Victim person.
g. Suspect car driver person.
h. Meth pipe.

4. *Search* Zone.

Step 2. Analyze the Scene

Scene Decision How does the scene work?

1. *Restrictiveness* The car scene is a restricted access hosting scene for its interior, but accessible for its exterior.

2. *Volatility* The scene is mobile, with the high potential to change, however many of the changes require technical skill and money to effect. Life protection supersedes all else, and ensuring a safe scene may mean closing an intersection with a patrol car which also helps preserve evidence. Uninvolved parties drive through scenes before police arrive, and sometimes they collide with the cars already in the scene.

3. *Function* The car scene is overall a subject scene, as it interacted with the driver (also a subject) and the other car and driver (both objects). The scene functions as a transporter in this case, but also as a place a person spends time. The suspect's fleeing action turned his car into a crime scene, as a crash

is not a crime by itself. The suspect took the car scene from the accident, making the investigation more difficult than had he remained. The car scene in this case was mobile, and identifiable by license plate, and thus he had little anonymity.

4. *Capacity and Interaction Points* The scene has the hosting capacity for DNA, fingerprints, and pattern markings to prove presence, and action. The information about the vehicle is hosted there too, and may be useful. A driver interacts with routine points in the car, while in control of it including a steering wheel, ignition, shift, and seatbelt. The exterior of a car will often have damage of interacting with another object and will exchange transfer evidence.

Step 3. Evaluate the Evidence Potential

Evidence Decision How would the evidence work in this scene?

1. *Production* The various other scenes had contact with the car, transferring evidence. This was car to car collision for paint transfer, car to person collision for seatbelt patterns.

2. *Proof Ability* The paint transfer show contact between cars. The suspect car's damaged driver seatbelt proves there was someone driving the car when it crashed, indicating enough force to leave a mark on the driver. The pipe shows actions indicating behavior. Collecting fingerprints from the suspect car may eliminate the claim the car was stolen by someone to be used at the time of the crash. All of those subscenes can be connected by evidence to other scenes.

3. *Quality* The evidence shows who controlled the suspect car scene, and what other scenes it interacted with. Paint chips are high quality, and the injuries will be fresh. The paint chips are also unique enough to support identification with a version of events. The pattern mark from the car made on the driver offers a very unique signature of a shoulder to hip injury and was the most relevant evidence because the pattern mark by the car seatbelt on the driver indicated driving during a collision.

4. *Timeline* This car scene timeline could provide pinpoint accurate actual times, if the collision set off one of the airbag systems and thus black boxes. There may third party video to timestamp the crash or catch someone leaving.

5. *Resilience* Injuries heal, making them time sensitive. The body car damage and paint chips are very hardy.

6. *Collection* The initial order of processing centered on the remaining car which could perhaps connect to the fleeing car. The fleeing car was unavailable for processing until it was found. After colleagues developed leads about the fleeing car it became the center of gravity, since it could connect the driver's presence to the actions of the crash.

The investigator processed both cars to look for contact evidence. Once the car is discovered, the scene can be processed in the routine order. It has already travelled, but the damage is still visible. The scene can be transported to a secure facility for processing. The standard CSI tools supported the investigator's efforts to get the evidence.

The investigator chose to process the suspect vehicle in the field rather than tow it. The investigator photographed the car's seatbelts, and collected paint chips. He later took photos of the suspect's injuries to match to the seatbelt in jail so as to control the suspect's movements.

Step 4. Work the Evidence

Evidence Decision How to obtain the evidence from this scene?

1. *Critical Thinking* The investigator thought about how the car scene played different roles in the case; as a transportation machine that collided with another scene, and protection for the driver who controlled the car which restrained him in the collision. There were two areas of interactions to prove presence and action; the car to the other car, and the car to the driver.

The investigator knew car interaction proof would come from an exchange of material like paint chips, and a matching pattern of damage. Car to person interaction would come from identifying evidence like DNA or fingerprint, which would be limited because the suspect was a regular presence in the car. The action of the collision provided enough force to deploy the airbag and mark the driver with a pattern of the seatbelt. The unique injuries injury indicated his presence, and action of driving the car.

Proving who was driving the suspect car is similar to determining who controlled a stolen car. The investigator explores the possibility or absence of evidence of other drivers. The controls of the car hold evidence of who controlled the car. The airbag could have DNA on it from hitting the driver in the face at the time of the collision had it deployed.

2. *Information* Witness information helps find evidence to solve the crime. Statements indicated who controlled the car, but the evidence proves the case.

The intersection map is included in this section because understanding how the collision happened assists in understanding where the potential evidence will be on the cars. The intersection was the response scene, but the cars held the key evidence of proving contact and action.

One sketch shows the damage to the cars, and how the car scenes interacted, supported by photographic, and paint chip evidence. The intersection scene sketch shows how the car scenes collided in the public scene. Photos, video, witnesses, and debris support the sketch. Both sketches explain the crime scenes.

The collision scene sketch showed where the event occurred, and the details of the site. The involved cars show the locations of intersection, and who drove each. Collision sketches range from basic to detailed, depending on the degree of injury or crime. The physics remain the same. The investigator practices skills with minor crashes for learning.

An expert collision investigator may work with the documentation. The case may require plotting everything in the scene and reconstruction remains an option if the case turns more serious. Orange spray paint allows an accident reconstruction expert to visit the scene and work through it. It also allows an investigator to preserve the scene regardless of seriousness and in anticipation of the worst. A minor collision might turn fatal for an elderly or fragile person. The investigator marked all four tire locations for all involved cars. He designated the fronts of cars with a V, with the small end pointing the way forward. Busy intersections may require simultaneous painting and photographing. Body locations do not need too much detail as an outline of a dead relative may disturb family members visiting scenes. Three dots near the head, and two for the feet indicates orientation with photographs.

3. *Photographs* Images of the damage on each car with scales can show how the two fit together. This pattern matching part of photography becomes relevant, as the cars will be returned to their owners.

4. *DNA* A person's regular presence in a car blunts DNA and fingerprint evidence to prove presence in the car during the event. The lack of anyone else's DNA or fingerprints in the car may support the argument of the sole contributor as the suspect. A similar appearing person could have driven the car. Standard methods work best for car scenes, by looking at the buckles, gear shift, and rear view mirror. DNA was an option to process to put a driver in the car, and eliminate other potential suspects. In this case, the airbag offers a promising DNA swab as the airbag is sealed prior to activation, and a car is not driven after it goes off.

5. *Fingerprints* The fingerprints may prove far more useful for identifying the most recent driver. Since both men drive the car, DNA does not determine who did the crime.

6. *Patterns* The investigator makes this case by pattern marks for car to car, and car seatbelt to driver. Corresponding damage on both cars means pattern or tool marks to be matched. Suspect cars often leave paint on the victim car or vice versa. Paint chips tie the car scenes together, and having them gives an investigator options. Analysis ranges for a lay person seeing the match with the chips to hiring an expert. The FBI has the potential capability to match paint to a car as a source, or provide specific car makes, models, and years for potential suspects.

Airbags injure people, break noses, and cause swollen lips. Depending on hand positions, airbags might throw the driver's arms into him and cause injuries also. The car tool of a seatbelt made a mark on the suspect during the crash. The pattern mark of the seatbelt on the suspected driver's person offers great proof he drove the car when the vehicle rapidly decelerated. The restraint caused the mark. He has a history of driving the car, and his evidence in the car will not prove he was just driving.

7. *Artifacts* The investigation should seek a suspect car identification, location, and connection to a driver. Witnesses and video footage of the suspect car overcomes this, but nothing substitutes having the instrument (car) of the crime. New cars come with *black box*. This recorder can provide indispensable information about car settings and events surrounding the crash. This may require a search warrant, and an investigator may tow the car a department lot in anticipation of obtaining a search warrant. An investigator can swab the meth pipe for DNA, or print it. The evidence may indicate a person connected with the car, or provide information about the owner.

8. *Report Production* The report structure covers an investigation emphasizing evidence by scene. The content includes the development of the case beginning at the large scene of the intersection, and evolving into the lead of the suspect car, and the suspect person scene. The victim's car and person scene was also a part of this investigation. The report documents the suspect's person scene with the seatbelt marks as a way to show the connection of driver to car, to the other car in the intersection.

12. Car Burglary

A car owner called 911 to report he parked his car in the lot of a store and returned to find the car broken into. He provided a basic idea about the stolen contents including a laptop computer and gym bag.

Summary
Burglary from car. No suspects or leads. Photos, fingerprints, evidence items recovered.

To Do
Fingerprints to Central ID
Evidence items to lab.
Cigarettes to lab for DNA

Investigation
The car owner said he parked and locked the car in the parking lot at 2:00 PM Friday, and went shopping inside. He returned at 3:40 PM to find the driver's window pulled out of the channel, the door open, and his backpack and laptop missing. His ignition lock no longer worked, and he showed me a piece of broken metal lodged in his trunk lock. There was no key in the ignition, but the car chimed indicating a key in the ignition. The owner provided no suspect information.

Area Description
The car was burgled in the parking lot of the Rapido Mart. The lot offers 50 parking spaces, with a high turnover rate of parkers in the lot. Landscaping obscured the location where the victim parked from within the store. No security cameras covered this area.

Scene Description, Victim Car
The victim drove a blue, four-door, 2009 X Car. It has no reported damage prior to the event. The victim paid cash for the car, and owes no money to a lender.

Entry Point
An unknown suspect pulled the driver's window, unlocked the door and gained entry into the car.

Suspect Activity
The suspect removed a blue gym bag and laptop computer (see Property Section of the report for details on make, model, and serial number). The suspect left in an unknown direction, by unknown means and remain at large. The suspect left behind a broken ignition lock, and a piece of metal in the trunk lock. He also bent back the door to access the gas cap.

Exit point
It appears the suspect left by the entry point; no other doors unlocked.

Evidence
I processed the car in the field and found items in the car.

1. Flashlight, yellow. Brand X. Front passenger floorboards. The victim denied ownership.

2. 16 cigarette butts, Sophisticant brand. The victim ruled out ownership and lawful presence of smokers in his car.

3. Metal piece from trunk lock.

Fingerprint Evidence
I photographed and fingerprinted the car and items associated with it. All windows were up. The driver's door window was crooked, and out of the channel. I dusted the driver door window, and passenger door window to develop fingerprints on the rear view mirror, driver's door window, and seat belt buckles. I used black powder applied with a fiberglass brush. I found and collected the following print cards.

Card #1 (large) Interior, driver's door window, top of glass.

Card #2 (large) interior, right side glass of rear passenger side window.

Card #3 (large) Interior, rear driver's side window, top edge.

Card #4 (large) Flashlight, no prints located.

See cards for orientation. I forwarded the cards to the Regional Police Department Identification Unit.

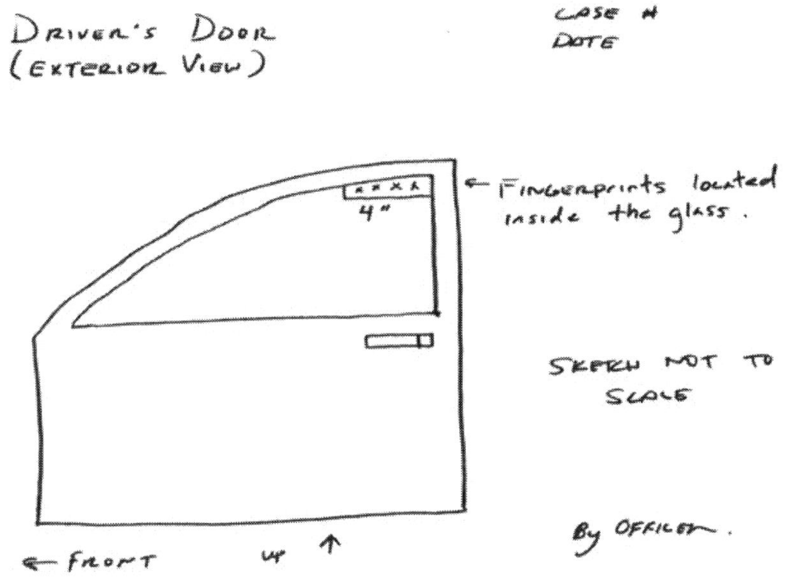

Step 1. Designate the Scene

Scene Decision Why is this a scene?

1. *Discovery* The investigator declared the scene by the victim's statement. The victim requested the investigation.

2. *Scene type* The car is the scene, and within the scene, the window bearing the fingerprints is the main subscene.

3. *Scene Group*
a. Neighborhood.
b. Parking lot.
c. Victim car.
d. Suspect.
e. Victim.
f. Flashlight.
g. Cigarette butts attributed to the suspect.
h. Broken metal piece from trunk lock.

4. *Search* Zone.

Step 2. Analyze the Scene

Scene Decision How does the scene work?

1. *Restrictiveness* The car scene is a restricted access hosting scene. Nobody should be inside the car without permission.

2. *Volatility* The scene is mobile, with some potential to change, however the broken glass kept the owner out.

3. *Function* The scene is an object scene. It was targeted and received evidence. The scene functioned as a transporter, but was a storage place for a person's things at the time of the crime.

This car was in a visible place limiting time for the suspect to act. The scene was controlled by the victim, so the suspect should have no prior evidence in the car. The suspect took available items after he attempted to steal the car. Unknown entry points represent fewer evidence opportunities in any car scene.

4. *Capacity and Interaction Points* The scene has the hosting capacity for DNA, and fingerprints to prove presence, and action. A car scene may have an outsider to connect to the scene. The owner has information about the vehicle too.

Knowing how a thief gained entry, and the area of entry aids in locating evidence. Options include the doors and windows, and the trunk or cargo area. Car entry methods include: door pry, providing marks for collection, a window pull, providing possible fingerprints, or a window smash, requiring no contact when a thief reaches in the car removing items without opening the door. A window smash may not trigger the alarm. Electronic keys allow a thief to open a car's lock, or alternatively, they overpower a lock signal when the driver thinks he secured his car. Burglars often use tools to enter cars, even throwing rocks. An investigator can often recover the tool marks for pattern matching. A method of entry should either show damage, or confirm an unsecured point of entry.

A suspect may ransack or search for an item with care.

The sole confirmed interaction points for this case are the broken locks and the window in the form of fingerprints. The damaged ignition lock indicates the thief tampered with the car with intent to take it during the process.

Step 3. Evaluate the Evidence Potential

Evidence Decision How would the evidence work in this scene?

1. *Production* The fingerprints were produced when a suspect touched the car.

2. *Proof Ability* The fingerprints on the car window show potential contact with a person scene. The items from inside the car are of limited value. The flashlight yielded no prints. The butts could have been transported to the scene, and may not prove presence by themselves through DNA. A fingerprint on an immovable part of the scene is more solid proof of presence and action.

3. *Quality* Fingerprints are excellent identification items when they are clear enough to identify a person. Fingerprints identify one person. The evidence shows who was controlling the car scene, and what other scenes it interacted with. In this case the most relevant evidence is the fingerprints on the window. The cigarettes are of dubious quality as evidence, but may not be of verifiable origin, as there are 16 butts for a short time.

4. *Timeline* This car scene timeline will remain all relative unless there is some way to timestamp it by an external source.

5. *Resilience* Quick processing of the fingerprints ensured they were not degraded by sun exposure, or any other weather conditions.

6. *Collection* The standard CSI tools will support the investigator's efforts to get the evidence. The investigator performed the evidence collection processes in the field.

There is nothing to alter the standard order. The weather does not appear to interfere, and there are no sprinklers in the parking lot.

Step 4. Work the Evidence

Evidence Decision How to obtain the evidence from this scene?

1. *Critical Thinking* The investigator thought about the car scene as the target for theft. The evidence artifact indicated the thief tried to take the whole car, and when he failed, he took items from within the car. The car probably had limited persons who had interacted with it at contact points, but there was little indication the person who stole from the car interacted with it in the control points. The damaged window did indicate where the suspect had interaction with the scene, and the investigator chose fingerprints to try to prove the presence of a person, while indicating his actions of tampering with

the window. The investigator also knew about the other evidence and its potential to not be valid as identification for the person who did the crime. The cigarette butts are questionable, as is the flashlight. The broken keys indicate an attempt to steal the car.

Thieves may peer into several windows before settling on a window to breech. Fingerprints on the outside of the car do not link the suspects to the inside of the car, but proximity to the point of entry may matter. A car scene's compactness may challenge the investigator's efforts to prove presence and action. A suspect can break a window and take items inside without touching the car, or leaving evidence in the form of DNA or fingerprints.

Car burglars seek electronics, such as GPS, stereos and their components, laptop computers, and personal items such as purses which may provide some trackability.

2. *Information* The victim provides little information beyond times and loss of items. He believes his car was burgled, which is true, but it was also the target of an attempted car theft. There are no witness statements to help guide evidence collection efforts. A neighborhood canvass may provide information about the car, occupants, or video surveillance of the scene.

A suspect may not plan on the car being found, recovered, or reported, and may not clean the car scene. Sketches may show actions and scene details and may save writing time. Door window tops may show signs of pulling the window from the frame to gain entry. Suspect damage door locks during thefts. The car owner determines if his key works in all the locks. Remote electronic entry locks can have a vulnerability to an electronic jamming device able to mimic the signals from key fobs. An unsuspecting driver believes he locked his car when in fact his car remains unsecured. The potential exists for an adept technician to intercept codes and send out false unlock codes to unlock doors.

3. *Photographs* Auto burglaries may not even get photos. Basic photos of fingerprints may suffice. Crime scene photography may capture fingerprint evidence as it moves to photography based collection and storage. This allows an investigator to take a few photos, reducing descriptive writing.

4. *DNA*. The unreliable evidence of cigarette butts negated the use of DNA for identification. They would be like blind swabs from the perspective of a crime lab.

5. *Fingerprints* The fingerprints on the window offer the best option at this stage.

6. *Patterns* The broken key is a potential identifiable pattern if it can be compared to the other half.

7. *Artifacts* The suspect removed the majority of involved items, limiting the remaining evidence to suspect fingerprints, or DNA. An investigator may decide to process the stolen items if recovered in the future. Evidence inside the car has more value than outside the car because it proves entry, but an investigator can work with either.

The broken metal piece is too small for prints, and a long shot for DNA. It may be useful to match if the other part is recovered.

The cigarette butts present a false opportunity to sequence, because the cigarette butts were in a car where the suspect spent so little time. While analysis could identify the DNA in the butts anyone could place the butts there as counter forensics. They are counter forensics instead of antiforensics because they do not disrupt the forensic process, but use it against the investigator. A stolen car where the thief spent more time might make the butts worth sampling for DNA. Burglars often use flashlights at night, but an investigator often looks at the crimes during the day, and may not consider tools for night crimes. The victim denied ownership making it the best piece of evidence.

If the thief had taken the car, the last parking place and surrounding area provides a low return on investment of time. The majority of the scene left, but tools or glass shards sometimes remain at the take scene. Security video may have recorded the events. The recovery scene gives limited return for time invested, aside from security video.

8. *Report Production* The beginning of a car burglary report establishes the details of the car and the scene when the owner left. With stolen cars, unless the victim has a specific suspect in mind, the majority of the evidence work happens post-recovery. The recovery often takes place in a different district, with different policies and procedures. Detailed documentation clarifies a crime, and safeguards against fraudulent claims.

13. Car Sex Crime Scene

A guidance counselor from high school called 911 to report a possible sexual assault. Detectives identified the man, and officers towed his car for evidence. He denied all allegations and gave his permission for officers to search his car for evidence.

Summary
Sexual assault in a car, cold case. Car towed and processed. Photos taken. DNA swabs. Fingerprints. Evidence items recovered. No victim or suspect SART due to elapsed timeframe.

To Do
Fingerprints to Central ID
Evidence items to lab.

Summary from Detectives who interviewed persons:
The 16 year-old girl reported she went out on a date with an adult man she met online two weeks prior. After going to a club and drinking, she felt tired. The victim said after they exited the club, she sat in the front seat of the suspect's car. She thought he was giving her a ride home, but woke up in a secluded spot, with him having sex with her in the back seat.

She described lying on the seat, with her head on the driver's side. She said she found her arms restrained by duct tape. but has little other recall of the night. The victim also said she did not remember ever sitting in the back seat. She could not recall where the assault took place, other than while there she looked down on the city.

The suspect said he met the victim online and they went to the club together. He said she never spent time in his car, and took care of her own transportation. He denied all allegations, and gave officers permission to search his car.

Scene Integrity

I obtained a search warrant for the car, and sealed it at the discovery location. Johnson Garage towed the suspected crime scene to HQ for processing in accordance with Vehicle Code 234433. They used a flatbed truck without entering the car.

Geographical Scene Description

The victim cannot name the geographical location of the crime. Supporting information aids in estimating the time and area variables.

Car Scene Description

The suspect car is a blue 2009, four door Speedster, with a trunk. License CA 123456. The upholstery is brown textured pseudo leather.

I created a sketch showing where I collected evidence items.

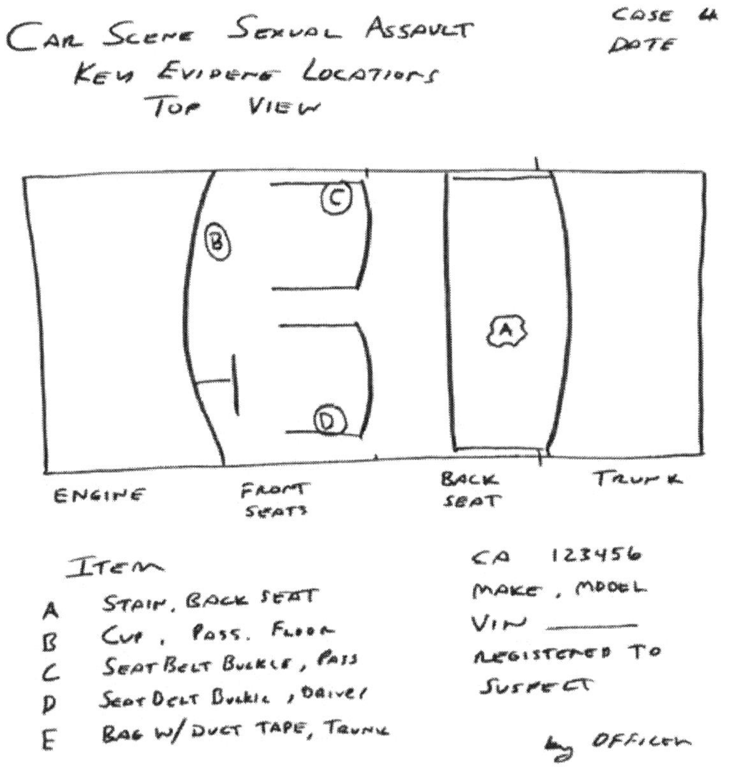

Photographs
I used a department issued camera for all photography. Natural light, fluorescent lights, flash, and alternate light sources illuminated the scenes for images.

Possible Staining Car Interior
I used an alternate light source, producing light at 750 nm frequency. This presents as bluish tinged photographs, indicating biological fluid. Images 52-59 show a stain in the back seat area, 3 feet from the driver's side, and near the center portion of the seat.

I tested a swab with the Roger Brand test and it tested positive for both vaginal fluid and semen. I cut a 6 inch by 6 inch square of fabric from the seat.

Possible Biological Evidence
I processed the seat near the stain by collecting swabs. Photos 60-72 show each swab's collection location.

I swabbed each area with a separate sterile swab with sterile water on it. I placed each swab in its own envelope and sealed as evidence. I changed gloves for each collection so no areas would have cross contamination. I sealed the items and placed them in the Crime Lab Freezer.

I took photos to show the exact locations of samples.

Swab 1 – plain swab with sterile water.

Back Seat
Swab 2 – stain area, driver's side.
Swab 3 – stain area, passenger's side.
Swab 4 – stain area, center.
Swab 5 – unstained area, driver's side.
Swab 6 – unstained area, passenger's side.
Swab 7 – plain swab with sterile water.

Front Seat
Swab 8 – unstained area, driver's side.
Swab 9 – unstained area, passenger's side.
Swab 10 – plain swab with sterile water.

Person Swabs
Swab 11 – The victim consented to provide a buccal swab as a sample.
Swab 12 – The suspect consented to provide a buccal swab as a sample.

Fingerprint Evidence
I completed the biological work and began fingerprinting. I dusted the passenger door window and seat belt buckle to develop fingerprints. I used black powder applied with a fiberglass brush. I found and collected the following print cards.

Card #1 (large) Interior, front passenger window.
Card #2 (large) Interior, front passenger seat belt buckle.
Card #3 (large) Interior, driver's seat belt buckle.

See cards for orientation. I forwarded the cards to the Regional Police Department Identification Unit.

Evidence
I collected the fabric square from the back seat. I packaged it in paper, and froze the evidence.

After completing processing, I removed the back seat to find any evidence lodged under the seat. I found a few coins, and a two year old movie ticket.

I found a small black bag in the trunk containing duct tape. I collected the bag and item to send to the lab for DNA testing as well as potential fiber evidence.

Step 1. Designate Car Scene

Scene Decision Why is this a scene?

1. *Discovery* The investigator declared the scene by the word of the victim, she did not control the scene.

2. *Scene type* The car is the scene. In this case, the victim is the outsider in the scene, and she indicates she spent time in the car's front and rear seats, providing the main subscenes of the car. The geographical scene is unknown.

3. *Scene Group*
a. Roads.
b. Club.
c. Unknown parking spot.
d. Storage areas for the suspect car.
e. Suspect car.
f. Suspect person.
g. Victim person.
h. Suspect's email and information tools.

i. Victim's email and information tools.
j. The items in the car.

4. *Search* Zone.

Step 2. Analyze the Scene

Scene Decision How does the scene work?

1. *Restrictiveness* The car scene is a restricted access hosting scene.

2. *Volatility* The case began with an unknown location, and may stay undetermined. A mobile scene is harder to find, with great potential to change. If the suspect understood there was some sort of crime, and he would want to eliminate as much evidence as possible.

3. *Function* The scene is an object scene, as it received evidence from the suspect and victim's persons. It can also be a subject scene as it was a tool used by the suspect to perform the task of transporting the victim. A car functions as a transporter, but in this case was a secluded place to perform a sexual assault after transporting the occupants to a secluded location.

This scene was controlled by the suspect, but it provided a way to identify him. Most cases where a suspect used his own car do not result in him getting rid of it. The initial complication in this case was finding the crime scene, as the car was mobile.

4. *Capacity and Interaction Points* The scene has the hosting capacity for DNA, body fluids, fingerprints, and evidence artifacts to prove the female's presence, and actions. The information about the vehicle is hosted there too, and may be useful.

The victim was and outsider, with no history in the car. Her actions of leaving body fluids, fingerprints, or evidence artifacts in the front passenger seat, and the rear seat the car prove her presence. She said she did not drive, but those interaction points may yield evidence showing presence also.

Step 3. Evaluate the Evidence Potential

Evidence Decision How would the evidence work in this scene?

1. *Production* The person scenes produced biological material and deposited it on the car, including DNA and fingerprints.

2. *Proof Ability* The fingerprints on the car could show contact with a victim person scene. The biological evidence within the car may prove victim presence.

3. *Quality* DNA and fingerprints identify one person. The biological fluid stains may be identifiable as to which part of the body they came from. The evidence could show who was within the suspect controlled car scene, and what other scenes it interacted with it. In this case the most relevant evidence is the biological evidence in the car, which could also indicate the type of activity if identified by its function. This becomes even more relevant if the suspect's biological material is collocated with the victim's.

Even if the car has been cleaned, biological material can be collected in quantities enough to identify a person.

4. *Timeline* This car scene timeline will remain all relative unless there is some way to timestamp it by an external source.

5. *Resilience* The owner has had several days to impact the crime scene, however while fingerprints are fragile to contact, biological evidence endures well, and may be found in the material below the surface, such as the stuffing in upholstery.

6. *Collection* The two weeks passing means there is no exigency to do the processing, and it should be according to standard procedure. The standard CSI tools will support the investigator's efforts to get the evidence. During the period of unaccountability, it may have travelled, and was stored somewhere. The owner must have impacted the car, such as removing or adding things. The car then would have a relationship to a garage where the car was altered.

Step 4. Work the Evidence

Evidence Decision How to obtain the evidence from this scene?

1. *Critical Thinking* The investigator thought about the car scene as a mobile scene for sex, where the female person had no historical interactions in the car. The car had limited persons who interacted with it before at contact points like any other car scene. The investigator knew his goal was to prove the female's presence in the car, and the action of having sex, without her consent if possible.

The investigator chose to show presence by seeking the DNA and fingerprint evidence. He paid special attention to the back seat where the victim said the assault occurred to seek the evidence of presence and action in the form of body fluids. The investigator also processed the rest of the car, since victims can get facts wrong, and just proving her presence in the car as a passenger is central to the case.

2. *Information* The victim in this case identified the suspect by forensics with her email, but many car cases can be solved by information agencies already have access to. Records can tie people to their cars, either by DMV, insurance or prior law enforcement contact. People post self-photos with their cars on the internet. A sketch compliments the photographs, and an investigator customizes it to show crucial elements. Officers protected the car scene's integrity as much as possible.

3. *Photographs* Photographic images showed the scene, and accentuated the evidence, such as stains. A car scene suspect may clean the car seeking to remove traces of presence and the action of the crime, while introducing new biological evidence from the detailers to the scene. Alternate Light Sources reveal collectible evidence in lower concentrations.

4. *DNA* The victim's biological evidence in the car offers the best chance to prove her presence as she had no history there. DNA can prove biological presence, but semen indicates sex.

Technicians cannot test all DNA swabs, but this allows for maximum flexibility as new information in the case comes to light. More information can lead to better decision making when choosing swabs to sequence. The detectives might test the back seat swab depending on the outcome of the SART DNA testing, and fingerprint outcomes.

The Sexual Assault Response Team (SART) had no involvement in this case, to the car became the primary scene. If the time frame was a day, the car would be secondary, but an important part off the case since it could provide an independent link.

5. *Fingerprints* The fingerprints still relate to a sexual assault case without DNA evidence conclusions. If a suspect cleaned the victim, DNA evidence might not exist. His denial of her presence in his car and her fingerprints inside the same car strengthen the evidence about conflicting version of events.

6. *Patterns* There are no pattern matching parts in this case.

7. *Artifacts* The sticky side of the tape collects matter, including fibers, as well as potential DNA evidence. The victim mentioned a restraining device, and duct tape qualifies as one. The investigator may never prove this part of the case, but the tape's presence supports it.

8. *Report Production* The investigator had to confirm or refute the presence of the victim in the suspect's car. As they did not have a prior relationship, the evidence in the restrictive place (his car) could indicate the crime much more than were it in a public place.

V. Person Scenes

Person scenes are well defined root scenes where ideas, and actions start as they impact other scenes.

Step 1. Designate the Scene

Scene Decision Why is this a scene?

1. *Discovery* The person scene most often comes to the investigator's attention by report from an involved party, or when the investigator notices the person independently.

2. *Scene type* Person scenes are the most intimate and complex crime scenes. A person is well defined as a scene, and controls many other scenes, including the hosting scenes, cars, and tools. A person is the origin of thoughts, ideas, actions and reactions which makes them also the root of all crimes. A suspect considered the situation, and took action in the form of a crime, and unless it is a crime against the state, there is a person scene as a victim.

Some examples of person scenes are suspects, victims, witnesses, and others. For investigative purposes person scenes can include animals as other life forms.

3. *Scene Group* Person scenes interact with all other scenes, and are central to cases as their own centers of gravity. They control and fit into larger public, private, and car scenes.

Persons also host and control tools as extensions of themselves. Clothing and other coverings such as hats, gloves, condoms, or shoes create barriers to entry for person scenes. These antiforensic tools are individual subscenes to be processed.

4. *Search* Persons are often searched from head to toe. The law differentiates between searches by purpose such as for safety, evidence, or inventory for custody, but this book is about evidence. Most investigations center on the

interaction points as centers of gravity. There may be multiple investigators involved in the search, with time and distance between the searches.

Step 2. Analyze the Scene

Scene Decision How does the scene work?

1. *Restrictiveness* Person scenes are often semi-restricted. Their exteriors are accessible, but they can provide internal restricted accessibility with privacy. Hard scene borders mean a strong layer of security to entry, and they are defined scenes with limits. Person scene exteriors often have layers like clothing to protect and serve as a barrier.

A person's thoughts and desires may be indicated by their actions with information machines, such as computers linked to the internet to search for knowledge.

2. *Volatility* Person scenes may change with higher volumes of scene interactions, since persons can decide to take actions. As person scenes are biological, they constantly change, either as part of living or in death. Person interiors are often protected from the changes. Fingerprints, body fluids, and DNA remain constant for persons. The scenes are mobile, making finding the person scenes themselves a challenge in some cases.

3. *Function* Persons come up with ideas, and act on them. A suspect (or victim) has his own body as a scene in whatever he does. They are host locations for crimes, and tools for crimes. They may support crimes by conveying people and things, or be at the center of gravity. The function of a person changes based what happens during a crime.

Person scenes function as either the subject, or the object of the crime. A suspect person scene is a subject scene because it is doing the action and presence, while a victim would be an object scene receiving the actions of the subject. Persons are often subject scenes when dealing with non-person scenes such as places, cars, or tools because they produce so much evidence; DNA in cellular matter, such as hair and blood, fingerprints, and patterns.

However, sometimes the subject will use tools as extensions of themselves to impact the object person scene. A pattern from tool scene interaction such as a hammer to the skull make the person scene the object of the subject (and suspect) scene using the tool as an extension of his own scene subject scene.

Every person scene has identifying features and predicable interaction points for committing crimes with the ability to plan, and execute the crime seeking to keep those features hidden. He can offset his person scene's interaction with other scenes by using tools to put layers between themselves and the objects of the crime. However, whatever a person puts between his person and the crime still is subject to evidence from both entities and can act as a chain to link the components.

The ways person scenes function creates challenges for the investigator:

a. Person scenes have their own motives, opinions, and reasons for actions and reactions. These can also be expressed in statements which may not contribute to solving a case.

b. Person scenes can change at any time. Persons can plan and take steps to mitigate evidence production and transfer. This hinders some evidence collection efforts, but fingerprints and DNA do not change.

c. Person scenes may not cooperate when an investigator works to connect them to other scenes, and may take actions to thwart connection.

d. Some person scene components are very restricted to the investigator.

Person scenes communicate with investigators during the investigation. Person scenes include the hazard of being able to impact the investigator's thoughts on the case. A common outcome of investigator interaction with a person is to sway the investigation away from evidence and to emotion.

4. *Capacity and Interaction Points* Person scenes are often great scenes for evidence collection and carrying capacities. They have predictable interaction points to provide evidence of presence, control and actions. The basic interaction points of body and mind of a person include:

a. The head has many sources of cellular material containing DNA such as hair, tears, mucous from the mouth and nose.

b. The hands provide both DNA, and fingerprints.

c. The genitals provide DNA in cells, and in seminal or vaginal fluid, as well as hair.

d. Feet can be identifying like fingerprints.

e. The entire body potential provides DNA.

f. The person can also interact with machines by choosing identification information, like passwords. This authentication can be used to identify a person by actions.

Step 3. Evaluate the Evidence Potential

Evidence Decision How would the evidence work in this scene?

1. *Production* Evidence can be produced by interaction of the person scene with another scene such as a person either driving or present, or event tools. The person scene is always producing cells laden with DNA, and discarding them. The person scene also touches the surrounding environment leaving fingerprints everywhere. The person scene uses tools to impact the other scenes.

2. *Proof Ability* Person scene evidence proves presence and action of a person in a hosting scene, or interaction with another person scene, or tool as an extension of the person.

3. *Quality* Person scenes are ever changing, producing, and replacing the quality and availability of material. Person scene evidence relates to showing how the person connected to another scene by presence or action. The person scene evidence may be very unique to a particular person, such as DNA, fingerprints, and many patterns.

4. *Timeline* Person scene timelines have no internal actual times, and rely on external time keepers for accurate times. Person scene relative times can be more revealing, such as certain things happen in order.

5. *Resilience* Person scene evidence can be less resilient because of the movement and constant change along with it being biological material, but some of the evidence is enduring.

Person scenes have a high likelihood of tainting given their activity levels. A suspect person scene is vulnerable to damage and alteration from his decisions and actions relating to evidence discipline, but victims can also damage the evidence in their person scenes.

6. *Collection* Person scene evidence fragility prioritizes the work. The accessible external person scene can be altered in seconds, damaging proof. The most vulnerable evidence is often foreign DNA, so it is often the highest priority in a person scene, since DNA is likely the only viable identification evidence.

Internal scenes are more restrictive, and the procedures may require medically trained persons to do the work, such as blood draws.

Some cases require different an investigator to work on the suspects and victims to prevent allegations of the investigators cross contamination by transferring the DNA from person to person. This includes being around a suspect, and going to any scene. SART nurses specializing in sexual assault exams overcome this by working on just one person in the case.

Step 4. Work the Evidence

Evidence Decision How to obtain the evidence from this scene?

1. *Critical Thinking* The first three decisions indicate person scenes function as host scenes and mobile, thinking, and acting scenes who are the cause, and feel the effects of crime. Persons fit into scenes, moving among them. Persons also present the investigator with two sets of decisions within one type of crime scene. Exterior decisions address accessible scene parts, while interior decisions address restricted access parts. Both parts are predictable, with recognizable and collectible evidence with evidence transfer points. Mobility of the scene type challenges the investigator to find it. Person scenes move among other scenes, all the while producing and collecting evidence.

Finding the suspect person scene can be the greatest challenge of all, and most of the time, parts are available before a full identification is made.

Evidence work coordination for person scenes varies given the challenge of securing and stabilizing the scenes. Persons change, as does the corresponding evidence. Cross contamination or the allegation of evidence travelling in either direction to connect suspect, victim, or any scenes together jeopardizes the case, and could convict the innocent.

Victims wash to clean up, or just recover from the crime. Suspects wash for the same reasons, and may want to blunt the forensic evidence capabilities. Medical necessity causes a reordering of the evidence steps as the preservation of life is the highest priority. Medical personnel alter scenes during treatment. Photographs move forward on the list of evidence work, as aid work taints evidence scenes.

The investigator may seek the substrate evidence from the person scene in the form of photos, DNA and fingerprints to compare to evidence found in other scenes. A person produces transfer evidence such as fingerprints, and DNA in the form of hair, skin, and fluids.

People come with a variety of changeable features. Plastic surgery changes a person's appearance. People modify their eye color, hair color, and skin tone. People describe others by clothing more than eye color. Changing clothing requires little effort, and people shed clothing to thwart identification.

Person scenes have predictable components DNA, other biological evidence fluids, fingerprints. Person scenes offer enduring and fragile evidence. Experts identify bodies after heat exposure inside burning buildings, burial, and decomposition, and partial consumption by other animals.

An investigator should know a person scene will often be compromised, and thus should take care to find redundant evidence, even if it is away from the person scenes. A suspect, victim, or third party may modify a person scene before investigators can start working. Some activity is intentional to derail the investigation. Suspects wear protective gear to keep their evidence from being left, including gloves, condoms, hats. They wear disguises, and may dispose of the countermeasures along their path of travel.

Lifesaving efforts address the specific sections of the body scene an investigator wants to remain pristine. Medics document interventions, and the ME addresses them in the death report. Medics document the lifesaving efforts, but the investigator should ensure documentation of the subtle alterations and impacts on the person.

2. *Information* Person scene information can be sparse or robust, but there are three main time frames; the past, the timeframe of the crime, and the results. Information about a person at the time of crime is a combination of stable measurements like height, and instable like pulse. Clothing is an unstable feature. A scene's history may include what the person owns and controls. Criminal history may provide insight into a history of how the person operated in the past. Since person scene integrity is almost always compromised, requiring more detailed information integrated into the description. Sometimes only results are available to an investigator.

Sexual assault kits supply human body sketch blanks. They prompt basic observed facts at the beginning. Height and weight measurements inform about physical dominance. The first person to report a crime between two people may not remain the actual and legal victim. An investigation starts with less information, and evolves.

Involved parties sometimes go to hospitals seeking treatment for injuries they obtained during a crime. An office person may call around asking about emergency patients. The person may go out of county and report a vague or unbelievable accident.

3. *Photographs* Person scenes change, and photographs show things at a particular moment in time, so multiple photographs over time can show changes. The longer the investigator delays photographing a scene, the greater the odds it could change to show something different.

Persons move around making photographs of persons difficult, unless deceased. Medics may display wounds for photography if it is safe. The victim may find starting up close more palatable. Injury evidence photographs should show the scene with and without a scale, or ruler, to show their size. Photographs should show the absence of injuries also; written reports denying injuries provide conclusions rather than evidence. Injuries change, and show up after time. Follow up photographs of the injuries two to three days after the initial set may show more detail.

Video recordings of interactions with persons preserve a person's statements and actions. Recordings also preserve the emotion, and delivery of the words.

4. *DNA* Persons can leave their biological material at other scenes, as well as their fingerprints and patterns, and can receive those areas evidence as well as patterns from any scene.

Person scenes offer opportunities to connect people through DNA. Most cells contain DNA so any contact could yield this evidence. DNA often includes a carrier substance, such as saliva, semen or mucous. Altercations between people often result in DNA carried in skin cells being lodged under the fingernails of the other person, and even whispering in someone's ear can leave identifiable cells with DNA.

Person to person contact means there will be two DNA samples to sort out in the scene. Finding and sequencing the right DNA challenges an investigator. Person scenes have DNA transferred for a variety of interactions, not just the alleged assault. More transfer options amplify the need to avoid cross contamination.

5. *Fingerprints* Person scenes are more apt to make fingerprints than receive them, but human skin can hold a fingerprint. This evidence must include the ME. The majority of fingerprints related to person scenes come from a person, deposited onto another scene such as a building, car or tool.

6. *Patterns* Person scenes can have pattern marks on them to be matched to a source. This can be general, like a cylindrical object used to cave a skull, or specific, like a burn pattern from a clothes iron used to torture. Bite pattern examination has come under scrutiny, but may corroborate details of a case.

7. *Artifacts* Most person scenes have several artifacts with their person. Some of them are tools, but the person wears clothes, and has things. An investigator should examine the scene, assessing the most vulnerable evidence requiring collecting before anything else. As with any fresh event, the person may wear the same clothing but the investigator should think about a change of clothing and document the facts.

A witness often identifies involved persons by clothing, and an investigator collects them as identification evidence. Robbers use distraction clothing, such as orange safety vests. The victims focus on the vest and give poor descriptions of the person wearing it. Suspects discard the vests along the way.

Clothing collection preserves the actual evidence, and the evidence the clothing carries. An investigator may overlook shoes as evidence items out of kindness in harsh weather. Shoes aid identification by appearance and tread. If the burglar wore gloves his shoe tread patterns may offer the best evidence left at the scene to match him. Shoe tops may also catch the victim's blood with the closeness of a suspect and victim in a stabbing.

People often leave their evidence artifacts at a scene. Mistakes happen and people forget to exercise proper evidence discipline in an act. Condom wrappers go in the trash out of habit, and hats fall off when suspects run from a scene. Items carrying the suspect's biological evidence tie him back to the scene. Missing persons leave their evidence, such as when suicides leave their car parked, and wander to their site.

Sexual assault processing captures evidence from a person scene in order to show proof of other persons, as both presence, and action. The evidence is cellular material like pubic hair, and semen, as well as photos for injuries, and drug screens.

A sexual assault kit for (male) suspects guides the investigator in collecting the evidence needed with assaults. (Typically, female sexual assault kits are collected by nurses.) An investigator should scrape under the fingernails of a suspect even if he has washed his hands.

8. *Report Production* Person scenes emphasize presence and action within other scenes, or to other scenes. The investigator often structures the report to describe the evidence from head to toe. Another option is by emphasis on key components. Time may become more relevant to a person scene because they change.

Person Scene Scenarios

14. Person Scene, Influence Suspect
15. Suspected Suicide by Shooting
16. Person Assault Scene, Robbery or Burglary Suspect
17. Domestic Violence Person Scenes
18. Sexual Assault Person Scenes

14. Person Scene, Influence Suspect

A man called 911 from the train station complaining he was being followed. He showed signs of drug intoxication, and an investigator ran a battery of tests which indicated he had several signs of drug use.

Summary
Influence report. The man was arrested based on objective signs and symptoms, and consented to a blood draw.

To Do
Evidence item to lab.

Investigation
At 1941 HRS, 9/23/06 (Friday) I was on patrol in a marked patrol car (#14) and in full uniform. A man reported being stalked and threatened by a homeless man in a black SUV in the area. He gave his name to Treeville Dispatch as Holden Vinson (2/29/82). I conducted an area check, and found no one matching the stalker description, nor an SUV.

At 2000 HRS in the Commuter Train Station, a man flagged me down. He said he was Vinson, and called 911. Vinson claimed involvement as the victim of a theft, a robbery, and an argument. He gave three different stories about what happened in less than a minute. He added the stalker took his wallet, and threw him out of his car. I asked for identification and Vinson gave me the wallet he just told me was taken from him. He was without CA ID, but told me his name was Ulysses Holden Vinson (3/29/80).

Vinson told me he argued with the man in the SUV, and the man told Vinson he was going to come to his house. Twice during the contact, Vinson misidentified uninvolved SUV's as the suspect car.

I noticed Vinson moved and fidgeted during our interaction. Vinson seemed nervous, and conversed with rapid speech. His skin felt cool and clammy. When Vinson spoke his breath carried a chemical smell, and the inside of his mouth was coated white. Vinson did not know the time, but knew he was in Treeville. I noticed discoloration on Vinson's right hand fingers with burned skin. He said he burned his fingers earlier in the day, but did not need any medical assistance. He did not elaborate on the cause.

Vinson told me he smoked crystal methamphetamine at 10:00 PM the night before. I told Vinson I thought he used drugs in the more recent past, and was going to test him. Vinson cooperated. Vinson said he was not under a doctor's care, nor was he prescribed any medications. Vinson did not wear glasses or contacts. I began to evaluate Vinson to determine whether he exhibited signs and symptoms of being under the influence of a controlled substance.

Field Observations
2000 HRS. Commuter Train Station with nearly level concrete sidewalk. Street lamps lit the area.

Radial Pulse, left arm.
2033 HRS 118 BPM
2036 HRS 120 BPM

Pupillary Comparison
Ambient light from street lights, and car lights. Officer Garcia's pupils compared to 4.0 MM in light, constricted to 3.5 MM in direct light. Vinson's pupils compared to 6.5 mm in diameter. I saw Vinson's pupils delayed reaction to direct light, and constricted to 6.0 mm, and returned to 6.5 mm.

Horizontal Gaze Nystagmus, Vertical Gaze Nystagmus, Non Convergence
Vinson did not stop moving his head long enough to measure.

Balance, Time Estimation
I asked Vinson to stand with his feet together and his arms at his side. I explained to him to lean his head back, and close his eyes and estimate in his head what he thought was 30 seconds. Vinson estimated 30 seconds after 3 seconds passed. His body swayed a few inches from left to right and front to rear. I confirmed the instructions, and Vinson performed the test again. Vinson estimated 30 seconds after 7 seconds passed.

Based on my training and experience I believed Vinson was under the influence of a controlled substance, a Central Nervous System (CNS) Stimulant. I told Vinson I was arresting him. I handcuffed Vinson, checked the handcuffs for a proper fit, and double locked them. I searched him incident to arrest at the station scene, and found no contraband. I placed Vinson in Officer Garcia's car for transport. Officer Garcia transported Vinson to Treeville PD HQ to obtain a blood sample.

Evidence
Vinson provided a blood sample. Licensed Medical Technologist Belseder took the blood sample at 2100 HRS. I booked the sample into evidence.

Recorded Statement
I advised Vinson of his Miranda Rights at 2130 HRS. Vinson said, *Yes*, to the four questions and said he understood his rights. Vinson agreed to talk with me, and signed the form.

Vinson said he smoked crystal methamphetamine alone on Friday night at 10:00 PM. He said after he completed his smoking, he decided to quit. Vinson said he broke the glass pipe in the name of Saint Michael.

I booked the recording into evidence.

Step 1. Designate the Scene

Scene Decision Why is this a scene?

1. *Discovery* The investigator declared the scene by the suspect's call to 911. The caller's role evolved from victim to suspect based on his activity in the officer's presence.

2. *Scene type* This person scene may be altered by drug use, which may produce objective signs and symptoms.

3. *Scene Group*
a. Train station.
b. Travel route of suspect.
c. Suspect home.
d. Suspect person.
e. Meth pipe.

4. *Search* Zone.

Step 2. Analyze the Scene

Scene Decision How does the scene work?

1. *Restrictiveness* The person scene is a semi-restricted access hosting scene. A person can be observed on the surface. The internal evidence of blood is restrictive. Urine could replace blood as the evidence holding the drug use proof.

2. *Volatility* The scene is highly mobile, with great potential to change. The person's exterior could change, but the symptoms' primary control factor in drug cases is time. The suspect likely understood there was some sort of crime and he would want to eliminate as much evidence as possible.

3. *Function* The body scene is an object scene in this case, as it has modified by the chemicals in the drugs, but also a subject scene, as it performed the action. The signs and symptoms may differ based on the drugs, but not the role. The person scene functions as the container of ideas and performer of actions. Sometimes the person is the unwilling object of drugs, in order to perform a crime, such as a sexual assault. In this case, the person is functioning as the recipient of drug use and intoxication.

The person scene is the suspect's only choice for a scene if he wishes to be under the influence. His behavior may gain the attention of an investigator independent of any calls for service.

4. *Capacity and Interaction Points* The scene has the hosting capacity for DNA, fingerprints, and evidence artifacts to prove presence, and action. The person is the scene for a drug intoxication investigation. The head is the center of gravity to show the presence and action through the specific points of the eyes, and mouth. The hands, and arms have arteries close to the surface, and an investigator can measure a person's pulse easier by them.

The drug interacts with the user's body, and is carried in the blood, and excreted in urine.

Step 3. Evaluate the Evidence Potential

Evidence Decision How would the evidence work in this scene?

1. *Production* The observable body reactions are produced by interaction with drugs.

2. *Proof Ability* The observable, and measurable evidence indicated Vinson was under the influence of a substance. The support built the case for a

blood draw to obtain definitive evidence. Some places use urine as a sample to test for drug use.

3. *Quality* The observation quality can vary based on persons, and the skill of the observer. There are often multiple sub exams involved, and redundancy helps to produce a preponderance of evidence. The information is relevant, as the methodology for the exams are scientifically verified. Most of the sub exams in the process produce specific results, which taken as a whole are relevant as indicators of a level of intoxication. The unique combination of facts may collectively indicate a condition of intoxication.

4. *Timeline* This person scene has no actual timeline, and can only be seen through external timing, such as the 911 call, police arrival, and arrest, and perhaps third party video.

5. *Resilience* The evidence in observation is solid, but time sensitive. Multiple drug use may skew results.

6. *Collection* The investigator processed the scene in the field, and then brought the person to HQ for a blood draw in a controlled environment. The blood was drawn by a technician to be sent to a lab for testing.

Everybody is different as a scene so most drug examinations of person scenes involve a series of tests to collect a preponderance of evidence. Despite differences, person scenes require a standardized process.

Step 4. Work the Evidence

Evidence Decision How to obtain the evidence from this scene?

1. *Critical Thinking* The investigator thought about the person scene as a place showing the interaction with other scenes on the exterior as well as interior. He set about to measure and document the person's statements, observable symptoms, and actions to see if indicated a pattern to indicate drug use. Patterns matching indicators of use could then be used to obtain a sample from the person scene to scientifically prove if drugs were present in his system.

This standard drug field examination follows accepted practices outlined in most legitimate training provider manuals.

2. *Information* Most of the information comes from the suspect himself.

3. *Photographs* Influence cases did not require photographs. An injury or visible evidence may require documentation. A person who uses intravenous drugs creates needle track marks. Body and dash cameras simplify collecting the footage evidence and may support or refute the allegations.

4. *DNA* The DNA is irrelevant.

5. *Fingerprints* The fingerprints are irrelevant for the case, but will be taken during booking.

6. *Patterns* Matching is used on an overall approach by measuring several signs and symptoms.

7. *Artifacts* The investigator considered Vinson may have had drugs or paraphernalia on his person. The investigator decided to find them before an arrest, through a search or even a conversation. A search incident to the arrest revealed no other evidence.

8. *Report Production* Influence cases begin with objective observations about the person's actions, such as violations. DUI and drug influence reports provide a methodical approach to treating a person as a crime scene, observable conditions and actions.

15. Person Scene, Suspected Suicide by Shooting

Multiple people called 911 when they heard a single gunshot in their neighborhood. Officers began to arrive into the area within a few minutes, and saw an elderly man lying on the sidewalk, with a wound to the head, and a pistol to his side. He remained alive, and transported to the hospital for treatment where he was declared dead a few hours later.

Summary
Fatal shooting, presented as a possible suicide. Photos taken. GSR kit collected on victim during treatment prior to being declared deceased. Firearm recovered by ME's Office.

To Do
GSR kit to lab.

Investigation
At 1200 HRS on 7/2/13 I found the victim in front of 644 Carney Dr., adjacent to his home at 648 Carney Dr. He lay on his back with his head pointed northwest, and his feet southeast. Blood flowed from the right side of his head, although I could not tell its origin.

Medics arrived when I did, and began treating the patient.

Scene Integrity
After providing medical aid to the victim, investigators secured the scene and victim's residence.

Scene Description

The neighborhood is a residential area with single family homes. The midblock scene is a low crime area, with no reports of drive by shootings in the area.

Photographs
I photographed the victim as I found him, clothed, and with a black pistol near his right hand. An aluminum walking cane was a few feet away on the front lawn. I canvassed the neighborhood and saw no security cameras.

Evidence
I attempted to collect gunshot residue (GSR) from his hands while the victim was still alive. At 1206 HRS I donned gloves. I swabbed the victim's left hand and his right hand with the appropriate collectors in the GSR kit. After I collected samples, medical personnel placed paper bags on the victim's hands.

Medical Examiner Investigator (MEI) Charlebois recovered a Wilder Arms, model 2342, serial number 234556, from beside the victim. It is a .357 caliber semiautomatic pistol, with a blue finish, and 4 inch barrel. MEI Charlebois showed me a 7 round magazine in the magazine well, with 5 unfired cartridges in the magazine. I saw an unfired cartridge in the chamber of the gun. She retained custody of the firearm for processing after the hospital staff declared the victim deceased.

Officers Smith and Birnkrantz used a metal detector to search the area for the shell casing from the fired bullet, but did not find it.

Victim Processing
After transporting the victim to the emergency room, I met with the physicians there (1230 HRS). He was still under the care of his physician. Dr. Vivian Chow allowed me to photograph the victim in the emergency room. I noticed a small cut in the webbing of the victim's right hand, between thumb and forefinger. See the Pathologist report.

Death
At 1330 HRS Dr. Chow declared the victim deceased. The Medical Examiner will conduct an investigation.

Step 1. Designate the Scene

Scene Decision Why is this a scene?

1. *Discovery* The investigator declared the scene by observing the person as a possible victim of violence due to the head trauma, and 911 calls.

2. *Scene type* This person scene appears to be altered by a gunshot.

3. *Scene Group*
a. Neighborhood.
b. Victim's home.
c. Victim's car.
d. Victim person.
e. Gun and potential casing.
f. Victim's computer or smartphone.

4. *Search* Zone. There will be a follow on search by a medical examiner, after treatment by medical personnel. The search becomes more relevant because the person will be transported in a body bag, and the evidence on the person will be shuffled. Although the Medical Examiner will have jurisdiction over the body, and will name the cause and manner of death, the scene while the person is still alive will be the best opportunity to look before things change.

Step 2. Analyze the Scene

Scene Decision How does the scene work?

1. *Restrictiveness* The person scene is a semi-restricted access scene. The exterior is accessible, while the interior is restricted. The damage from the firearm could be achieved by someone well outside the scene, and the bullet was not restricted from entering into a body and may be within the restricted person scene's body.
The weapon was next to the body.

2. *Volatility* The person scene is mobile, with great potential to change.

3. *Function* The injured person scene is an object scene, as it received the action of the gunshot, but is potentially a subject scene if it is a suicide, meaning the victim did the shooting. The scene functions as the manifestation of the idea of violence, although it is undetermined if it is suicidal violence, or homicidal violence in this early phase

The person scene received the action, prompting the questions of who did the action. The body scene resents a robust opportunity for documentation but the body transport process alters the scene. Also, the person scene will not have evidence from another person scene on him.

There appears to have been no efforts to eliminate evidence at the scene, as the gun remained.

4. *Capacity and Interaction Points* The scene has the hosting capacity for DNA, limited fingerprints, patterns, and evidence artifacts. This person scene has the classic interaction points, the head, and hands. The dying man has what looked like a bullet wound to the head, which may provide evidence to connect to a firearm. His hand also had a minor injury.

The potential information about the gun may connect to the person.

Step 3. Evaluate the Evidence Potential

Evidence Decision How would the evidence work in this scene?

1. *Production* The bullet damaged the victim's skull, the cycling action of the firearm may have injured his hand. GSR may be a product of the firing of the gun on the victim's hand.

2. *Proof Ability* The gun next to the victim, and lack of information about a suspect shooting at the victim give supports the idea the victim was shot at close range, possibly by himself.

3. *Quality* The investigator arrived after the gunshot, and collected GSR soon after. The handgun was on scene, collected by the MEI. The information about the lack of an identified or suspected shooter is relevant. The gunshot to the head, and hand injury from an awkward shooting grip may indicate a self-inflicted wound.

The bullet from the victim may be unique enough to match to the gun at the scene. The hand injury may also correlate with the slide of the pistol. GSR is not always reliable by itself, and has been criticized lately, so it may not be a reliable primary evidence.

4. *Timeline* This person scene has no actual timeline, and can only be seen through external timing, such as the 911 call, police arrival, medical treatment, and perhaps third party video.

5. *Resilience* The evidence for GSR is fleeting, but the wound pattern is more stable, and the metal bullet will hold its shape.

6. *Collection* The investigator processed the person scene in the field. The gun went with the MEI, as does the body for autopsy. This person scene requires a standardized process, and there is nothing to indicate evidence is in jeopardy beyond time.

There is no reason to believe the person's car is involved, however people can use cars for storage also. Cars are the usual means to go to meetings, and sometimes there is evidence from the meeting in the car which may provide some insight into the victim's environment before the incident.

Step 4. Work the Evidence

Evidence Decision How to obtain the evidence from this scene?

1. *Critical Thinking* The investigator thought about the person scene as a place to show interaction with other scenes. He saw the injured person was injured in two interaction points; the head with the bullet holes, and the hand with the cut on the webbing. The investigator also knew the injured man would probably die, but the question in such cases is when death will happen. If a person is stabilized on life support for two weeks, the Medical Examiner will probably not investigate, and the body scene's most fragile evidence could be gone, damaged, or contaminated.

The investigator's role would be limited with the body scene, but he would still have to work the case, but without control over how the body scene would be handled after the person was declared deceased. The Medical Examiner controls the body scene upon death. The investigator chose to collect as much evidence as possible before the person died.

2. *Information* The elderly man on the sidewalk is the main scene. He was 80 feet from his home, and investigators found his gun near his right hand. The ME Investigator checked his home for other potential victims, and safety reasons, and found nothing suspicious. No witness reported other persons in the area, and the weapon was next to the man when encountered by personnel. Factual observations help prevent accusations of an investigator rushing to a judgment or conclusion. A simple wound description provides enough information to establish the seriousness. A Medical Examiner will later give an expert explanation of the wound, and detailed information about the body. The description explains the victim's gunshot head injury, and the gun next to him indicates self-inflicted violence, but an early conclusion of a self-inflicted gunshot will not help investigate the case.

3. *Photographs* The photographs provide time stamped evidence documentation for the events in this investigation. All scenes change after the pivotal event of the gunshot. Some people modify body scenes in the post crime period before investigative stabilization.

4. *DNA* Person scenes may include fragile DNA evidence collected by the ME. Medical personnel often have instructions to bag a victim's hands,

preserving evidence under a person's fingernails for collection. Any indication of violence indicates the need to swab the person's hands. Fingernail scraping may yield the best evidence for the deceased's final fight. A victim of close up violence often has another person's DNA under his fingernails. As the man died as the result of violence, the ME will scrape under the deceased's nails at autopsy to provide trace evidence. What the ME found on the firearm may yield DNA. The DNA may connect the two persons together, or eliminate other potential persons, and narrow the persons to the victim.

5. *Fingerprints* The ME coordinates fingerprint collection. The investigator may collect suspect prints on a deceased person scene with ME permission prior to the body's transportation, or request one of the ME's assistant perform the procedure.

6. *Patterns* The bullet hole, and marks on the bullet provide good pattern matching evidence. The person has a small cut on the webbing of his hand, which is sometimes a result of shooting a semi-automatic pistol when it is held in an awkward way.

7. *Artifacts* The ME's Office handled the firearm scene, reducing the investigation workload. The focus shifts to locating evidence at the scene to indicate what transpired at the scene in the form of presence and action. Suicides may have a note on their person outlining their actions and reasons.

8. *Report Production* The report format should cover what roles the various investigators have in the case, and how they control particular evidence. The content of the report covers the evidence itself. In this case there may be no evidence to support more than a single person's involvement. An investigator should limit death case conclusion to the most general terms at the outset given the limited information.

16. Person Scene, Assault Suspect

A man called 911 to report his 27 year old son stabbed him with a knife, and left the family home about 2 minutes prior. One of the arriving officers noticed a man matching the description walking away from the area of the home, and detained him.

Summary
Assault with deadly weapon. Father victim, major injuries, stabbed in back. Son suspect, in custody. Photos taken. Both parties swabbed. No weapon recovered. Clothing of both collected.

To Do
Evidence items to lab

Investigation
At 4:45 PM on 10/14/14 I arrived to the suspect stop location. Officer Mattington briefed me.

Suspect Detention Location
Officer Mattington stopped Suspect Wong at the southeast corner of Barnes Ave. and Ordonez St. at 4:08 PM, 8 minutes after the 911 call. I measured 0.3 miles from the home the suspect shares with his father (3343 Tarex Dr.) to the detention location. The exact detention spot is a street corner with landscaping in the nearby yards. The area is a residential neighborhood with single family homes. Most of the homes have yards ranging from 6000 square feet to 9000 square feet, with fenced backyards. There were many cars parked on the streets.

Officers Wilson and Smith conducted a search of the stop area and did not find a knife. I retraced the possible suspect routes and did not find the knife. (See the attached map for locations and routes).

Initial Suspect Field Processing
I processed the suspect at the detention scene, prior to placing him in a patrol car. Officer Mattington handcuffed suspect Wong prior to my arrival. I noticed several red stains on his shirt, pants, shoes and hands.

I collected possible biological samples from the suspect at the detention site. Prior to swabbing I donned fresh gloves to avoid cross contamination. I placed the sealed swabs in the Crime Lab Evidence Freezer.

Item 1 Swab, sterile water.
Item 2 Swab, S. Wong Right Hand, and sterile water.
Item 3 Swab, S. Wong Left Hand, and sterile water.
Item 4 Swab, S. Wong shirt, and sterile water.
Item 5 Swab, sterile water.

Follow on Processing – Suspect Wong
I processed Wong in the Spartanburg HQ Holding Facility, Cell #5. Start time 1650 HRS. I photographed the suspect from different angles during in the process.

Item 6 Tee shirt, blue short sleeved. It had several reddish stains on the front. (See photos.)
Item 7 Jeans, blue dark red stains on both upper legs.
Item 8 Shoes, athletic, red trim. Size 9.

I used the sexual assault kit to collect the listed evidence from the suspect's body.
Nail scrapings Left Hand.
Nail scrapings Right Hand.
Pulled Head Hair.
Anatomical Drawings Page (Copy in General file).

Visible Evidence of Injuries and Struggle
I photographed the suspect after he removed his clothing. I also used the Anatomical Drawings section of the Sexual Assault Exam to document injuries. I filed the document in general file.

Wong had a fresh cut one quarter inch on the webbing of his left hand between his index and middle finger. He also received a half inch cut along the side of his thumb. I saw blood stains on his left pocket, and right thigh, and mud stains on his knees.

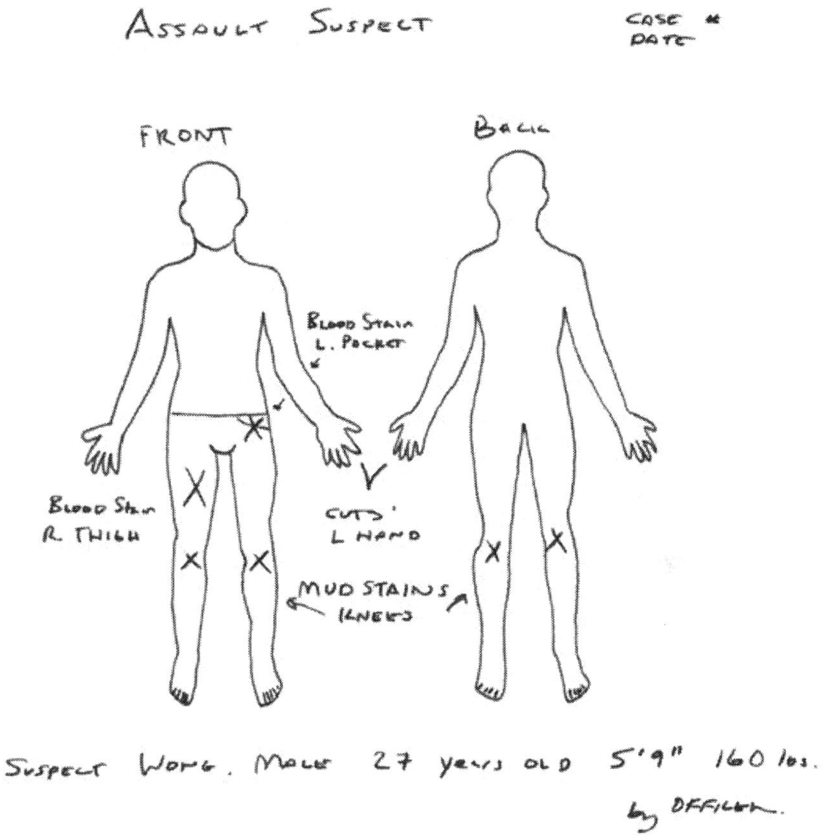

Step 1. Designate the Scene

Scene Decision Why is this a scene?

1. *Discovery* The investigator declared the scene by the victim naming his son as a suspect, and his being located close to the hosting scene. The suspect and victim know each other, solidifying the identification. He also had visible blood stains.

3. *Scene Group*
a. Neighborhood.
b. House assault scene.
c. Detention scene.
d. Transit scenes.
e. Fleeing suspect person.
f. Injured victim person.
g. Outstanding weapon.

h. Suspect's computer or smartphone.
i. 911 call of the injured person.

4. *Search* Zone.

Step 2. Analyze the Scene

Scene Decision How does the scene work?

1. *Restrictiveness* The suspect person scene is a semi-restricted access hosting scene. His exterior is accessible, while his internal components like body fluids and DNA are restrictive.

2. *Volatility* The person scene is mobile, with great potential to change. The suspect left and may have cleaned himself along the way.

3. *Function* The scene is a subject scene as the person did the actions, and an object scene as it may have received evidence from the actions. The scene functions as the manifestation of the idea of violence.

4. *Capacity and Interaction Points* The scene has the hosting capacity for DNA such as victim blood, and artifacts to prove presence, and action.

The suspect scene offered better evidence opportunities than the victim because the suspect's person scene was captured nearby after little interaction with other scenes. The suspect's hands are a center of gravity to show the presence and action from interactions with other scenes. The visible blood stains offer evidence to connect the two scenes. The victim received treatment from medics who cut off clothing and closed wounds.

The two person scenes in this scenario have the routine body interaction points of the head and hands, as well as the stab site, but they are also connected via the weapon as an extension of the assaulter.

Step 3. Evaluate the Evidence Potential

Evidence Decision How would the evidence work in this scene?

1. *Production* The puncture in the victim's body scene was the result of a tool being pushed into it. The investigator presumed the blood on the scenes was from the injury.

2. *Proof Ability* The victim scene had a stab wound, and the suspect was found a short distance away, with blood on him. The weapon was not recovered.

3. *Quality* The evidence is good quality as it was collected soon after the events, and verified by at least the victim. The blood is a unique identifier, and blood on another scene answers questions of action and presence. The quantity of the injured person's blood, who was injured in the back is very relevant to showing an assault rather than incidental blood collection from people who cohabitate. The information of the injury is relevant. The stabbing tool is also relevant, but had not been found.

The 911 call established the stabbing was malicious. Statements about the injury may change in court, and the spontaneous statement about the injury is a snapshot of what happened.

4. *Timeline* This person scene had no actual timeline, and can only be seen through external timing, such as the 911 call, police arrival, medical treatment, and perhaps third party video.

5. *Resilience* Blood evidence can be frail, but the investigator collected it at the detention site with limited tainting. The injuries were treated, changing them quickly.

6. *Collection* The investigator processed the suspect person scene in the field, and then brought him to HQ for more thorough follow up in a controlled environment.

This person scene requires a standardized process. The blood and DNA evidence is attached to the suspect, but can be tainted through touching other scenes, or washing. This may prioritize the documentation and collection of evidence before it can be destroyed.

Step 4. Work the Evidence

Evidence Decision How to obtain the evidence from this scene?

1. *Critical Thinking* The investigator thought about the person scene as it would interact with another person scene in an assault. The head might control the action, and have some involvement, but the hands interacted with the tool or other person during the fight. The attack involved a stabbing tool as an extension of the person doing the stabbing. The tool often cuts a person or persons, releasing blood onto the scenes. The simultaneous discovery of multiple scenes, (with a list of evidence to collect in each) sets up the decisions about how to prove transferred evidence among the entities of place scenes and persons. The knife is outstanding, but the suspect has blood on his clothing which can be tested to determine if it belongs to his father.

Anonymity is not an issue as both person scenes were identified. This allowed the transferred evidence between them to be focused on proving an assault, and how it happened.

The suspect scene resembled a sexual assault suspect, but with far less intimate evidence. Assault, robbery or burglary suspects as scenes include a lot of common processing.

2. *Information* Officers detained the suspect scene as he fled. The investigator analyzed the distance travelled in the elapsed time. An investigator captured the suspect around the time and location of the event, and he documented him by words, photos, and swabbing at the stop. Information will be necessary to see if the blood came from another incident, or could only be from the stabbing. Recordings can offset conclusions about what happened later.

3. *Photographs* The hospitalized victim increased investigator access challenges to take photographs, and process the person for other evidence. Documenting the suspect at scene anticipates potential witnesses, as well as shows his condition. People often downplay injuries and situations, but photos provide visual proof of damage.

4. *DNA* A suspect often has evidence on him indicating recent action, such as blood in a stabbing. The victim and suspect's fingernail scrapings may yield DNA. The nature of skin being trapped under fingernails may indicate a struggle.

5. *Fingerprints* The fingerprints are unnecessary on this suspect person scene, although the private scene of the stabbing should be searched for prints. A known suspect reduces but does not eliminate the usefulness of prints. There is no challenge to identification in this case.

6. *Patterns* If the outstanding weapon is found it could connect the suspect and victim by both presence and action. The artifact may provide a distinctive mark, or even a reasonable possibility, such as a near fit.

7. *Artifacts* The missing weapon creates a challenge for linking the suspect to the action of the assault as it could possible prove presence and action. An investigator retraced the route, and looked for discarded evidence including the weapon, but found none.

If the two persons in case were strangers, and the suspect took an article from the scene, or left one there, he has simplified the investigator's effort to connect him to the scene. The suspect might have the victim's property in his possession, or have discarded it nearby.

8. *Report Production* This report was structured to cover the investigation in chronological order of discovery. Geographical elements are strong in the organization, but it flows in a way to emphasize how the case unfolded. The evidence content addressed efforts to avoid contamination, which will likely be a part of the case.

17. Person Scene, Domestic Violence

A neighbor called 911 to report shouting in an apartment. She believed she heard a slap, and a scream. Officers contacted the husband and wife residents. Officers spoke with each person alone. After determining the husband grasped the wife on her upper arms and shook her, they arrested the husband for domestic violence.

Summary
DV, visible minor injury with complaint of pain. Suspect in custody. Photos taken. Victim damaged clothing collected.

To Do
Follow up photos of victim

Investigation
On 3/17/14 I arrived to the scene and spoke with Officer Martoch who briefed me on the call. He spoke with the wife at her kitchen table. He recorded her statement with a hidden digital recorder. She said she was married to her husband for five years. After the birth of their child, Susie, one year ago, their relationship became difficult. She felt her husband did not contribute to Suzie's care, and they argued about money. Over the past month the arguments have grown worse and today after arguing for about an hour her husband grabbed her on the upper arms and squeezed while yelling at her. He said if she left, he would ensure she would not receive a Green Card.

Officer Jones spoke with the husband. He recorded his statement with a hidden digital recorder. The husband stated he did nothing wrong, and only spoke with his wife.

Evidence

I recorded all conversations with citizens in my investigation. I booked the recordings into evidence.

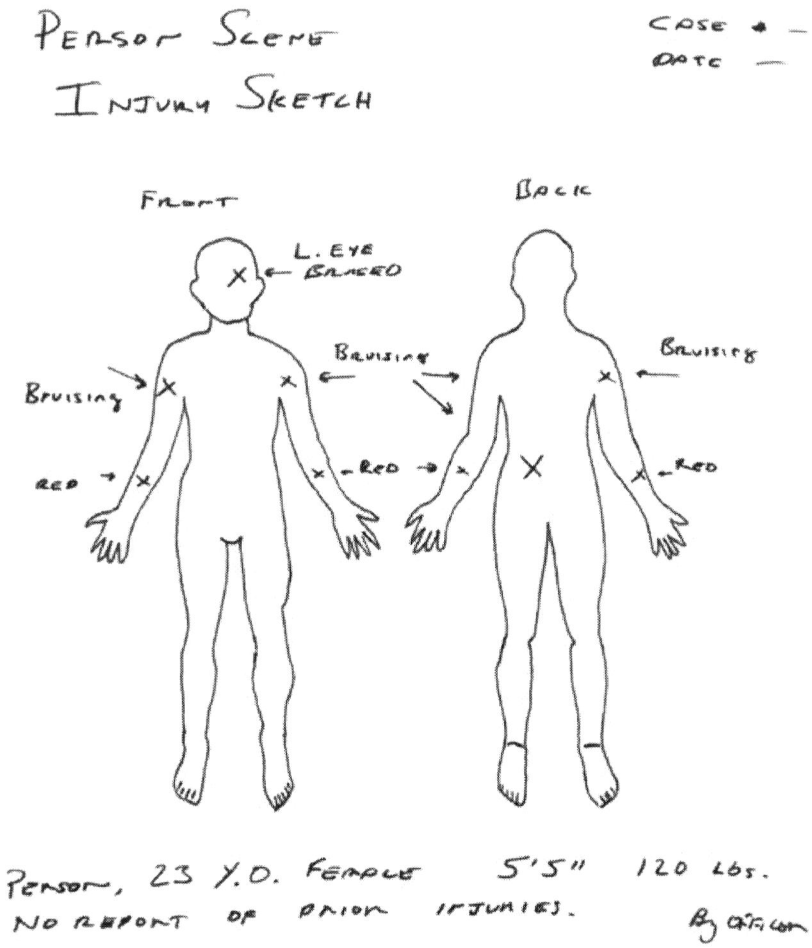

Photographs

Officers detained the husband (suspect) in the driveway before I arrived. I photographed him there. I photographed the baby on the walkway as she was held by Officer Jones. I photographed the victim in her home. She wore a sweater when I arrived, but at my request, she changed to a yellow shirt to show her upper arms. I photographed the room of the fight with the wife's permission.

Wife Visible Injuries (See sketch)
Redness / bruising on upper arms, elbows and forearms, front and back.
Left eye / cheek bruised.
She reported pain with all injuries.

Husband, no injuries.

Daughter, no injuries.

Evidence
I photographed the victim wearing her tee shirt with the neck stretched from the fight. The victim attributed the damage to her husband grabbing her about the collar. I collected the item as evidence.

Follow Up Images Advisement
I advised the victim of the need to photograph her injuries after 24 hours. We made an appointment for her to come to HQ on 1/26/12 around 1:00 PM for follow up photographs.

Investigation Continued
I believe the husband injured his wife by grabbing her upper arms based on the statements of both parties, and the visible injuries. I placed him under arrest for domestic violence. Officer Jones transported husband to headquarters for booking.

Follow up
On 1/26/12 I was working for Newtown Police Department as a Crime Scene Investigator. At 2055 HRS I met with the victim at the Newtown Police Department Headquarters to take follow up pictures of her injuries.

Visual Evidence of Injuries
Victim – photographed in room 201, the conference room.

Bruising left eye. Bruising on the outside of her left and right upper arms. She attributed the injury to being grabbed by the suspect.

Unreported prior invisible bruising on her left lower back.

She reported reduced pain with her injuries, and stated her back did not have pain.

Digital Images, Preserved on the digital photo file via the server as evidence. See metadata for camera settings. Lighting: with natural light, artificial lighting, and a flash. I photographed in different formats.

Victim 66 digital images. Image Quality JPEG FINE format for images 05 through 45.

I used the Department issued alternate light source employing the wavelengths of light, 430 – 470 nm wavelength blue light for images 26 to 39, and 43 to 45. I saw darker blue areas in the locations where the victim complained of visible bruising, but I did not see significant bruising invisible the unaided eye.

Step 1. Designate the Scene

Scene Decision Why is this a scene?

1. *Discovery* The investigator declared the scene by the victim's declaration she was involved in a crime.

2. *Scene type* The female victim's injuries on her person are the center of gravity. The suspect is also a person scene, but he is uninjured, and shows no evidence.

This scenario could be modified to a child abuse case given the person scenes. In child abuse cases there are often special interviews conducted by experts.

3. *Scene Group*
a. Neighborhood.
b. Home assault scene.
c. Uninjured male person.
d. Injured female person.
e. Injured female's shirt.
f. Child.
g. The 911 call.

4. *Search* Zone.

Step 2. Analyze the Scene

Scene Decision How does the scene work?

1. *Restrictiveness* The female person scene is an accessible scene as it is entirely exterior. There is no indication of any restriction as the internal workings of her are not part of this case.

2. *Volatility* The person is mobile and while it produced evidence of presence and action, it also healed to change the evidence. The damaged clothing is an example of how a scene can change, as the female could have changed clothes, and valuable evidence indicating actions would have been eliminated from the case.

3. *Function* The person is an object scene, as she received the actions of the subject scene or suspect. However, it is possible she fought back, and injured the suspect, and has subject qualities also. The female person scene functioned as a carrier of thoughts, and a doer of actions, just as the male person scene did.

This crime involves both persons' bodies as crime scenes. Identification is not in question, but showing injuries without conclusion is required to allow others to conclude who the aggressor was. Persons in a relationship have a regular evidence of presence, and persons get injured all the time by unrelated actions. Sometimes investigations require more work to navigate those situations.

4. *Capacity and Interaction Points* The female person scene has hosting capacity for DNA, pattern marks as injuries, and evidence artifacts. The female person scene offered better evidence opportunities as she was injured.

Both parties interact with the standard points, head and face, hands, and body.

Step 3. Evaluate the Evidence Potential

Evidence Decision How would the evidence work in this scene?

1. *Production* The observable body reactions of bruising are produced by interaction of force upon a body scene.

2. *Proof Ability* The observable, and measurable evidence of visual injuries supports the theory the wife was hit. This does not establish whether she was innocent or guilty, only she was injured.

3. *Quality* The injury quality can vary based on a person's body, the type of injury, and the skill of the photographer to show the injury. Facial injuries are relevant to any assault case. Eye injuries tend to indicate a fight, and since the area around the eye is so sensitive, it shows injuries. Vision is an important sense, and people are more apt to see a doctor for an eye injury, which can provide excellent documentation for the investigation. Information is

relevant and with the photographs provides indication of events. The damaged clothing supports a fight also.

Experts such as physicians can sometimes identify injuries as defensive or offensive. Injuries may be pattern matched to a source. Facial injuries are pretty unique to altercations.

4. *Timeline* This person scene has no actual timeline, and can only be seen through external timing, such as the 911 call, police arrival, and perhaps third party witnesses. The follow up photos put the injuries and their healing on a timeline.

5. *Resilience* The injury was changing and healing.

6. *Collection* The female person scene received the violence, causing injuries, and the since the bruising injuries will change with time photographing them is a priority. The investigator processed the scene in the field with photos, and then rephotographed the victim at HQ for follow up to show similar injuries, but also changed injuries in a controlled environment. The victim requested the investigation, and her cooperation indicates consent.

Domestic violence is not typically something a person plans on, and the value of searching a computer scene for information about it might only yield a potential motive for the fight, such as an affair, pornography, or money problems.

Step 4. Work the Evidence

Evidence Decision How to obtain the evidence from this scene?

1. *Critical Thinking* The investigator thought about the person scene as it would interact with another person scene in an assault where there no weapons. The head might control the action, and have some involvement, but the hands interacted with the tool or other person during the fight. The attack involved only person body weapons, but also impacted the victim's clothing. The lack of weapons, and cutting the body reduced the scenes, and injury levels for evidence.

The persons are the two main interacting scenes. The victim remained the priority as she received the assault, had damaged clothing, and her body as a scene remained unaltered by treatment. The suspect was available in jail. A domestic violence case indicates known parties, but requires an evidence agenda to prove the presence and action. Uncooperative involved persons may necessitate identification, and their actions should contribute to decisions about evidence.

2. *Information* The information corroborates presence. Statements establish the crime and pointed the way to finding injuries and bruise evidence. The victim's first statements with her emotions still active about the events, make revision and fabrication more difficulty and less natural. Recordings of her statements memorialized the information, making them valuable artifacts to present in court. The surrounding environment showed circumstances, such as a party, or broken doors. Scene architecture relates to the case later. A trapping scene may provide an excuse for violence by a person trying to escape.

3. *Photographs* Scene photography showed the suspect before transport, and contact with additional unrelated scenes. Visible injuries on the person scenes along with photos of the surrounding environment clarify the fight scene. The investigator photographed persons from multiple angles by removing clothing one piece at a time throughout the process. He also photographed the scene locations for any possible improvised weapons. The investigator photographed bruises at the time, and in a state of healing 48 to 72 hours later.

Sometimes one party will advise the investigator he or she has no injuries. The best course of action is to take photos of both parties. If a person claims no injuries, and then later develops them it could cloud the case. Photos in the beginning document the presence and absence of injuries.

4. *DNA* There is no need for DNA in this case.

5. *Fingerprints* The fingerprints would also not prove anything in a case like this. If there were a weapon, locating prints on it to show the most recent user could have great value.

6. *Patterns* There are no pattern marks in this case to match, however the victim's bruising on her upper arms could be from when she said she was grasped by the suspect; the front of her arms bruised by his thumbs, and the backs by his four fingers. This is not something for a preliminary investigator to diagnose, but it is something to look for to present the visual evidence of bruising. It is rare for a person to be bruised on both sides through an accident. The injuries should be documented without concluding it is from something or someone.

7. *Artifacts* The investigator collected the victim's clothing with signs of a struggle as evidence, or a carrier of evidence. Had the suspect's clothing been torn it would have been evidence also.

There were no weapons in this case, but in some cases, the weapon may appear in the background of scene photographs, but an investigator might not know it functioned as a weapon, such as a can of hairspray. This may become significant later to match the tool mark of the weapon to the injured person. People use improvised weapons in domestic violence cases, such as kitchen utensils, alarm clocks, etc.

Both involved parties may change their versions of events, or refuse to testify, causing an evidence-based trial.

Victims may keep a journal of events. Some abusers do not stop even after an arrest, and create trackable events. Electronic devices simplify the victim's evidence collection for all emails, texts and phone calls related to the abuser. Social media contributes to the evidence. The evidence also prepares for a follow on stalking case with correspondence evidence.

8. *Report Production* This structure of the report compares the two involved persons' injuries, and corroborates them with information from statements, injuries to the persons, and damage to the female's clothing. The victim also gets follow up photos taken, as she has suffered greater injuries.

18. Sexual Assault Person Scene

A bystander called 911 about a woman screaming for help. She reported being assaulted by a man. Police took a suspect into custody six hours after the event at a nearby restaurant.

Summary
Stranger sexual and physical assault. Suspect in custody, SART kit performed. Victim to ER for minor injuries, SART kit performed. Photos taken. Evidence items recovered.

To Do
SART kits to lab.
Send blond hair to lab for confirmation or refutation it belongs to victim

Investigation
At 0100 HRS on 4/11/13 LT Jones briefed me on arrival to the scene.

Victim Photographs and Evidence
Officer Tong photographed the victim in the ambulance. Officer Tong told me she was bound for the Emergency room, and to the Sexual Assault Examination. Medical services document her injuries and collect the evidence recovered from her person. I did not have contact with the victim until later in the day.

The victim said she fought back during the assault, and kicked the suspect with her heeled shoes. She thought she made contact with his chest.

The victim later provided hair samples for comparison to the hair collected from the suspect's person at the time of apprehension.

Suspect Evidence collected at Sit Down Restaurant Detention
At 0700 HRS, investigator Pfenton and I arrived to Sit Down Restaurant, 802 N. Lucas. The restaurant is located at the north side of the hotel grounds. It is a standard family restaurant with booths and chairs in an open, well-lit dining room.

I photographed the suspect at the Sit Down Restaurant detention. He wore a dirty shirt and pants. I saw a long blond hair on the suspect's shirt in the abdomen area, lower front left. Images 363 and 364. At approximately 0715 HRS I collected the hair (Item 1).

Biological Evidence
I collected possible biological evidence from the suspect's person before he was placed in a police car. I sealed the swabs in their own envelopes. I donned fresh gloves each collection to avoid cross contamination. I booked the sealed items into the Crime Lab Freezer.

Officer Upton had physical contact with the suspect during a search of his person.

Item 2 Swab, sterile water.
Item 3 Swab, Alberg Right Hand, and sterile water.
Item 4 Swab, Swab, Alberg Left Hand, and sterile water.
Item 5 Buccal swab voluntary, Alberg, Luis.
Item 6 Buccal swab voluntary, SPO Upton.
Item 7 Swab, sterile water.

Officer Upton transported the suspect to HQ, where I processed the suspect in jail.

Sexual Assault Kit, Suspect
I processed a sexual assault kit for Alberg in the Coffeetown HQ Holding Facility, Cell #3. Start time 0745 HRS. Alberg has an uncircumcised penis. He has dark skin tones, and he had light discolorations on the top of his penis. Image 401.

Clothing Evidence, Suspect
Item 8 Shirt, black short sleeved polo style. I saw a reddish stain near the left breast area, on the large white horizontal stripe. Images 406 to 408. Image 363 shows a large stain on mid abdominal area.
Item 9 Jeans, blue dark red stains on the right upper leg. Visible in images 364, 390, and 398.

Item 10 Gravel I collected from the back pockets of the suspect's jeans. It might place the suspect in another location upon discovery of additional scenes.
Item 11 Shoes, black lace up.
Item 12 Tan belt.
Item 13 Socks, white athletic.
Item 14 Boxer shorts, tan, discolored.

Additional evidence
Item 15 Alberg's cash, $427 total. Denominations; four $100 bills, one $20 bill, and seven $1 bills.

Item 16 Sexual Assault Kit contents, Suspect
Known saliva sample.
Penis swab A, outside foreskin.
Penis swab B, beneath foreskin.
Nail scrapings Left hand.
Nail scrapings Right hand.
Pubic hair combings.
Pulled pubic hair.
Pulled head hair.
Anatomical drawings page (copy in General File).

I replaced the kit's swabs with the SwabRight brand used by Coffeetown PD.

Item 17 the leftover parts of the Sexual Assault Kit, including instruction sheet.
Item 18 the 3 foot by 3 foot sheet of brown paper Alberg stood on during the collection.

Biological Evidence collected in the field
I collected swabs from the suspect at the stop scene.

Visible Evidence of Injuries, Suspect
I photographed the suspect during the Sexual Assault Exam. I made a copy of the Anatomical Drawings section of the Sexual Assault Exam.

Right ear, lower, one inch scratch, possibly an older mark. Images 374 to 376.
Right wrist, redness after wearing handcuffs. Images 377 to 384.
Left bicep, an old bruise. Images 390 to 392.
Right chest, ½ inch circular bruise. Image 393.
Right upper back, two scratches possibly older marks. Images 394 to 397.

Digital Images
I collected 129 digital images as evidence and transferred them to the Coffeetown PD digital photo file via the management system.

Step 1. Designate the Scene

Scene Decision Why is this a scene?

1. *Discovery* The investigator declared the scene by the words of the victim. The suspect was also near the hosting scene, and identified himself as having some connection.

2. *Scene type* The sexual assault body scene furnished the investigator with the best potential source of evidence to prove presence and action.

3. *Scene Group*
a. Overall neighborhood.
b. Porch assault scene.
c. Hotel meeting scene.
d. Restaurant apprehension scene.
e. Victim medical intervention site.
f. Transit scenes.
g. Victim body scene.
h. Suspect body scene.
i. Suspect's outstanding car is a potential scene.
j. The male person's possession such as a smartphone.

4. *Search* Zone.

Step 2. Analyze the Scene

Scene Decision How does the scene work?

1. *Restrictiveness* The suspect scene is an externally accessible scene with restricted access internal components. The sexual assault accusation makes the exterior of the body accessible for investigation. The suspect's interior is restricted access, such as blood, and potential diseases within the body.

2. *Volatility* The person is mobile but producing evidence of presence and action. In this case the suspect's person scene moved around for several hours, providing time, and additional scene contacts.

3. *Function* The suspect person scene is a subject scene, as it delivered evidence to the object scene, but also an object scene, as it can hold the victim's evidence on him. In this case the suspect's person was the scene.

Intimacy of the person scenes indicate a greater amount of biological evidence potential. A crime involving sex means the scenes will include the bodies of the involved persons; often at least one person is missing from the initial investigation, making it difficult. The victim in this case is a sex worker, which could make getting a match through DNA very difficult as there may be multiple unrelated DNA samples on her person scene. This means looking for more restrictive subscenes to connect the two. The suspect may have multiple DNA profiles in the evidence on his person, but not as many.

4. *Capacity and Interaction Points* The person has the hosting capacity DNA, Fingerprints, pattern marks, and evidence artifacts, but can also receive each of those. The scene produces and holds evidence. Both person scenes have presence in the other, and their actions may reflect upon one another. Both parties interact with their head and face, hands, genitals, and the rest of their bodies. The male person scene offered better evidence opportunities as he was available, versus the female who received medical attention. The male scene was fresh.

Step 3. Evaluate the Evidence Potential

Evidence Decision How would the evidence work in this scene?

1. *Production* The observable body reactions of bruising is produced by a tool used with force to produce trauma. The exchange of body fluids is a part of sexual intercourse.

2. *Proof Ability* The SART exam of the suspect should provide evidence toward proving or disproving sexual contact between the suspect and victim scene. The sexual activity of each scene is not definitive by itself for action of sex as a crime, but does show intimate presence. The unwanted action may be supported by the injury. The hair collected may provide an evidence link between the two if the other evidence fails to show the link.

3. *Quality* The victim's SART was within an hour of the assault, and may be great quality. In contrast, the suspect had six hours to tamper with the evidence. His body scene may not provide perfect evidence, but it was good enough. Injuries will usually have varying quality. The collective quality of the injury evidence was pretty good. The suspect's injury on his chest may corroborate the victim's claim of injuring him in self-defense, just as the hair could show close contact between two people who had no history together.

The DNA within the sexual intercourse realm of biological material may not be definitive since the victim has had multiple partners, and the suspect's history was unknown. The hair could provide a direct link like an artifact that sidestepped the multiple donor problem with the SART exam. Even if the DNA is not sequenced, an examiner could compare hair through a microscope to determine a match or not. The circular injury may match the victim's shoe heel. The combination of multiple evidence areas could provide unique proof of interaction.

4. *Timeline* This person scene has no actual timeline, and can only be seen through external timing, such as the 911 call, police arrival, and perhaps third party witnesses.

5. *Resilience* The evidence is resilient. if there is no effort to remove it. The suspect appears to have had little time to clean up.

6. *Collection* The investigator processed the suspect in the field for the most fragile and changing evidence of the hair, DNA on the hands, and photos. Investigators arrested him and then brought to HQ for a detailed examination in a controlled environment.

The fragility of the scene makes it a priority scene. The hands and genitals are prioritized because they have fragile biological evidence. The suspect's head has limited value given the elapsed time, where the suspect was eating in a restaurant.

The female was a second scene to be processed as the two person scenes may have traded evidence, with both showing evidence of the other.

Step 4. Work the Evidence

Evidence Decision How to obtain the evidence from this scene?

1. *Critical Thinking* The investigator thought about the person scene as it would interact with another person where the two scenes fought, and had sexual intercourse. The obvious head, hands, and genitals would be involved, but also many other body parts could have been involved in the interaction of scenes.

The suspect remained the priority as he was available for processing. He also knew his colleagues would transport the suspect in a contaminating environment of a patrol car. Collecting the evidence at the beginning meant at the least contaminated point possible.

Investigators searching persons to check persons for weapons and other evidence holds the potential to impact the evidence at the scenes. In this case, the officer had close contact with the suspect. He volunteered his DNA sample to have it ready to deflect allegations of cross contamination. Those allegations jeopardize the evidence and the overall case.

The hair offered great biological evidence for analysis to show interaction between the two persons.

2. *Information* The suspect eluded police for hours, creating evidence voids. The suspect had not showered during the time he was on the run. The evidence collection of the suspect begins with the first observation. The process began with investigator observations, and notations of conditions. Unique suspect features aid identification, and may provide leads for other cases. The penis bumps may indicate a motivator for anger if the victim wished to avoid venereal disease and refused the suspect. A standard person sketch would help to note details on the suspect's person.

A Sexual Assault Response Team (SART) Nurse processed the victim. The SART nurse examiner is a civilian trained medical professional who performs medico legal examinations on victims of sexual assault. She starts with an interview. She takes photographs and collects the victim's clothing. The nurse documents the victim's physical condition. The nurse collects biological samples of debris under the victim's fingernails, swabs from the mouth, anus, vagina or penis. The nurse also constructs a report on the findings. The property department stores the evidence in the freezer, and books the report into evidence to preserve victim confidentiality.

3. *Photographs* A police officer processed the male suspect. He photographed him, as he collected evidence. Early photos of the assault victim captured the scenes best. An investigator may alienate the victim by taking photos of her as she receives treatment if done without sensitivity. Scene photos aid in context development. A trained sexual assault nurse will examine and report on the victim with photographs of the victim's injuries hours later, when the wounds have changed.

4. *DNA* Biological evidence can connect the two person scenes. At the time of processing the SART exams for both persons does not indicate DNA findings to identify, so it is very important the investigator pursues as many avenues of DNA transfer as possible. If the hair is the sole DNA evidence connecting the two, it still does job. Also, more DNA may indicate a different suspect, and exonerate an innocent person. The investigator who interacted with the victim did not interact with the suspect, avoiding cross contamination, or the allegation of it. Biological evidence centers on person to person scene transfers. The suspect's DNA collected during the victim SART proves presence, and action. The suspect processing collects the victim's presence on him. An uninvolved person may come into contact with

a suspect necessitating an elimination DNA sample. The investigator documents this by noting the details and obtaining the swabs.

5. *Fingerprints* The person scene fingerprint is not a factor in this case.

6. *Patterns* The victim said she kicked the suspect in the chest with her shoe. He has a small circular bruise on his chest that could be a pattern mark from the shoe, and should be documented by the observable facts. When the shoe becomes available to investigators it should either be collected, or photographed with a scale to show a possible pattern mark connection.

7. *Artifacts* The investigator was ready to collect evidence when the suspect was captured. The investigator addressed the more vulnerable evidence at the scene. The blond hair on the suspect's clothing may have a mitochondrial DNA match to the victim.

8. *Report Production* The report structure covers the body scene processing contents of the suspect while corroborating the information from the other components of the case.

VI. Tool Scenes

Tool scenes are extensions of person scenes designed to do a job.

Step 1. Designate the Scene

Scene Decision Why is this a scene?

1. *Discovery* The tool scene most often comes to the investigator's attention by either a person's declaration, or by its connection to or possession by a person.

2. *Scene type* Tools are subscenes to persons because a person controls them to bring a change to another scene. An investigator needs to prove what result the tool delivered, and how it changed the scenes.

Some examples of tools are hammers, guns, drugs, and computers. Cars can be used as tools, but they have hosting capabilities.

3. *Scene Group* Tool scenes interact with other scenes. Tools are subscenes, existing as components of public, private, car, or even on a person scene. They often bridge two scenes, as a person controls a tool to make a change on another scene. This means there should be two distinct evidence transfers associated with the tool.

4. *Search* Tools tend to be smaller subscenes and require zone searches, but some tools involve larger areas. A hand tool might require basic zone search of a single zone, while a data system might require multiple locations.

Step 2. Analyze the Scene

Scene Decision How does the scene work?

1. *Restrictiveness* Tool scenes' restrictiveness can be based on what greater scene they are in, and their structure. Tool scenes can provide internal restricted accessibility with privacy, but may be very accessible externally. Tools tend to be smaller scenes, but in the microscopic world of evidence, tools are as big as any other scene.

2. *Volatility* Tool scenes may change with higher volumes of scene interactions. People may be willing to discard tools or destroy them. Some tool interiors are often protected from the changes. The scenes are often mobile, making finding the tool scenes themselves a challenge in some cases.

3. *Function* Most tool scenes are subject scenes acting as extensions for the person subject scenes (suspects). Tools can either be the subject scenes of a crime, or the object of the crime. A suspect tool scene is often a subject scene because it is doing the action and presence, while a victim would be an object scene receiving the actions of the subject. Sometimes the victims control pattern-making tools, and they end up leaving their evidence on the offending scene, making it the object of the case.

Tool scenes function as extensions of the subject scenes, as they impact the object scenes on behalf of the subjects. Tools may support crimes by conveying people and things, or be at the center of gravity. A tool has value as an item to perform a function, or for its own value.

Portable, functional tools offer reduced anonymity and vulnerability of identifiability and potential loss of the tool. Suspects using tool scenes trade off the ability to complete a job with the liability of leaving evidence. A tool bridges the gap between a person scene and the scene he wishes to work on; meaning if it is found it can tie the two together by evidence, however, if the tool is not found, there is a missing link in the chain proving action.

Tool scenes may need a knowledgeable person to explain their function. A victim may be able to explain how a suspect controlled tool scene.

The ways tool scenes function creates challenges for the investigator:

a. The only way to identify a tool may be by its mark, as the tool is often gone. Tool scenes give a narrow window of opportunity to collect evidence of transfer between the scenes.

b. Tools can be moved, challenging locating them. The tool may be in a place where the investigator cannot get to.

c. A suspect who stops using or discards a tool reduces the odds of solving the case.

d. Several people may have legitimate history with the specific tool.

e. Some tools rely on non-suspect third parties, such as internet tools, and require integrating them into the evidence work.

f. Tools may still require an evidence connection to a suspect when found in their possession.

g. Some high technology tools may exceed the capabilities of the investigator or even the investigator's laboratory personnel.

4. *Capacity and Interaction Points* Tool scenes are often great scenes for evidence collection and carrying capacities. Tools are usually human-made, (although anything can be used as a tool) and there are often predictable evidence transfer points. Tools have evidence of presence, control and actions. This is often DNA, fingerprints, and pattern marks. With a lower volume of scenes interacting, the odds of relevant evidence go up, thus an isolated tool scene could have a high capacity for evidence. Tool evidence is easier to discern when the functional purpose is clear.

Tool scenes are defined scenes with limits and tend to be smaller. Since tools are used by persons or subject scenes to achieve specific ends, they may have had fewer interactions with other object scenes. Subject thoughts and plans may be indicated by tools, such as lock picks, or information machines, such as computers.

Tools have three areas of evidence; external providing controller contact evidence, internal providing action, and sometimes contact or pattern evidence. A key factor in the evidence potential is the stand-off ability of the tool. Longer range tools have more challenges to prove scene interaction.

Step 3. Evaluate the Evidence Potential

Evidence Decision How would the evidence work in this scene?

1. *Production* Evidence can be produced by interaction of the tool scene with another scene such as a tool changing it, and often making a mark or pattern. The tool scene is often solid and impacts the other scenes.

2. *Proof Ability* The tool scene evidence may prove who controlled the tool as an extension of the person scene proving who did what.

3. *Quality* Tool scenes are often hardier than the scenes they are pitted against to change. For example a club is stronger than a skull. This imbalance of sturdiness leads to one scene marking another, which is good quality evidence. The same hardness reduces the changes of patterns on the tool, or evidence adhering to it.

Tool scene evidence relates to showing how the tool connected to the case as a way to make things happen. Tool scene evidence may not be very unique on a regular scale, but if it is magnified enough, the uniqueness can be seen.

4. *Timeline* Tool scene timelines vary based on tool sophistication. The simpler tools have no internal mechanism, and may only be timed by external means, or relatively. Sophisticated tools with information handling capabilities can provide timelines for actual times, and relative times.

5. *Resilience* Tool scene evidence on the scene can be less resilient because tools may have little ability to retain evidence, but often some of the evidence is enduring.

6. *Collection* Tool scene evidence collection covers the inside and outside, and tracks the sophistication of the tool. Outside is accessible, while the inside may be restricted, and the hosting scene has relevance to collection. Finding the suspect tool scene can be the greatest challenge of all, and most of the time, parts are available before a full identification is made.

Step 4. Work the Evidence

Evidence Decision How to obtain the evidence from this scene?

1. *Critical Thinking* The first three decisions indicate tool scenes function as extensions of persons, and host scenes for evidence. Persons control tool scenes. Tool scenes have three predictable components of evidence decisions. The exterior decisions often center on who controlled the accessible exterior part of the tool (presence). The interior decisions often look at what was inside the tool if there is an interior, and how the tool was used (action). The action of the tool often creates decisions about whatever pattern was made by the tool, or in some cases was received by the tool. Control connects the tool to a person scene, and function connects the tool action to another scene with the pattern. Tools have recognizable evidence transfer points, while the mobility of the scene type challenges the investigator to find it.

Most cases include tools, since few crimes do not have someone performing a function with a tool. An investigator may find there are a dozen potential tools in a case, and has to reduce the number of tools in order to concentrate on the best tools. The most valuable tool connects persons to other scenes.

Tool scenes often have smaller, well defined parameters, but nontraditional tools span large areas, as seen with the internet. The tools also have more routine evidence work coordination, given their ease to secure and stabilize, and smaller size. The investigator addresses individual scene work in routine order without much need for change. Capabilities tell a lot about the item, and its use. The investigator should define the intended functions of the tool scene when design differs from the use function.

The investigator needs to connect specific tools, to other scenes, as well as the tool to the hosting public scenes, other tools and sometimes private scenes. The investigator may be able to prove presence and action simultaneously, but they may be separate evidence components.

Pattern matching often connects tools to other scenes. Evidence for tool scenes proves who touched and controlled the tool, connecting it to the crime by action. Suspects often take tools away from the crime location to avoid discovery. Suspects may use tools found at the scene, and improvisation eliminates prior cases with the tool. The cheaper the tool, the easier a suspect disposes it; and stolen tools are cheapest.

The more specialized and abstract the tool, the greater difficulty the investigator might have understanding it.

2. *Information* Tool scene information includes a tool description and its history. The greater the defining of characteristics, the more individualized the tool. Basic identifying class characteristic information includes; make, model, and serial number, along with specific characteristics, such as dimensions weight. The internet provides excellent background information on tools but may require verifying the information for accuracy. Individual characteristics of markings and imperfections make the tool unique among all similar tools.

3. *Photographs* Tool photographs start in the host scene, and continue as subscenes. Evidence close ups show class characteristics and individual characteristics, highlighting the distinctive marks.

4. *DNA* Restrictive scenes may increase chances for a successful identification. Compact tool sizes present DNA opportunities by reducing the guess work of a blind swab. Crevices in the tool trap DNA. Finding the right DNA still challenges the investigator. Tools have a smaller population of contact people.

5. *Fingerprints* Tool scene fingerprints have a lot of the same challenges as DNA. An investigator may consider their fragility as a relative indicator for timing, even if one cannot determine the age of fingerprints. Smooth metal collects fingerprints well.

6. *Patterns* Tools impact scenes by changing them, and thus pattern marks are often the defining evidence of tool scenes. Every tool has a function, and can leave a mark on the scene it contacted. The investigator must match the tool marking to the tool, and connect the tool to a person, but often the tool is missing, or unrecognized.

7. *Artifacts* Tool scenes can be artifacts, but they may carry collectible evidence artifacts. Tools often leave trace evidence showing contact between scenes. Tools often leave trace evidence showing contact between scenes. Trace, debris or material transfer attaches to tools and the reverse holds true as evidence detaches. The investigator eliminates potential tool scene damage through transportation by processing it in the field.

The tool scene may carry the substrate evidence of material or patterns to compare to impacts found in other scenes.

8. *Report Production* Tool scenes reports are structured to emphasize the content relating to the controller of the tool and the function of the tool in the crime. The tools are tied to people who control them to commit their crimes. An investigator should explain how the tool relates to the scenes, and the people involved.

An investigator integrates the information into the circumstances of the contact, such as time and distance from the main physical scene, and activities since the initial crime. A limited tool scene report should include basic details on the location and collection for each tool and each mark.

Tool Scene Sections

There are four categories of tool types covering the different tool crime scenes.

A. Hand Tools
B. Gun Tools
C. Drug Tools
D. Information Tools

A. Hand Tools

Basic hand tools deliver physical force as an extension of a person.

Step 1. Designate the Scene

Scene Decision Why is this a scene?

1. *Discovery* The tool scene most often comes to the investigator's attention by either an involved person or witness declaration, or by its connection to or possession by a person.

2. *Scene type* Hand tools are compact scenes used to deliver a change to another scene, while being controlled by a person. They have few secrets about them, but there is no guarantee the person using the tool will use it in the prescribed manner.

Some examples of tools are hammers, and screwdrivers, but a person can improvise and use anything as a hand tool. All sorts of things have been used as bludgeons such as toasters, cellphones, and TV remote controllers.

3. *Scene Group* Hand tools are portable, controlled by person, and found within greater scenes. Basic hand tool scenes interact with other scenes. Tools are subscenes, existing as components of public, private, car, or even on a person scene.

4. *Search* Zone searches work best with hand tools.

Step 2. Analyze the Scene

Scene Decision How does the scene work?

1. *Restrictiveness* Basic hand tool scenes' Restrictiveness can be based on what greater scene they are in, and their structure. Tools tend to be smaller scenes, but in the microscopic world of evidence, tools are as big as any other scene. There is often no internal restricted part.

2. *Volatility* While tools are often hardier than what they interact with, basic hand tool scenes may change with scene interactions, like a shoe tread wearing down for

a runner. People may be willing to discard hand tools or destroy them. The scenes are portable, making finding the tool scenes themselves a challenge in some cases.

3. *Function* Basic hand tool scenes are subject scenes, often used by the subject on the object of the crime. A suspect tool scene is a subject scene because it is doing the action and presence. It may receive evidence from the other scenes.

Hand tools leverage a person's actions by penetrating, cutting, prying, and delivering force. Hand tools are short range tools requiring contact between scenes. They deliver force to change another scene. They may be used in crime, as for legitimate purposes. The investigator may be able to prove presence and action simultaneously, but they may be separate evidence components.

Hand tools offer availability, ease of use, and afford user anonymity, while unique characteristics make the tool unique and identifiable. Hand tools are often large groups of scenes with common attributes, but on a microscopic scale they may be unique. The ways hand tool scenes function creates challenges for the investigator:

a. Most people have hand tools not specific to particular crimes.

b. Portability of hand tools.

c. Hand tools' simplicity and similarity makes differentiation of tools challenging.

d. Most hand tools do not have dedicated forensic systems, (except guns). Tool scene pattern matching requires both scenes as evidence.

4. *Capacity and Interaction Points* Basic hand tool scenes are often great scenes for evidence collection and carrying capacities as they bridge a person scene controlling them, and an object scene they deliver action to. Most hand tools are human-made, (although anything can be used as a tool) and they have predictable evidence transfer points of control points or handles, and function points or blades, heads, or tips.

Step 3. Evaluate the Evidence Potential

Evidence Decision How would the evidence work in this scene?

1. *Production* Evidence can be produced by interaction of the harder hand tool scene with another softer scene, often making a mark or pattern.

2. *Proof Ability* The tool scene evidence acts as a link to prove who controlled the tool as an extension of the person scene. Control is presence, and whatever action the tool did was on behalf of its controlling person scene.

3. *Quality* Hard metal hand tool scenes are slower changing, with high quality mark, and often include some retention of evidence on them to provide good quality evidence. Hand tool scene evidence show how the tool connected to the case as a physical way to make things happen, indicating a transfer of force. The hand tool scene evidence may not be very unique on a normal scale, but can be magnified to show its uniqueness.

4. *Timeline* Hand tool scene timelines have no internal mechanism, and may only be timed by external means, or relatively.

5. *Resilience* Hand tool scene evidence on the scene can be less resilient because those tools may have little ability to retain evidence. The tool scene pattern making parts are often very resilient.

6. *Collection* Tools tend to be simple extensions of person scenes, and are often handled in a conventional order, outside in. The steps to collect the evidence are basic, but the hosting scene dictates the level of accessibility. Tool scenes have a high likelihood of becoming tainted from activity levels. The evidence processes are similar to those of other scenes, but privacy is dependent on where the scene was located.

Step 4. Work the Evidence

Evidence Decision How to obtain the evidence from this scene?

1. *Critical Thinking* The first three decisions indicate hand tool scenes function as extensions of persons, and host scenes for evidence. Persons control hand tool scenes to interact with the object scenes a few feet away. Tool scenes have three predictable components of evidence decisions. The exterior decisions often center on who controlled the accessible exterior part of the tool (presence). The action of the tool, often creates decisions about whatever pattern was made by the tool. Control connects the tool to a person scene, and function connects the tool action to another scene with the pattern. Tools have recognizable evidence transfer points, while the mobility of the scene type challenges the investigator to find it. The more generic the tool, the more it can be used as an improvised weapon or tool of opportunity, but specific purpose tools have been used to bludgeon also.

2. *Information.* Statements or other corroborating information helps identify and contextualize tool scenes. Hand tool information documentation follows the simplicity of the tool.

3. *Photographs.* Pictures show the tools and their parts. Photographs document tool scenes well. Photos document the distinguishing characteristics of hand tools.

4. *DNA.* Depending on material, biological evidence is often collected on tool control and function areas. DNA sloughs off the person using hand tools, so even with a non-print bearing tool handle might hold skin, and DNA.

5. *Fingerprints.* Depending on material, fingerprints may be collected on parts off the tool. Tool use smears or wipes clean fingerprints, but show the newest smears and prints.

6. *Patterns* Tools often leave pattern marks on the object of their function. Pattern matching connects two scenes by a mark one leaves on the other. Hand tools often leave marks on other scenes.

7. *Artifacts.* Trace materials are evidence artifacts on a microscopic scale. Tools may leave material samples on a scene, or collect *material* from the scene they deliver a function to. Trace evidence material often transfers to hand tools.

8. *Report Production.* The tool scene report is short and structured with a content of basic evidence details. It often exists within larger reports.

Basic Hand Tool Scenarios

19. Knife
20. Hammer

19. Knife

An investigator recovered a knife at a fight scene.

Summary
Knife recovered. Photos taken.

To Do
Fingerprints to Central ID
Evidence item sent to lab to be swabbed, and fingerprinted.

Investigation
I photographed and collected the knife at the stabbing scene. The knife is a five inch long, one inch wide, fixed blade; a smaller version of a combat knife. See photos showing its appearance, and features. The knife had no serial number.

Evidence
The blade side of the hilt had dried blood in the crevices.

I used Phenolphthalein to test the tool for the presence of blood, and saw the swab turned pink, indicating the knife had been in exposed to blood.

I sealed the knife in a knife box. I requested the county crime lab perform DNA swabbing and testing, and fingerprinting on the knife.

Step 1. Designate the Scene

Scene Decision Why is this a scene?

1. *Discovery* The investigator declared the scene by locating the weapon in the crime scene of violence.

2. *Scene type* A knife with blood on it is a tool that may connect two person scenes, just as a screwdriver, or pry bar would connect a person scene to the object scene like a home, or car.

3. *Scene Group*
a. Neighborhood.
b. Assault scene.
c. Injured person.
d. Knife controlling person.
e. Knife.
f. Clothing from the injured.
g. Clothing from the controller.

4. *Search* Zone or point.

Step 2. Analyze the Scene

Scene Decision How does the scene work?

1. *Restrictiveness* The knife tool is an accessible scene as anyone could operate it.

2. *Volatility* The tool is durable, portable and easy to hide.

3. *Function* The tool is a subject scene as it changes other scenes under the control of a person. A person may have had legitimate contact with the knife in the past, increasing the importance of showing its functional evidence as well as presence.

4. *Capacity and Interaction Points* The tool has the hosting capacity for DNA, fingerprints, and can produce pattern matching evidence. The handle and the blade are two distinct points of interaction. The handle often holds the evidence of the controller to prove presence, and the blades and hilts of the tools hold evidence of the object scene the tool modified.

Step 3. Evaluate the Evidence Potential

Evidence Decision How would the evidence work in this scene?

1. *Production* When the knife functions as a cutting or puncturing tool it may retain evidence of contact. Blood on the knife implies someone being injured by the weapon. Knives often hold the evidence of blood in crevices, and fingerprints on the flat surfaces which can be identifiable DNA of good quality. A person who controlled the weapon may leave fingerprints.

2. *Proof Ability* The knife was its own crime scene within a crime scene. The knife may be matched to an injury, but the key evidence is the blood and DNA. That DNA on the knife could indicate who bled on it. The stabber

could also be placed there by DNA. Another key evidence feature would be fingerprints to connect the blade to a handler.

3. *Quality* The knife appeared to have blood on it, and was found by an officer within a stabbing scene soon after arrival. In cases where the knife is one among many knives, the investigator can test the knife in the field for the presence of blood to narrow the collection of evidence to potential weapons.

4. *Timeline* A knife tool scene timelines have no internal mechanism, and may only be timed by external means, or relatively. The fingerprint can provide insight into relative timing, and even more so if it is in blood.

5. *Resilience* The fingerprints evidence can be wiped off, but the blood based DNA remained in the cracks.

6. *Collection* This subscene has fragile evidence, and the investigator chose to protect it early by photos, and sealing the scene in a box away from the elements. The investigator chose to seal the evidence at the scene, and send it to be tested as its own scene. He outsourced the collection of the blood for DNA and fingerprints to reduce his workload for other more time pressed scenes to process.

Step 4. Work the Evidence

Evidence Decision How to obtain the evidence from this scene?

1. *Critical Thinking* The investigator thought about how the tool scene with the capability to cut, penetrate, or pry could play a role in a case. The investigator sought to confirm it was blood on the blade, and then ensure preservation of the evidence to identify persons who had contact with the tool. In some cases the action part of tool can be used to match with other scenes in a pattern. The investigator could have collected the evidence in the field, but opted to preserve it in order to provide time for other tasks which often come with violent crimes.

Knives are not always good at making signature marks in cutting. The combination of evidence can make for uniqueness to indicate presence and action.

2. *Information* Contextual information about how the tool works helps find the evidence in the crevices.

3. *Photographs* Close up photography shows details for the case.

4. *DNA* Knives have the potential to carry DNA of different persons on the handle and blade. A controller of a knife may injure himself in the process of wielding the knife, resulting in leaving his own blood evidence. The knife required contact with both stabber and target to do damage, so it may carry the DNA of both parties.

The investigator tested the blade with phenolphthalein and found the presence of blood. This provides some verification the knife was related to the crime.

5. *Fingerprints* Metal blades hold fingerprints well.

6. *Patterns* Depending on how the knife was used, it may leave a pattern mark. Stab wounds can represent the item used to penetrate, but as the human body is pliable, the injuries may not exactly match. The blade can cut flesh, making the injury larger than the blade. The more unique the stabbing tool, the easier it is to match. Slicing provides fewer ways to identify a pattern. The injury begins to change as it heals.

7. *Artifacts* Parts of a knife trap debris, whether biological or general trace. There was no debris in this case to provide artifact evidence.

8. *Report Production* This is a limited report within a greater report structured to present the content of the evidence by types.

20. Hammer

A man was dropped off at an emergency room with severe head trauma. The hospital called 911. During the course of an investigation at the inured man's home, the scene yielded a blood-stained hammer with hairs stuck to it.

Summary
Hammer recovered in assault case. Bloody hairs collected from the tool head. Photos taken.

To Do
Evidence item to lab for DNA, hair testing.

Investigation
Upon learning of the potential assault at the apartment, I responded there. The manager provided entrance. I investigated the hammer only. Officer Lockwood investigated the overall scene. See his report for details.

Hammer
The hammer was on the floor, 8 feet south of the north wall, and 5 feet east of the west wall. I photographed it prior to touching it. I wore disposable gloves inside the crime scene.

The hammer has a 12 ounce head, 1.5 inches across the waffle patterned face. The other side of the head is a claw designed to pry nails. The handle is a 16 inch wooden piece, oval in shape. The hammer has no serial number. See photos showing its appearance, and features.

I noticed several dark hairs attached to the claw side with blood. I noted bloody hairs on the head, and no fingerprints in their vicinity. I collected the hairs for their preservation, and froze the evidence for lab testing.

I packaged the hammer in a knife box, and secured it to the box with ties to prevent its movement. I requested the county crime lab perform DNA swabbing and testing on the item.

Step 1. Designate the Scene

Scene Decision Why is this a scene?

1. *Discovery* The investigator declared the scene by finding the weapon inside a hosting crime scene of violence.

2. *Scene type* The hammer was within a greater scene, and appears to be the link between the victim and suspect scenes.

3. *Scene Group*
a. Neighborhood.
b. Assault scene.
c. Injured person.
d. Hammer controlling person.
e. Hammer tool.
f. Clothing from the injured.
g. Clothing from the controller.
h. Phone or computer of injured.
i. Phone or computer of controller.

4. *Search* Zone.

Step 2. Analyze the Scene

Scene Decision How does the scene work?

1. *Restrictiveness* The hammer tool is an accessible scene as anyone could operate it within the restricted access scene.

2. *Volatility* The tool is durable and mobile.

3. *Function* The tool is a subject scene as it changed other scenes while under control of the subject person. The scene functioned as a striking tool or improvised weapon as an extension of the person wielding it. The hammer was effective in injuring the victim, but identifiable as the weapon. The tool was left at the scene, making it a key piece of evidence.

4. *Capacity and Interaction Points* The tool has the hosting capacity for DNA, fingerprints, and pattern matching. This hammer modified the person scene by damaging the body with the force of a hard object against bone. The tool was an extension of a person controlling it.

The two interaction points are the handle for the controller of the scene, and the head for the object scene.

Step 3. Evaluate the Evidence Potential

Evidence Decision How would the evidence work in this scene?

1. *Production* The suspect grasped the hammer, possibly depositing DNA and fingerprints, on it. The impact of the hammer on the victim caused trauma in the form of a pattern matching the hammer, and drew blood, and collected a hair in the blood, both DNA potentials.

2. *Proof Ability* The bloody hammer in a bludgeoning assault scene is central to proving a link between the victim and suspect. If this case involved persons who lived together, everyone's evidence could be on the weapon without proving anything other than common living, so the blood and hair support the connection to violence.

3. *Quality* The hammer scene appeared to be the bludgeon tool, and the bloody hair on the action end, offering proof of presence and action securing its value. The material is good quality since it was protected, and the tool has limited assault use. DNA is unique, and the pattern is a good back up. Construction accidents can be common, but not often with hair.

4. *Timeline* Hand tool scene timelines have no internal mechanism, and may only be timed by external means, or relatively. Hair stuck to the hammer by blood indicates the blood was drawn, and was still wet when the hairs were available to stick to the hammer. Those facts in a relative timeline indicated the hammer was involved in injuring a person in the head.

5. *Resilience* The hair stuck in blood is fragile evidence.

6. *Collection* This subscene had fragile evidence, and an investigator protected and collected it early. The scene is protected from the elements, but the apartment scene had several officers working, thus exposing the evidence to potential tainting.

Step 4. Work the Evidence

Evidence Decision How to obtain the evidence from this scene?

1. *Critical Thinking* The investigator thought about how the tool scene with the capability to smash could be used in a case, given its control part of the handle, and its action part of the hammer head. The investigator knew bloody hairs were the evidence artifacts to carry DNA. He also knew the potential fingerprints in blood would indicate which person touched the tool after the assault. The hammer head also have left a pattern mark on the person scene.

2. *Information* Hammers function as specialized club weapons to deliver force, whether pounding a nail, or crushing a skull.

3. *Photographs* Images showing the features of the object with a scale allow an investigator to compare the tool with patterns on scenes.

4 *DNA* Hammers have the potential to carry DNA on the grips, as well as the hammer head. It may carry both parties' DNA.

5. *Fingerprints* The handle may carry fingerprints, as could the metal head.

6. *Patterns* The hammer head leaves a tool mark to be matched with an object scene. Photos with scales can be used against x-rays with scales on the victim.

7. *Artifacts* The investigator decided to collect and freeze the hairs prior to packaging the weapon to avoid losing fragile evidence.

8. *Report Production* This is a component report within a larger report structured to show the evidence from the hammer.

B. Gun Tool Scenes

Gun tools deliver physical force as an extension of a person in a specific form.

Step 1. Designate the Scene

Scene Decision Why is this a scene?

1. *Discovery* Gun tool scene most often comes to the investigator's attention by either an involved person's declaration or by its connection to or possession by a person.

2. *Scene type* Gun scenes require an investigator prove controller or presence, and action or what result the tool delivered, and sometimes how it changed the scenes. Guns perform a specialized function, and create several other evidence-laden scenes in the process. A handgun provides the delivery of violence in a portable and concealable package. The presentation of a gun often gains compliance when people recognize killing tools.

3. *Scene Group* Gun tool scenes interact with other scenes, but they must be used by a person and are subscenes of a person. Guns always exist within host scenes, indicating corroborating evidence within host scenes, and are controlled by person scenes. They often bridge three scenes, as a person controls a tool to make a change on another scene, and the evidence such as a bullet or casing is left at a hosting scene.

4. *Search* Zone.

Step 2. Analyze the Scene

Scene Decision How does the scene work?

1. *Restrictiveness* Gun tool scenes' restrictiveness can be based on what greater scene they are in, and their structure. Gun tools are always within host scenes, which may restrict access to them; both for suspects, and for investigators.

2. *Volatility* Gun tool scenes are stable because they continue to make similar patterns on cartridges, and bullets. People are often less willing to discard guns tools, destroy them, or change out barrels. The portable scenes make finding them a challenge in some cases.

3. *Function* Gun tool scenes are used by the subject on the object of the crime. Gun tool scenes function by delivering force to change another scene. They differ from hand tools used for violence by virtue of their stand-off distance, which can be close or several hundred feet away, and in a separate host scene.

Guns offer availability, ease of use, standoff capability, and effectiveness with vulnerability to forensics, and identifiability. The ways gun tool scenes function creates challenges for the investigator:

a. People move guns with ease, and they have value.

b. Guns often require experts to build cases.

c. Upon firing the gun, there are multiple separate scenes.

4. *Capacity and Interaction Points* Gun tool scenes are often great scenes for evidence collection and carrying capacities as they bridge a person scene controlling them, and an object scene they deliver action to. A person who uses a gun may choose to use evidence discipline or antiforensic methods to avoid revealing his identity.

Guns have several interaction points. A gun is a tool the controller holds by the handle, but must touch other parts to operate, such as the slide, magazine, or cylinder. The gun also mark bullets as they travel through the barrel receiving pattern marks and the target sometimes holds the spent projectile with marks from the barrel. The firing pin marks cartridges carrying the bullets. Gunpowder is ignited to set off a chemical reaction necessary to propel the bullet from the gun. Guns have unique features including serial numbers, model number, and styles. Gun tools have long range capabilities requiring no physical contact between scenes. Some persons use guns at short range providing more evidence.

Guns are unique tool scenes because using them multiplies the number of scenes and geographically expands the scenes. Every time the gun is fired the investigator must consider the scenes produced by that act.

Step 3. Evaluate the Evidence Potential

Evidence Decision How would the evidence work in this scene?

1. *Production* A person controlling a gun scene will leave evidence on it and the gun leaves its mark on the projectile bullet, and the casing if there is a casing. Sometimes the object of the gun leaves evidence on the gun. If the target is close to the gun, body fluids can splash onto the gun.

2. *Proof Ability* The gun scene evidence may prove a connection between the controller person scene, the bullets fired from the gun, and the target or object scene.

3. *Quality* Gun evidence material varies in quality. Ballistics are a robust discipline to identify pattern marks but require high quality raw evidence to compare. The bullet goes through a lot before it can be tested. It travels several hundred feet per second, and may stop in a hurry, damaging it beyond recognition. A good sample of material can identify a patterned connection.

4. *Timeline* A gun tool scene has no internal mechanism for actual time, and may only be timed by external means, or relatively. The relative timeline is the firearm must be controlled (this is touching) then it can be fired. The bullet leaves the gun, and hits the target.

5. *Resilience* The evidence is subject to great forces so the projectile may be fragile. The gun itself is very resilient, but the tool can be wiped clean.

6. *Collection* Gun tools are often collected by the investigator, and processed in varying degrees. The investigator must protect the tool in order to prevent damaging or ruining the evidence. The technical procedures of matching the gun are the domain of an expert working with patterns. The DNA and fingerprints can be part of processing to connect the gun to a person, but an investigator may wish to process for identifying evidence prior to sending the gun off given the increased likelihood of damaging the evidence.

Step 4. Work the Evidence

Evidence Decision How to obtain the evidence from this scene?

1. *Critical Thinking* The first three decisions indicate gun tool scenes function as extensions of persons, and host scenes for evidence. Persons control gun tool scenes, and can interact with other scenes at a standoff distance. Gun tool scenes have three predictable components of evidence decisions. The exterior decisions often center on who controlled the accessible exterior part of the tool (presence).

Control connects the tool to a person scene, and function connects the tool action to another scene with the pattern. These decisions mirror hand tools but include the bullet as a part of the proving decisions.

An investigator decides how to use gun evidence to prove presence and action by connecting the gun scene to a controller, a target, and location.

Some guns have a long history in other crimes more serious than the present one. Crime guns have the possibility of being involved in other crimes in other jurisdictions. The lab may tie the gun to other crimes. Gun laws vary by region. The investigator should consider how ammunition, proximity, and storage enter into the case.

2. *Information.* Most gun scene investigations work with modern firearms, assuming a factory built firearm, with factory ammunition using smokeless powder in a metal shell casing. The gun may be a revolver, or semiautomatic.

Gun evidence work involves IBIS, a robust, national forensic identification system to connect guns to crimes through pattern matching. IBIS (Integrated Ballistics Identification Network) is the platform for NIBIN (National Integrated Ballistics Information Network) evidence. NIBN is the government program including the IBIS technology.

3. *Photographs.* Images document gun scenes well by showing their circumstances when found. The examiner will take more detailed photos of the firing pin, and other key parts.

4. *DNA.* The gun's controller deposits DNA on the grips, and among the tool's crevices by manipulating the weapon.

5. *Fingerprints.* Fingerprints show recent users, and smooth metal can hold prints from manipulation.

6. *Patterns* Examiners seek to match bullets to the rifling pattern in the barrel of the gun, as well as the firing pin on the cartridge. Sometimes the gun deposits a pattern of gunpowder on whatever it shot at if it was done at close range.

7. *Artifacts* Firing guns produces evidence transfer material or trace. Guns also have ancillary equipment such as spare bullets, and ejected casings. The lack of casings found at a scene does not guarantee a revolver, and finding them at a scene does not guarantee a semi-automatic.

8. *Report Production* Gun cases are often partial reports covering how the weapon was found, and collected as well as the processing done before it is sent on to be processed by an expert. The structure of gun scene reports deconstructs the parts of the weapon as they connect the content evidence.

Gun Tool Scenario

One scenario covers gun tool crime scenes.

21. Gun

An officer recovered a gun on a car stop.

Summary
Gun recovered on a car stop, Photos taken. Gun swabbed. Serial number ground down preventing identification.

To Do
Evidence item to lab for serial number restoration, and ballistics testing (IBIS).
DNA swabs to lab for testing.

Investigation
Officer Thompson conducted a car stop, and requested my involvement. Upon arrival he showed me a backpack containing the firearm, magazines, and ammunition. I photographed the scene throughout the process.

Firearm
Predator Arms, 9mm semiautomatic pistol, with a 5 inch barrel, and chrome finish. Model 43433234 Serial number 12345567.

9 mm Magazines
a. Predator Arms, 9 mm magazine with a 16 round capacity. The magazine held 10 unspent bullets. Inside the middle pocket of the backpack.

b. Predator Arms, 9 mm magazine with a 10 round capacity. Empty. See Officer Jilton's report for details.
Predator Arms, 9 mm magazine with a 16 round capacity in the handgun. The magazine held 8 unspent bullets.

9 mm Ammunition
I found unlabeled ammunition in the magazine in the 9 mm pistol (15 bullets) and the other 16 round magazine (10 bullets). The owner reported the gun stolen a week prior with 25 total bullets. (Blythe PD Case 12-3344) The hollow point ammunition included a copper jacket, and brass casing.

I will send the firearm to the County Crime Lab for processing to recover the serial number, and investigate the ballistic features.

Biological Evidence
I processed the evidence in the field for DNA evidence. I swabbed each area with separate sterile swabs with sterile water on it. I placed each swab in its own envelope and sealed as evidence. I placed the sealed items in the Crime Lab Freezer.

Item 1 – Blank Swab with sterile water.
Item 2 - Swab of pistol trigger with sterile water.
Item 3 - Swab of pistol grip with sterile water.
Item 4 - Swab of pistol slide with sterile water.
Item 5 - Blank Swab with sterile water.

Fingerprint Evidence
The pistol had no smooth surfaces suitable for printing. I dusted the three 9mm magazines after removing ammunition to develop fingerprints. I collected two fingerprint cards.

Card #1 (large) the left and right sides of the magazine inside the pistol.
Card #2 (large) the left and right sides of the magazine inside the black backpack.
I forwarded the firearm to Big City Police Department Identification Unit.

Step 1. Designate the Scene

Scene Decision Why is this a scene?

1. *Discovery* An investigator declared the scene by finding to the weapon scene within the hosting scene.

2. *Scene type* The gun was in a backpack and does not connect to a crime beyond possession.

3. *Scene Group*
a. Neighborhood
b. Transit scenes.
c. Person residence.
d. Car scene.
e. Person scene.
f. Backpack scene.
g. Gun scene.
h. Ammunition.

i. Smartphone.

4. *Search* Zone.

Step 2. Analyze the Scene

Scene Decision How does the scene work?

1. *Restrictiveness* The gun tool is an accessible access scene as the gun has no restrictions by itself. It was found in the backpack which may be restricted to investigators.

2. *Volatility* The tool is mobile but sometimes attached to the owner by records information. The evidence is often recent but can be very enduring.

3. *Function* The gun tool is a tool to deliver force. As a subject scene as it impacts other scenes and makes evidence; as an object scene it collects evidence. In this case it is a possession, and collects evidence. In this case it is unknown if the tool constitutes a crime beyond possession.

A gun can be an effective tool to perform a function, but they may not be easy to part with. This weapon remained in the area to be found, and presents an opportunity to link scenes. If a firearm tool has had multiple owners, it has had multiple interactions with persons' evidence. The ground-off serial number may seem like a way to make the gun anonymous, but it may be restorable, and just the grinding makes the gun a crime gun, thus exposing the possessor to charges.

4. *Capacity and Interaction Points* The tool has the hosting capacity for information about it to show ownership. It also can host DNA and fingerprints, and pattern matching evidence to prove presence, and action. The ground-off serial number reduces information about the gun.

Any operator, controller, or possessor could have interacted with the handle and trigger, the firing pin interacts with the cartridge, and the bullets interact with the barrel.

Step 3. Evaluate the Evidence Potential

Evidence Decision How would the evidence work in this scene?

1. *Production* The controller of the scene manipulates the scene by touching the grips, depositing DNA and fingerprints on it. Firing the weapon produces evidence in the form of chemicals sprayed out from the tool, a projectile bearing marks of the barrel, and cartridge bearing marks of the firing pin. In

this case, the gun was not fired in association with a crime, and the evidence produced with the gun is deposited on the gun, rather than from it.

2. *Proof Ability* The presence of a gun may be a crime, and require investigation, even if it was not used. The gun should be connected to a person through DNA or fingerprint evidence.

3. *Quality* The material is moderate quality given the tool was loose in a back pack. Some of the protected areas, like the trigger were protected. DNA is unique, and the fingerprints on the magazines are strong evidence for recent contact. The gun as a tool is relevant as an extension of a person, so the evidence showing who had contact with the weapon indicates action as well as presence.

4. *Timeline* This gun tool scene has no internal mechanism for actual time, and may be timed solely by external means. The relative timeline relies on witnesses seeing the weapon, and the gun was not fired as a part of the incident.

5. *Resilience* The DNA and fingerprint evidence is fragile. The ballistics are stable, but not central to the case.

6. *Collection* The investigator processed the scene in the field due to the evidence fragility.

Step 4. Work the Evidence

Evidence Decision How to obtain the evidence from this scene?

1. *Critical Thinking* The investigator thought about how the gun tool scene would interacted with a person when there was no indication the gun was fired. The investigator decided to field process the firearm for more delicate evidence. In most cases field processing offers a better chance to collect evidence before it is bounced around. The investigator chose to collect DNA and fingerprints as they can show a presence of a person scene, while the pattern marks of the bullet can show the actions such as firing the gun at something.

2. *Information* A lab will work to identify the weapon to connect it with persons and crimes. Some guns have documented historical information, which is complicated by the serial number being ground off this weapon.

3. *Photographs* The standard photos showing how the weapon was on encountering it are useful. Showing whether it was loaded, and how it was configured, safety off, etc. can have value in the investigation.

4. *DNA* The pistol grips and trigger offer an opportunity for DNA collection.

5. *Fingerprints* The smooth metal and composite parts of the weapon offer opportunities for fingerprint collection.

6. *Patterns* The firing pin marks each cartridge it fires, and the barrel marks each projectile or bullet it sends through it, in this case no shots were fired.

7. *Artifacts* The accompanying items such as spare bullets of the same brand and caliber, and a holster help solidify ownership.

8. *Report Production* This gun report is structured to prepare the evidence for processing by a technical expert, but also focusing on the content of the evidence as found.

C. Drug Tool Scenes

Drug tools are valuable chemicals used to bring about a change for a person.

Step 1. Designate the Scene

Scene Decision Why is this a scene?

1. *Discovery* The tool scene most often comes to the investigator's attention by either an involved person or from witness declaration, or by connection to or possession by a person.

2. *Scene type* Drug tools are used by persons to perform a function to bring about a change.

Some drug examples are alcohol, cocaine, marijuana, and licensed pharmaceuticals.

3. *Scene Group* Drug tool scenes chemically interact with persons, and otherwise interact with containment scenes. They are tool subscenes for a person. Drugs exist as components of public, private, car, or even on a person scene.

4. *Search* Point, zone searches around them.

Step 2. Analyze the Scene

Scene Decision How does the scene work?

1. *Restrictiveness* Drug tool scenes' restrictiveness is based on what greater scene they are in. The drug tools themselves are small scenes, often stored within a private place, like a pocket.

2. *Volatility* Drug tool scenes are stable chemical compounds. Drugs often create recognizable symptoms when the drug is introduced to the user's system. People are often less willing to discard drugs tools or destroy them

due to addiction and their value as commodities. The scenes' portability make finding them a challenge in some cases.

3. *Function* Drug tool scenes are used by the subject as an extension of the subject to achieve the crime. Drugs have a lot of purposes, but possession is the action, whether during use, or transport. Even when used as an exchange medium, drugs do not receive action. Drug tool scenes function by delivering a chemical change to a person scene. They may be used in crime, as for legitimate purposes. They also are items of value, so they also function as currency.

Drugs function as tools to achieve goals of sensation or trade. The drug possessor's usage plans can range from self-administered drug use, to malicious incapacitation of another, as with date rape drugs. Drugs may contribute to cases, or can be the whole case. People use drugs as an alternate form of currency. Drugs are made, possessed, consumed, or traded. They are portable within host scenes. There are several examples of drugs including amphetamines to stimulate and speed up the nervous system, depressants to slow things down, analgesics to kill pain, and hallucinogens to trick the brain. Drugs evolve based on consumer taste, and market forces.

Drug tool scenes offer high value for a small size and their prohibition increases their value. Prohibition also increases the drug tools' need to be controlled scenes, thus they are often tied to persons by possession. Presence is the action of possession.

The ways drug tool scenes function creates challenges for the investigator:

a. The investigator may not find or identify the drugs.

b. Given the small size of drug scenes, they are often carried in restricted access scenes, such as in a person's clothing.

c. Evolving drug tools require skills, training, and experience.

4. *Capacity and Interaction Points* Possession and chemical composition are central issues for drug cases. Drug tool scenes are chemicals, and rely on supporting scenes of packaging, and administration paraphernalia for use. Drugs on their own are poor scenes for evidence collection and carrying capacities. They are often too small for fingerprints, and DNA is a blind collection. The packaging and paraphernalia provide better opportunities.

Drug tool scenes have the two components, the control, and the function. Control proof often comes from packaging, or paraphernalia. Function comes from biological chemical testing on the user, or drugs. The investigator also proves presence by seizing the material, or developing the information to determine a person consumed the drug. Drug tools are short range tools requiring contact between scenes when a person consumes them, but mere possession or use as an item of value requires no contact.

Step 3. Evaluate the Evidence Potential

Evidence Decision How would the evidence work in this scene?

1. *Production* Drug scene evidence is limited given its size, but cases are less dependent on a person's evidence, and rely on recognition and critical thinking. The component chemicals can be analyzed to identify the materials.

2. *Proof Ability* Possession is action and presence. Intoxication by drugs is a related area of investigation. Proving possession when the possessor is not collocated, relies on evidence from the packaging to prove a connection.

3. *Quality* Observation notes circumstances to indicate drug tool possession. The packaging holds most of the identifying evidence. The chemical material is of varying quality, but identifiable, making it high quality. The chemicals in a particular drug are identifiable, thus the effects the drug will have on a person are identifiable.

4. Drug tool scene timelines have no internal mechanism except when they are a prescription drugs with a timestamp for the sale. Most timelines are relative.

5. *Resilience* The evidence is often carried in a person's pockets, and subject to a lot of contact. The chemicals are very resilient, while the fingerprints may not be.

6. *Collection* The investigator often obtains the drugs after touching them to remove them from their storage location. Search has a high potential to destroy the identifying evidence.

There are many ways to identify drugs, but the investigator can look at the contextual clues of packaging, storage, and appearance to decide if he thinks a substance is a drug. Drug tools often require an initial chemical test, measurement, and sending the material to a lab for further confirmation. They are often handled in a conventional order.

Drug scene evidence procedures include precision measurement of the materials, meaning minor mistakes can damage a case. Uncalibrated scales giving bad readings create a fact problem in court. The drugs are processed by an outside organization to identify them.

Step 4. Work the Evidence

Evidence Decision How to obtain the evidence from this scene?

1. *Critical Thinking* The first three decisions indicate drug tool scenes function as extensions of persons to either serve as an item of value, or bring about a desired state of being for a person. Other scenes host drugs and persons control drug as tools. Drug tool scenes have three predictable components of evidence decisions even though the exterior decisions often center on identification by sight. The action of the tool often creates decisions about determining the chemical composition. Control connects the tool to a person scene, and function connects the tool action to another scene with the pattern of symptoms from use. Presumptive testing requires laboratory expertise for confirmation.

Choosing material for its defined functions can imply purpose. Drug facilitated crimes use drugs to incapacitate or reduce the resistance of a victim. Alcohol is a common tool in such crimes.

2. *Information* The internet provides a lot of information to document drug tools. The report should list substance identifiers, packaging, and discovery location. The substance packaging often indicates its purpose. The actual substance appearance, color, texture, and odor also provide information about its origin. Manufacturers stamp prescription pills an identification number.

Exotic or new drugs may need explaining.

3. *Photographs* Images document including the context. Photographing the drugs on the scale showing weight, the chemical test showing the reaction colors, and the sealed evidence can create a storyboard.

4. *DNA* Biological material to identify a person in contact with drugs might play a part of a drug case, with packaging and paraphernalia. Generally, the possession makes this redundant, but the drugs may be with a person who has died from an overdose or problem with the drugs. Then testing the drugs to find a person who provided them is relevant to the case.

5. *Fingerprints* An investigator may find fingerprints do not always stay on contact with paraphernalia, as a user may put the tool in his pocket. The same concepts for DNA with fatalities may apply to fingerprints with drugs.

6. *Patterns* Drug pattern matching seeks the impact or mark the chemicals have on another scene, often a person. Chemicals metabolize in a person, and leave a chemical pattern mark. Technicians may analyze the molecular chemical composition of a substance to identify the material. Scientists identify precursor chemicals as part of a pattern.

Sometimes the patterns are as simple as matching photos from reference books about drugs and production methods with the scene.

7. *Artifacts* Paraphernalia may be or carry evidence artifacts as transfer material. Paraphernalia, scales, baggies, and a ledger demystify drug tools. An investigator can process the bags or any storage container for DNA or fingerprints.

8. *Report Production* Drug scene reports structure the evidence contents to explain all of the basic things any report would, such as discovery, and details about location and description. They also need to confirm the drugs are in fact drugs and how they are against the law.

Drug Tool Scenarios

22. Illicit Drug
23. Pharmaceutical Drug

22. Illicit Drug

An officer located an unidentified substance on the front seat of a car during a stop, and believed it to be drugs.

Summary
Drug possession case. Photos taken. Evidence items recovered, presumptive positive test for substance, methamphetamine.

To Do
Evidence items to lab for testing.

Investigation
At 14:45 HRS on 6/7/09 Officer Martinez found the below mentioned items, and showed them to me on the front passenger seat of CA 454987655. The car is registered to Kramer, who was alone in the vehicle.

The item was a sandwich baggie containing a crystalline white powder. Based upon my training and experience, I believed the crystalline powder could have been methamphetamine. I transported the material to HQ for processing. I tested the powder with a field presumptive test kit. After breaking the three chemical vials from left to right, I saw the liquid substance turn yellow, a presumptive positive for methamphetamine. I recognized the controlled substance as a usable amount. The content weight was 21.7 grams including the baggie.

I photographed the substance during testing and weighing. See photos for documentation.

I was unable to locate fingerprints on the baggies.

Also within the car were 15 empty small baggies with skulls and crossbones on them.

I requested the county crime lab test the substance for confirmation of methamphetamine.

Step 1. Designate the Scene

Scene Decision Why is this a scene?

1. *Discovery* The investigator declared the scene by report of his fellow officer identifying it as a crime scene.

2. *Scene type* Illicit drug scene packaging is often the source of evidence to identify a possessor. The product itself does the action. The illicit drugs are often identified by how they are packaged. They will be sent for precise testing.

3. *Scene Group*
a. Neighborhood
b. Transit scenes.
c. Person residence.
d. Car scene.
e. Person scene.
f. The drug scene.
g. The packaging scene.
h. Smartphone.

4. *Search* Point, the zone search around the seat yielded the 15 baggies.

Step 2. Analyze the Scene

Scene Decision How does the scene work?

1. *Restrictiveness* The tool is in a restrictive access hosting scene as the car would either have to be operated by someone with a key.

2. *Volatility* The tool is mobile but attached to the car. Its chemical composition is very enduring.

3. *Function* The tool is a subject scene, and always an extension of a person scene. The scene functions as an item of value during transactions, and the additional bags at the scene point to the tool being connected to trade rather than just sensation. This size of a drug package can be hidden on a person, but there are only so many places to hide it. Also, its scent may not be concealable. Even though the substance is inside a person's car, it still must be connected to a person by evidence. The car's owner could deny the drugs, and say perhaps another occupant dropped it in his car.

4. *Capacity and Interaction Points* The tool has the hosting capacity for evidence to prove presence, and action limited to what is on the packaging. Packaging

may provide some identification evidence, and the drugs may analyzed for specific chemical presence. The packaging is also the interaction point between a person and the drugs.

Step 3. Evaluate the Evidence Potential

Evidence Decision How would the evidence work in this scene?

1. *Production* The controller of the drugs creates the evidence by possession. While there may be transfer of DNA or fingerprints from the controller touching the packaging scene, they may not be collectible.

2. *Proof Ability* The presence of drugs in a car is a strong case against the car owner based on information alone. Identifying evidence could help the case, but is not attempted.

3. *Quality* The drugs in the car of someone a unique circumstance for possession. The information evidence is the most relevant, from identifying the evidence to covering the circumstances of the evidence in the car. If the bags are tested, the DNA material can be of high quality, but not of the current possessor or even prior possessor. Fingerprints are lower quality because drugs are often carried in a way to brush against pockets.

4. *Timeline* This drug tool scene timelines is relative, and is limited to knowing the drugs came into the suspect's possession prior to investigator arrival.

5. *Resilience* The evidence attached to drugs is often fragile.

6. *Collection* This is a solo scene, and provided no indications of changing the order of processing. The investigator processed the scene in the field to the point of identifying drugs. He transported the material to the lab for presumptive testing to prove it, and weighing.

Step 4. Work the Evidence

Evidence Decision How to obtain the evidence from this scene?

1. *Critical Thinking* The investigator thought about how the drug tool scene would have interacted with the possessing person. He concluded possession indicates who owns the drugs. But a person might deny owning the drugs, or the pants he wears. Information shows who owns the car, and photos show the orientation of the contraband.

An investigator may find it more possible to collect evidence from the drug packaging to connect a suspect to the tool such as by fingerprints on the packaging or even DNA. Alcohol bottles provide excellent packaging for evidence work, DNA at the mouth, and fingerprints on the glass. An investigator could also process paraphernalia to connect it with a person scene, proving presence and action by indicating the supporting evidence of drug use tools.

2. *Information* Cocaine and methamphetamine can look alike, and may have different laws governing their possession, making identification relevant to an investigation. While marijuana has a reputation of being natural, laboratories have found other drugs such as PCP or chemical pesticides with the marijuana. This case involved a single package, but drug packaging in 15 small baggies may support the assertion the drugs go beyond personal use. The drug bag decoration can be considered branding.

3. *Photographs* Showing drugs in context saves time, and answers questions by showing results.

4. *DNA* Biological evidence is not a part of this case.

5. *Fingerprints* Most cases will not need fingerprinting the bags, but in some cases, the skill will become relevant, and practicing on bags may prepare the investigator for more serious cases.

6. *Patterns* There is no pattern matching part of this investigation. Should other investigations reveal similar baggies with skulls and crossbones they may be a pattern. The bags by themselves are available to anyone, limiting their evidence value.

7. *Artifacts* The packaging accompany the drugs.

8. *Report Production* This is a short report on the drug component of a case structured to show the content of the evidence, and the logic of its possession. It highlights the location of the drug, and presumptive testing.

23. Pharmaceutical Drug

An officer arrested a woman for outstanding warrants. During the booking process, he located undocumented prescription drugs in her purse along with paraphernalia.

Summary
Prescription drug possession case. Photos taken. Evidence items recovered, presumptive identification for substance via reference materials.

To Do
Evidence items to lab for testing.

Investigation
On 1/5/10 I was working for Whatachee Department of Public Safety as a Crime Scene Investigator. At 1730 HRS I met with Officer Manfred at WPD HQ. He briefed me on the details for the case. He handed me items #1 and #2. He explained he found no prescription information on the arrestee's person, and she did not provide contact information for a medical provider to confirm a valid prescription.

Evidence
I processed the evidence in the Police Department HQ CSI lab.

Item #1. Unmarked amber pill bottle containing 7 white tablets marked XV57. According to the 2009 Book of Drugs Reference, page 393, this designates the drug, ___. The ingredients are __ 500 mg, __ 5 mg. The federal government classifies it as an Analgesic, Schedule III drug, and refers to it as a member of the opioid family.

Item #2. A scorched glass pipe with white residue. I recognized the device as used to smoke drugs.

I photographed all evidence prior to booking.

I booked the items into property. See property section of report for further details on items #1 and #2.

Step 1. Designate the Scene

Scene Decision Why is this a scene?

1. *Discovery* The investigator declared the scene by the word of a fellow officer who brought the scene to him.

2. *Scene type* The illicit drugs, and the tools to divert them to illegitimate use.

3. *Scene Group*
a. Neighborhood
b. Transit scenes.
c. Suspect home.
d. Car scene.
e. Suspect person scene.
f. Drug scene.
g. Drug packaging scene.
h. Smartphone
i. A fake prescription may bring another scene into the investigation.

4. *Search* Point, zone.

Step 2. Analyze the Scene

Scene Decision How does the scene work?

1. *Restrictiveness* The drug tool is in a restrictive access hosting scene of the suspect's purse.

2. *Volatility* The tool is mobile but also valuable to the possessor so she probably chose to keep the drugs rather than attempt to get rid of them.

3. *Function* The drug tool is a subject scene for evidence. The drugs are a subject scene, changing the object scene of a person's body. The packaging is an object scene in this state, as it receives evidence, and is controlled by other scenes. Drugs function as a tool to provide pleasure, feed an addiction, or may be an item of value to trade. The pipe indicates active drug use, rather than commerce.

Prescription drugs offer the possessor and user reassurance of quality, and authenticity, thus their values are reliable. While some pharmaceuticals are obtained illegally such as by robbery, many of them are obtained by false pretenses. Either way, they transition from legitimate to illegitimate, exposing their controller to legal troubles. Packaging provides context. If a possessor were to have a legitimate looking prescription, there is no evidence to show any crime.

4. *Capacity and Interaction Points* The tool has very limited hosting capacity for evidence like DNA and fingerprints on the packaging. This lack of capacity is offset by possession. The packaging could hold information about the drugs, but has been altered to remove information.

The drugs may have specific chemical presence. The packaging may provide some identification evidence, and by the interaction of the person controlling the drugs. The container may hold fingerprints or DNA. The action of diverting the drugs may have required another tool such as a forged prescription.

Step 3. Evaluate the Evidence Potential

Evidence Decision How would the evidence work in this scene?

1. *Production* The controller of the drugs touches the packaging scene, but in this case the evidence is presence, with the circumstance of no prescription.

2. *Proof Ability* The possession of drugs by the person lacking authorization along with the paraphernalia for using the drugs is strong factual evidence based on information and lack of information to indicate proof of presence and action.

3. *Quality* Pharmaceuticals are high quality chemicals, packaged with markings to be identifiable. The absence of authorization in the form of a prescription is the critical thinking evidence.. Unique identifying numbers make the drugs identifiable, and the drug function provides insight. Since person possess drugs for their functionality, the chances of illegal possession of anti-fungal cream are a lot lower than possession of pain killers.

4. *Timeline* This drug tool scene timeline is relative, and is limited to knowing the drugs came into the suspect's possession prior to investigator arrival. The pharmaceutical component provides no time, and would not be reliable if it did.

5. *Resilience* The chemical evidence is stable and resilient.

6. *Collection* The investigator processed the scene in the field to the point of identifying it as probable contraband. He transported it to the lab for presumptive testing to prove it, and weighing.

Step 4. Work the Evidence

Evidence Decision How to obtain the evidence from this scene?

1. *Critical Thinking* The investigator thought about how the scenes would have interacted when a possessor converted a legal drug tool into an illegal drug tool. The investigator researched the drug to establish it as a legitimate drug which the suspect's actions diverted. The investigator sought to prove presence and control of the drug, and sent it for testing to locate more technical evidence.

2. *Information* Pharmaceutical drug tablets include stamped identification information. An investigator in the field can use reference books, or access the internet by smartphone to obtain the details. Every pharmaceutical drug has a scientific name, a marketing or trade name, and a relevant street name. The investigator uses published information to identify the drugs, although laboratory analysis may be necessary.

3. *Photographs* Images show the markings on the medication. They also show how the drugs are kept, which may indicate a lack of legitimacy. A pill bottle in the purse seems more legitimate than a pill wrapped in a nondescript baggie in someone's bra.

4. *DNA* Biological evidence is not relevant for this case at this time.

5. *Fingerprints* Identifying evidence is not relevant for this case at this time.

6. *Patterns* Chemical testing could identify the components of the drug to match.

7. *Artifacts* The scorched pipe is a common delivery method for illegal drugs, and there is no legitimate reason for it possession. The lack of evidence artifacts such as prescriptions is relevant to showing the illegality.

8. *Report Production* This is a very limited report as the evidence showed up at the investigator's workspace when a colleague brought it. The report is structured to show how the investigator approaches pharmaceutical drugs just like the illicit drugs, by gathering information, and documenting the results. Explaining drug paraphernalia and its function defines how it relates to the case as additional content.

D. Information Tools

Information tools control information flow as an extension of a person.

Step 1. Designate the Scene

Scene Decision Why is this a scene?

1. *Discovery* The tool scene most often comes to the investigator's attention by either an involved person's declaration, or by a person's connection or possession.

2. *Scene type* Information tools, such as computers, cellphones, or anything defined by its ability to process information. The simplest information tool could be pencil and paper, but electronic tools are the majority of the group, and the scenarios are geared toward the higher technology. Information tool investigation evidence work seeks the information contained in the device, and the evidence of controller. Information tools function by handling information. The scenes can be small, local, and portable as well as have global reach through communications networks.

Computers process information through a series of instructions. The computer processes information by instructions with an algorithm, or formula. The general public uses computers as the research portal of choice, portable libraries logging all browsing. Computers track a person's interests by search. Computers and cell phones converge as they both have massive computing power and communication ability. Many electronic devices have features such as GPS and internet connectivity. Social media crime exploded the last few years. An investigator should consider most copiers as computers containing evidence from an information tool. Every person has the exploitable vulnerability of either their own computers, or inclusion in a third party computer system.

Some examples of information tools include complicate smartphones, laptops, and even simple tools like paper and pencil.

3. *Scene Group* Information tool scenes interact with other scenes, as controlled subscenes of a person. Persons operate information tools within public, private, car, or even on person scenes. Information tools operate as part of a chain including; the tool, the conduit of information, often served by an Internet service provider (ISP), and a host or cloud service.

4. *Search* Tools tend to be smaller, and require zone searches, but some tools involve larger areas.

Step 2. Analyze the Scene

Scene Decision How does the scene work?

1. *Restrictiveness* Information tool scenes' restrictiveness can be based on what greater scene they are in, and their structure. Their exterior may be accessible, but complexity and legalities restrict an investigator from internal searches of information tools.

2. *Volatility* Information tool scenes are stable as they continue to make similar patterns, but they can be programmed to discard information, or password protected to keep unauthorized users out.

The scenes are often portable making finding the information scenes themselves a challenge in some cases. However, people are often less willing to discard information tools or destroy them.

3. *Function* Electronic information tool scenes are often used by the subject on the object or target of the crime. Information tool scenes function by processing and handling information on behalf of other scenes. The tools follow algorithms or instructions, which implies a control. They may be local, or remote in function, but they often connect to other information tools, or sensors.

While the tool functions to execute the actions of the subject scenes, it can also be impacted by the object scenes and receive action from them. A suspect tool scene is a subject scene because it is doing the action and presence. Sometimes the tool is used to gather information from third parties about the target or to collect information about something related to the crime, such as techniques.

Information tool scenes offer communication, convenience, and access to massive amounts of information, in a small, portable package with trackability, excellent records of actions, contacts, and locations. Privacy software alters the tradeoff, obscuring the information an investigator seeks.

Most persons in society will have at least a smartphone, which provides access to many other information tools. The ways information tool scenes function creates challenges for the investigator:

a. These tools allow great access, but record all actions of the user, meaning a glut of information.

b. People often build or load antiforensics into their information tool.

c. With the popularity of these tools, everyone has them, and it will not always be clear how necessary they are for the case.

d. Sophisticated information tools require training and experience. An investigator can fail to keep up with the technology and may not recognize the scene.

e. The courts recognize information tools as private areas of a person's life, and restrict searching.

4. *Capacity and Interaction Points* Information tool scenes have two distinct parts. The exterior collects physical evidence like DNA, fingerprints, or material to show presence. The interior of the tools have massive capacity to collect, process, and save information.

Information tools have the control points or external physical scene, and the function, or internal information scene. An investigator must decide how to prove presence and action with information handling tools by proving who controlled the devices, what the device did, and what pattern marks it exchanged with another scene. Information tools have long range capabilities but still require a form of contact between scenes.

The tool operator interacts with the exterior to control the inner workings. The tool interacts electronically with the outside world often by the internet, or even a private data link. The tool have built-in recording of electronic interactions as the scenes processes information for the uses. The tool can have great stand-off distance for use with a connected system.

Hardware and software work together, but are not always found together. Hard drives and removable drives store information. Local wireless technology allows for detached hard drives to serve the computers. The identified tool may not hold the records.

Computers are converging with smartphones and they all have contact with many of the same systems. Some laptops record locations by GPS, cell phone tower, and Wi-Fi. An investigator may trace web activity to a wireless internet hub, such as a restaurant. Remote cloud computers log access, and actions, making for an additional tradeoff device functions being performed by third party vendors. Networked computers make up the cloud, and parts of the suspect's computing, or information tools function at a distance. Devices serve as gateways for what lies beyond including the individual's computers, smartphones, third party tools, and software. Social media requires communication between entities.

Step 3. Evaluate the Evidence Potential

Evidence Decision How would the evidence work in this scene?

1. *Production* The controller of the device touches the exterior, depositing DNA and fingerprints on it, but they may not be collectible. The controller's thoughts and ideas are often recorded when the tool works with the information as instructed by the user.

2. *Proof Ability* DNA and fingerprints show physical control and contact with other scenes and who was present with the scene, but the flow of information shows what the ideas and action were. The massive information available to the phone controller can be compared to the facts of the crime, to show commonalities.

3. *Quality* The exterior evidence of DNA or fingerprint can be good given the smooth surfaces and a limited pool of users. A shared information tool offers the same challenges as any scene with multiple persons interacting with it. Electronic information is often of high quality if it can be harvested. Internal evidence is central for information tools and the highest quality information is specific to time, and location.

4. *Timeline* Information tool scene timelines vary based on tool sophistication, but most of them have an internal mechanism to establish timelines and by extension relative times. Non computational information tools, like credit cards, checks, or other hardware may not provide actual times by themselves, but can be timestamped by third party information tools.

5. *Resilience* The physical evidence is fragile since an information tool is touched a lot. The data are very resilient, but connectivity may provide an opportunity for a person to alter the information tool scene anytime remotely, so even if the device is in custody, it may not be stable.

6. *Collection* Information tools are complex extensions of person scenes. They can often be processed for exterior evidence by an investigator who first

encounters the tool, and are later forwarded to laboratories for more involved searches by technical experts. The fragile evidence of DNA and fingerprints might be processed in the field, but the data evidence might be obtained elsewhere by a specialized technician in a lab. While a tool's screen can show information, an investigator's best course of action is to use a tool to extract the information stored in the tool.

Step 4. Work the Evidence

Evidence Decision How to obtain the evidence from this scene?

1. *Critical Thinking* The first three decisions indicate information tool scenes function as extensions of persons to process information, make it, obtain it, or send it. Information tools can also destroy information records; either by accident, or by design. Information tool scenes have three predictable components of evidence decisions. The exterior decisions often center on identification of a physical controller. The interior decisions revolve around who controlled the information machine. Information tool control connects the tool to a person scene, and function connects the tool action to another scene with the pattern of information flow from use.

2. *Information* The internet supplies information to document information tool tools. Sometimes the labels on the tools have the information. Computer processing may mean the difference between successful prosecution and exclusion of evidence. Computer handling methods evolve, requiring training. Computer forensics exceeds the scope of *Crime Scene Decisions*, but the FBI publishes expert advice in the area how to collect the equipment without hindering the investigation. The local crime lab has guidelines. A specialist maximizes the evidence collected from the equipment.

3. *Photographs* Images show configuration of the tool, and may be the only way to preserve what the machine shows on its screen and does to other scenes. This is important at an early phase. Persons may alter information scenes easily, and the early phase may be the only time to capture the tool working.

4. *DNA* Biological evidence may show a connection between the tool and a person.

5. *Fingerprints* Prints may show a recent connection between a tool and a person.

6. *Patterns* Information tools create transfer material including data logs and digital trails. The electronic interaction may show a connection between a

person and other entities. Pattern matching for information tools seeks the pattern the tools leave on other tools they interact with. Most tools require log-ins, a pattern, and the tool connects to another tool in the cloud. The two exchange information, leaving pattern marks with each other.

7. *Artifacts* The peripheral items may have evidentiary value, such as built in memory.

8. *Report Production* Information tool reports are structured to be subscene reports about tools used to bring about a change. Their content shows how the tool fits into the overall case as evidence. They are often partial, as the forensic examination may take months.

Information Tool Scenarios

24. Personal Computer
25. Smartphone
26. Car Black Box
27. Financial Information Tools

24. Personal Computer

A homicide victim's husband was out of town during her murder. He denied the detective permission to search his computer. The detective wrote a search warrant for the computer, and a judge signed it. The detective called an investigator to assist with the investigation.

Summary
Homicide case involving a computer. Search warrant served for a laptop computer. Photos taken. DNA and fingerprints collected from device to prove user.

To Do
Computer to lab for forensic search.
DNA and fingerprints to lab.

Crime Scene Investigation
Detective Milligan provided me a copy of his signed search warrant. I reviewed the document to ensure I understood what I sought, and was entitled to collect.

Scene Description
Officers secured the residence before I arrived. I saw the computer in the northwest corner of the living room on the north side of the apartment. The front door is against the south wall. The TV is on the west side, and the couch on the east. The kitchen is to the north east corner.

The laptop computer was off. The electric service stopped around the time of the homicide, and remained off. There was no backup power. I photographed the scene as I encountered it.

Laptop Computer Description
The laptop is a Smith brand, model 234. It has a 1TB hard drive. Color blue.

Investigation

I wore single use nitrile gloves throughout the investigation and changed several times.

I saw several papers of indicia in the area around the computer, including suspect mail addressed to the location. One spreadsheet showed a column of names and a corresponding column with a series of numbers. I photographed the documents in place.

Possible Biological Evidence

I collected possible DNA evidence from the laptop. I designated the swabs in the Property Section as ES (for Evidence Swab). Prior to swabbing I donned fresh gloves to avoid cross contamination. I used a sterile swab for each. I designated swabs collected with sterile water as +SW. I placed each swab in its own envelope and sealed as evidence. I placed the items in the Crime Lab Freezer.

ES1 +SW control swab with sterile water
ES2 +SW swab of keyboard
ES3 +SW swab of mouse
ES4 +SW swab of speaker controls
ES5 +SW control swab with sterile water

Latent Fingerprints

I dusted the exterior of the face of the laptop to develop fingerprints. I used black powder applied with a fiberglass brush.

Card #1. Large. Face of laptop housing of the computer. Collected after swabbing the equipment.

See card for orientation. I forwarded the card to Large Regional Police Department Identification Unit.

Evidence

I tagged each cord and its receptacle on the equipment prior to unplugging it and packaged each component in its own box, and sealed the box. I will forward the equipment to the regional high tech lab for forensic examination into the use of the tool.

Step 1. Designate the Scene

Scene Decision Why is this a scene?

1. *Discovery* The investigator declared the scene by recognizing its relevance to crime, and knowing it was within the hosting crime scene.

2. *Scene type* A computer offers an opportunity for a person to explore the world of information by querying millions of databases worldwide. In this case the investigator has other evidence to consider the husband may have used a computer to access information.

3. *Scene Group*
a. Neighborhood
b. Residence.
c. Husband.
d. Wife.
e. Computer.
f. Smartphone..
g. Third party accounts such as email or social media.
h. E-mail.

4. *Search* Zone.

Step 2. Analyze the Scene

Scene Decision How does the scene work?

1. *Restrictiveness* The computer as a tool is in a restrictive access hosting scene of the residence. The scene's exterior is accessible, while the tool's interior data handling parts are very restrictive.

2. *Volatility* The tool is mobile but attached to the home, the information is very enduring, and may be duplicated elsewhere as the information was transferred to the device from other locations. The tool will do as instructed, so fragility or hardiness can be built in to the operating instructions.

3. *Function* The laptop is a subject scene as it performed the action on behalf of the subject person. It is an object scene when it receives information from external sources. The scene functions as an information processing tool with recording capability to save evidence.

This laptop offered the user access to the world's information. It is small, portable, and cheap enough for most people to afford. It records actions it could be very revealing as to the user's questions, and intentions.

While the main computer was easy to find, this may not be the sole computer. Most people have access to several devices, including a smartphone, another computer, a work computer, a rental, or library computer.

4. *Capacity and Interaction Points* A laptop has the hosting capacity on the exterior for DNA and fingerprints. The device holds evidence of who controlled what data was sought and obtained through logins and password requirements. The machine interacts with external data systems through local networks, or phone lines.

Step 3. Evaluate the Evidence Potential

Evidence Decision How would the evidence work in this scene?

1. *Production* The controller of the device touches it, depositing DNA and fingerprints on it, but they may not be collectible. Information exchange is recorded as is travels to and from the machine.

2. *Proof Ability* Information tools are extensions of person scenes just as hand tools are. Information tools can yield physical evidence of contact and thus identification, and the paths of information can show ideas, and actions of the controller of the phone. Fingerprints on the machine are more recent than DNA and are the better choice for the purpose of proving recent contact. The traffic coming and going from the machine shows what the controller of the device sought and found.

3. *Quality* The exterior will probably yield identifying evidence and fingerprints are very unique and strong evidence for recent contact. The interior will also be of high quality with digital forensics. If the controller visited his e-mail while logged in, he is tied to the activity.

The digital evidence indicating what the suspect was seeking is the most relevant, but should be supported by a way to attach the activity to a person. Digital evidence indicating what the suspect was seeking is the most relevant, but should be supported by a way to attach the activity to a person.

4. *Timeline* This information tool scene can provide very detailed timelines when a technician extracts the data. The fingerprints may provide a more relative timeline in the short term, and could indicate who recently touched it.

5. *Resilience* The DNA and fingerprint evidence can be pretty enduring if protected. The digital evidence is fragile and could be wiped, but often remains.

6. *Collection* The investigator processed the scene in the field to the point of collecting fingerprints. The forensics will happen elsewhere by a specialized technician. The priority for processing requires attention to a potential destruction of information, thus shutting the device down may be a priority to preserve internal data.

Step 4. Work the Evidence

Evidence Decision How to obtain the evidence from this scene?

1. *Critical Thinking* The investigator thought about how the information tool scene would have interacted with the other scenes. He sought to prove external presence and internal control of the information tool since both husband and wife likely used the same computer. This evidence will be internal and external, and will require he send it for testing to locate more technical evidence in the form of data.

A computer hosts information handling processes including searches, and the investigator thought perhaps those searches would provide insight into what the husband was thinking about, and seeking information to do. The computer is in the husband's presence, but the investigator has find evidence to prove if he used it and if his use was for criminal purposes.

2. *Information* The owner may have registered the serial number in the manufacturer's database. Information on the tool may show who owned and controlled the device. Sometime there are photos of the suspect with his computer.

3. *Photographs* Basic images showed the contextual information of the case, such as the indicia paperwork.

4. *DNA* Biological evidence will not play a central role, but it will be available in the event it is necessary to clarify who touched the tool.

5. *Fingerprints* Interaction with the scene goes some distance, but the internal scene search shows the contact evidence between the computer as a scene, and the external information accessed, such as internet searches performed with the tool. A fingerprint of the husband on the tool indicates he touched the equipment, but it proves his truthfulness about the issue. If his fingerprints are connected with bad intent searches, the evidence indicates thoughts and actions.

6. *Patterns* The lab can create a mirror image of the information on the computer and run sophisticated forensics programs to determine the contents and use. This includes log in, which indicates an intentional act by a specific person.

7. *Artifacts* There were no additional items to be collected.

8. *Report Production* The report is structured to cover the context of the computer, and the steps to collect it without damaging it for the detailed forensic examination to be performed by an expert later.

25. Smartphone

An officer found a smartphone in a stolen car on a car stop and requested an investigator assist him.

Summary
Stolen car, three suspects in custody. Smartphone as potential evidence in stolen car. All occupants deny ownership. Photos taken, DNA swabs, fingerprints collected. Data extracted from phone.

To Do
Fingerprints to lab for analysis. Consider DNA sequencing.
Contact police who took the home invasion case with information about this case, and the two who had the phone.

Investigation
At 0330 HRS on 1/26/16 I arrived to the intersection of Wilmont Ave. and 4th St. to assist Officer Hunter with a stolen cellphone he had recovered on a car stop. He detained the two occupants of the car who denied ownership of the phone.

Description
The phone was on the hood of Officer Hunter's patrol car when I arrived. See his description of the scene.

Newtown Police Department dispatch researched the identifying information for the cell phone. They reported Watertown PD list the phone as stolen five days earlier in a home invasion robbery. WPD case number 12-12344.

Evidence
I wore single use nitrile gloves throughout the investigation and changed several times and photographed the phone. I processed the evidence in the Newtown PD HQ CSI lab.

The cell phone is High Technology brand, model number CEP 27894, serial number 2279848E 26. IMEI number 35 647101 295782 2. Phone number 888-555-1212.

Possible Biological Evidence
I collected possible DNA evidence from item #1. I designated the swabs in the Property Section as ES (for Evidence Swab). I donned fresh gloves to avoid cross contamination. I used a new, sterile swab for each. I designated swabs collected with sterile water as +SW. I placed each swab in its own envelope and sealed as evidence. I placed the items in the Crime Lab Freezer.

ES1 +SW swab with sterile water.
ES2 +SW swab of cell phone.

Latent Fingerprints
I dusted the exterior of the smartphone. I used black powder applied with a fiberglass brush. I collected one sample from the cell phone.

Card #1. Large. Face of cell phone. Collected after swabbing the phone.

I forwarded the card to Large Regional Police Department Identification Unit.

Data Harvesting
I used the Data Grabber 4400 to create a copy of the cell phone data. I collected call logs indicating several phone calls to the phone number 555-5555. This phone number belongs to suspect's home phone. See attached call logs for details on times of calls.

I viewed photographs of two suspects smoking cigars, drinking beer, and attending a house party. The images were timestamped from 8 hours before the car stop. The camera program for the phone included the GPS locations of each photograph taken. I included a map in the general file showing the dates, times, and locations of photos to cross reference with potential crimes.

I took digital photos of the party pictures.

Step 1. Designate the Scene

Scene Decision Why is this a scene?

1. *Discovery* The investigator declared the scene by thinking about the scene as an unclaimed tool.

2. *Scene type* This phone is an information tool of value taken in a violent theft. The camera function made it a recording device the suspects used to capture their (bad) ideas with photos at a party.

3. *Scene Group*
a. Neighborhood.
b. Home where phone was first taken.
c. Suspect homes
d. Car.
e. Suspect person scenes.
f. Victim person scene.
g. Phone.
h. Computer the phone may have been synchronized with.
i. Third party internet scenes to be searched as a result of the phone search.
j. Phone company records.

4. *Search* Zone.

Step 2. Analyze the Scene

Scene Decision How does the scene work?

1. *Restrictiveness* Smartphone have varying restrictiveness based on their placement, and the password protection for the device. The tool is a restrictive access scene as the phone is owned and operated by one person with a password, an unlikely to be hacked.

2. *Volatility* The tool is mobile, as it was designed to be. Data systems can store information, and erase it, making it changeable. A copy of the data often resides elsewhere, providing an opportunity.

3. *Function* The tool is subject scene as it is an extension of the subject (person) scene. When the suspect used it to record photos, he used the device as an extension of himself, or subject. However, he did not use the tool to modify another scene, and it only recorded the events, and actions of the controller. The phone holds more evidence of interaction than it imparted on other scenes, and is an object scene.

Smartphones function as personal black boxes by integrating networked computers, cameras, and communication devices. The scene functions as an information recording tool producing evidence. Phones store information, such as contacts, and photos. The device can be used to seek specific information indicating thoughts and plans.

This portable device offers massive amounts of information. The device has value on the resale stolen goods market, but it also is trackable, and its true owner can be found. Gadgets are often very tempting to people who want to play with them, but everything an operator does on a phone is tracked. In turn those records of actions can sometimes be challenging for the investigator to access.

4. *Capacity and Interaction Points* The tool has the hosting capacity for information and data to prove presence, and action. The phone can also host DNA and fingerprints to show person presence. The device holds evidence of who controlled it physically, and used it. The images showed it was used by persons not the owner.

The phone's housing, including its glass face is the main exterior or physical interaction point. The interior interactions points are with all the networks a phone can connect to, and what the parts of the phone can capture. In this case the camera part of the phone was used to document what people were doing. GPS can indicate location history. Cell tower connections may also help. Internet history can also provide insight.

Step 3. Evaluate the Evidence Potential

Evidence Decision How would the evidence work in this scene?

1. *Production* The physical controller of the device touched the outside, depositing DNA and fingerprints on it, but they may not be collectible. The images are stored inside the phone as the result of the deliberate act of taking photos.

2. *Proof Ability* The phone's exterior may indicate presence and physical control of the tool. Fingerprints imply recency more than DNA, and are the better choice for the purpose of proving recent contact. The DNA will probably indicate several profiles, which may not provide any answers for the case. The phone's interior scene of internet and communication traffic coming and going from the machine shows what the controller of the device sought. The images on the phone are information, and show who was in the phone's presence.

3. *Quality* The exterior evidence may not have survived the handling by the suspects and then the officer. Photos will be of high quality, and matchable to the persons at the scene. The digital photo evidence is also immediately available, since the phone will not have to be sent anywhere for lab results. The photos may indicate a group of people interacting with the stolen phone, but there may not be a selfie photo to indicate a specific person, which is where the fingerprint evidence becomes more crucial.

Fingerprints are very unique and strong evidence for recent contact. If the photographs include persons who were in the presence of the phone at the time of investigator contact, it shows long term presence, and control.

4. *Timeline* The smartphone information tool scene timestamped everything, from communication, to information searches, to photos.

5. *Resilience* External evidence is pretty enduring if it is not touched. The digital evidence is also enduring as long as it is not deleted. People who steal phones and take photos may not exercise caution about erasing evidence, but sometimes the owners will reset the phone to wipe everything off it out of identity theft concerns.

6. *Collection* The investigator processed the phone in the lab. The priority for processing requires attention to a potential destruction of information, thus shutting the device down may be a priority to preserve internal data. The forensics will happen elsewhere by a specialized technician.

Step 4. Work the Evidence

Evidence Decision How to obtain the evidence from this scene?

1. *Critical Thinking* The investigator thought about how the information tool scene would have interacted with the other scenes, knowing smartphones are portable, networked computers. He sought to prove external presence and internal control of the information tool since the persons who possessed the device denied owning it.

This phone was taken in a violent crime, and has the role of stolen property at the car stop, but it provided a link between two sets of person scenes in another case. The initial owner of the phone was connected by records, but the investigator chose to use forensics to connect the person (s) who stole it can be used to show their presence, and actions, as possession of the phone is a crime. At the preliminary stage, the phone was connected to both suspects who occupied the car.

The investigator used fingerprints to seek a physical connection of suspect scenes to the phone, and the data to seek the digital connection of suspects through actions such as photos and calls.

Cellphones are not isolated scenes, and securing them sometimes requires anticipating invisible problems. Faraday boxes isolate signals from phones, while providing a plug for power, preventing a suspect from altering information on the phone from elsewhere. Cloud computing applies to smartphones making evidence available via third party sources. The greater number of third parties involved equates to more search warrant work, and a greater chance of locating information.

2. *Information* The car scene where the phone was found was stolen, and two suspects were in it along with the phone. No one claimed ownership of the phone. Photos in the phone could prove interaction. Connecting the tool to a person starts at the scene with documentation of relevant phone recovery details, including the location and proximity to persons and other relevant evidence. Packaging and appearance, including personalization assist with identification. The setting may indicate it facilitated illegal activities of drug sales, or weapons crimes.

The photographs taken with the phone may include geotagging providing locations of activities.

3. *Photographs* Images can show context of where the phone was found. Photographs documented the tool serial number and appearance. Contact lists reveal a lot about the owner as well. Smartphones are also wallets, with a person's purchases in person visible. Internet access provides inside views of a person's buying habits through internet stores. The phone's users deposited their DNA on the phone, as they held the device to their face and spoke into it. The phone yielded fingerprints due to its smooth face used to dial. Data is an evidence artifact for a crime in this case. Information technology moved laboratory based processes to the field. Forensic devices search phones for data and save a copy of the data on memory sticks etc. Extraction may require a technician.

4. *DNA* Externally, the smartphone has the standard challenge of fingerprints vs. DNA to prove presence, and (assumed) action.

5. *Fingerprints* The fingerprint evidence will be better evidence to connect a person due to the recency of evidence. The prints have known suspects to compare to, and they are in custody speeding up the processing.

6. *Patterns* Forensic examination can show the use patterns. Matching the persons in the images to real persons is a form of pattern matching.

7. *Artifacts* There were no other artifacts connected. Photos of the suspects and scene may later reveal evidence artifacts present in some photos.

8. *Report Production* The phone tool report stands alone, and fits into the overall case. The report is structured to show what the phone evidence content to connect persons to the device.

26. Car Black Box

Several people called 911 to report a fatal traffic collision. Witnesses gave contradicting statements about the actions of the cars prior to the crash. The physical evidence also lacked enough information to determine fault.

Summary
Undetermined fatal collision. Black box data collected by technician. Photos taken.

To Do
Review data.

Investigation
On 12/12/13 I arrived to the Smalltown PD Impound Lot with Officer Wilson. He showed me a signed search warrant to search CA 123FSFDD and collect the data from car.

Evidence: Car Data Harvesting
I photographed the car, and the black box in the trunk.

Patrolman D. Farmigian of the State Police used his agency's device, the Car Data Collector, Model 8523. Serial number 54345jj455. I observed him connect the device to the data port in the trunk. See photos for exact location. He saved the data to a new 8 GB memory stick. He repeated the process. I signed for the memory sticks. I booked one stick into evidence, and forwarded the other copy to the Accident Reconstruction Team for analysis.

Step 1. Designate the Scene

Scene Decision Why is this a scene?

1. *Discovery* The investigator declared the scene because the car was involved in a collision. The search warrant provided entry to the scene.

2. *Scene type* The black box provides factual information about what was happening in the moments preceding a collision. As they advance, the black box provides more information, and may keep long-term recordings of actions.

3. *Scene Group*
a. Intersection.
b. Car.
c. Driver.
d. Black box.
e. Third party data scenes.

4. *Search* Zone.

Step 2. Analyze the Scene

Scene Decision How does the scene work?

1. *Restrictiveness* The tool is in a restrictive access hosting scene as the car would either have to be operated by someone with a key, or hacked.

2. *Volatility* The tool is mobile but attached to the car. The information is recent and enduring.

3. *Function* The tool is an object scene as it received and recorded information about a car's actions, and driver choices. Black boxes are designed to show what was happening right before a crash, the data may evolve to be a running record of driver choices, and car activities.

4. *Capacity and Interaction Points* The tool has the singular hosting capability for information about what the car was doing just prior to the collision. The device interacts with the car electronically, and is not subject to suspect contact. Its connection is data.

Step 3. Evaluate the Evidence Potential

Evidence Decision How would the evidence work in this scene?

1. *Production* The device records driver actions, and car actions.

2. *Proof Ability* The information evidence obtained from the black box shows what the car was doing right before and at the time of the crash.

3. *Quality* The information about the car's actions indicate the physics in the crash. The information can also refute or support statements made by parties.

The digital forensics will probably be of high quality, but a limited period of time. The data are very unique as they come from the car.

4. *Timeline* The black box information tool scene timeline should be timestamped, or provide relative times between events to be corroborated.

5. *Resilience* The evidence is enduring, as the device was designed to survive crashes.

6. *Collection* The specialized technician investigator processed the scene in the field to collect the data to be analyzed in a lab.

The data often requires the expense of an expert, which could save money in the long run given the high costs of investigations. Departments often hire an expert to interpret and explain the evidence. Outside experts have the skills and equipment to obtain the data evidence artifacts. Most large agencies provide mutual aid for this. Private contractors also cater to black box investigative work.

Step 4. Work the Evidence

Evidence Decision How to obtain the evidence from this scene?

1. *Critical Thinking* The investigator thought about how the information tool scene of the black box recorder would have kept records of what happened with the driver and the car before and during the collision. He knew the data was the evidence he sought, and it was created as a result of recording sensor collected information.

2. *Information* A car's *black box*, functions as a specialized information recording tool. The device may not prove who drove the car, but it preserves a history of what happened with the car as information recorded on the black box provides many answers to an investigator questions by providing many snapshots of different aspects of the car, before, during, and after the collision. The black box records vehicle speeds, as well as driver behavior. The black box gathers data from sensors within the car. It takes information from the braking system records about car the driver's application of acceleration and brakes. It also collects data from the seats, seatbelts and airbags, to report occupant locations and choices. Other data includes not just driving performance, but car locations by times. Electric cars might share additional data on locations and times of recent charging. Other sources of route information may include smartphone or web application data. Information corroborates or refutes the owner's statement and may provide the sole source of pre fatal collision facts.

3. *Photographs* Images show the device as installed, and untampered.

4. *DNA* Not relevant to this case.

5. *Fingerprints* Not relevant to this case.

6. *Patterns* Not relevant to the black box part of this case to show presence, but pattern matching may come into play to show how things fit together.

7. *Artifacts* Not relevant to this case.

8. *Report Production* The report is a small part of the main case structured to show how the investigator obtained the contents of the device to help explain the events that preceded the crash.

27. Financial Information Tools

A retail store called 911 about a shoplifter in custody. An officer arrested a professional thief for shoplifting and discovered financial crime tools in the suspect's car.

Summary
Shoplifter / ID theft and fraud case.
Suspect in custody.
Photos taken. Fingerprints collected. Evidence items recovered.
True owners confirmed unauthorized transactions.

To Do
Send electronic data storage items to lab for testing.
Fingerprints to lab.
Contact persons and credit card companies to determine if more victims.
Further lab analysis to investigate alteration of the checks.

Investigation
Store loss prevention arrested Suspect Naranda for shoplifting and a records check revealed he had previously received a criminal court sentence of supervised probation for a check fraud conviction. Naranda parked his van in the parking lot before the crime, and officers searched it post-arrest finding evidence of financial crime.

Suspect Van CA ZXC-QWER – Evidence Notes and Photographs
I found the suspect's van in the store parking lot. The probation grant included a clause for Naranda's van. Naranda outfitted his van as a movable office with many electronic devices and the ability to print media. I took photographs of evidence in situ, prior to removal and collection. See metadata for detailed information on the images. I placed numbers by the items to show their evidence booking number.

Initial Case - Shoplift Evidence
1. The shoplift evidence in a white plastic bag I received from Totally Electronics Loss Prevention at scene. A copy of the receipt showed a value of stolen items ($567.56).

2. The Totally Electronics Loss Prevention security video of Naranda during the crime showing deliberate actions, and misrepresentations. See the internal report for details.

Car Evidence – collected during the search, photographed in place prior to collection.
3. The check from Ruralto Valley Construction, made out to *Totally Electronics.* The back of the check bore the inscription; *To be deposited in to the Totally account at Domination Bank, CDL #345634676576.* Naranda's California Driver's License number.

4. Credit cards from *Phillip T. Jepson.* Officer Fong collected the cards while booking Naranda. I called Mr. Jepson and he said he gave no one permission to possess his credit cards. He reported the cards stolen in his hometown. See attached police report for detailed information.

5. A card credit card embosser and magnetizer, boxed in the back seat, driver's side. The device embosses credit cards by raising the printing on the card and it loads a code on the magnetic stripe on the back of credit cards.

6. A box containing 124 cards with magnetic stripes; both hotel room keys, and used credit cards.

7. Printer from the cargo area. Star Brand, SN 123456.

8. Laptop Computer. Star Brand, SN 58776858, and a USB memory stick.

9. Checks, credit cards, load documents, bills, and blank check stock, from the rear cargo area. Several of the blank checks have faded coloring, with faint writing on back. I found several different versions of check stock, blank checks, but I found no blank paper, or blank envelopes in the car.

Person Evidence – Collected during booking
10. Naranda's address book. This small handmade book contained several names, social security numbers, birthdates, driver's licenses, addresses, and account numbers.

11. Naranda's cell phone.

12. CA Driver's License, Michael Deetz.

Evidence Processing
I photographed the scenes using natural light, artificial light, a flash, and an Alternate Light Source.

Alternate Light Source
I looked at the Deetz CA DL with the suspect's photo when I shined a UV black light on it. The light revealed a false hologram. See photo showing this.

Fingerprint Evidence
I used black powder to develop fingerprints on the embosser, laptop, and printer. I applied the powder with a fiberglass brush. I found and collected the following fingerprints. See cards for orientation.

Card #1 (large) Front face of embosser.
Card #2 (large) Left side of embosser.
Card #3 (large) Right side of laptop.
Card #4 (large) Top side of laptop.
Card #5 (large) Top side of printer.

Chemical Print Development
I used heptane ninhydrin to develop fingerprints on paper items, including the blank checks. I bathed the papers in the solution for 20 seconds and hung them to dry in the fuming chamber with humid air. I photographed the prints with a scale to preserve the evidence, and sent the disc of photos with the fingerprint cards.

I forwarded the cards and CD to the Square County Identification Unit for processing.

Step 1. Designate the Scene

Scene Decision Why is this a scene?

1. *Discovery* The investigator declared the scene by recognizing the suspect had control of several tool scenes used for fraud.

2. *Scene type* The printers, checks, and credit cards come together to be tools of information to commit crimes.

3. *Scene Group*
a. Store.
b. Parking lot.

c. Suspect residence.
d. Prior victims' residences.
e. Suspect car.
f. Suspect.
g. Tools; computer, peripherals, printer, credit card embosser, blank cards, paper records, checks.
h. Suspect phone.
i. Third party data scenes

4. *Search* Zone.

Step 2. Analyze the Scene

Scene Decision How does the scene work?

1. *Restrictiveness* The tools are in a restrictive access hosting scene as the car would either have to be operated by someone with a key, or broken into to plant the tools. The laptop is accessible on the exterior, but the interior is restrictive. The printer has a similar situation. The embosser / magnetizer, the partially finished and fully finished tools like the checks and credit cards are accessible.

2. *Volatility* The tools are portable and enduring.

3. *Function* The tools help achieve the acts of fraud. Some of the tools are subject scenes used to perform the function of making things. Tools like the fake credit cards are object scenes receiving the markings. The user brings information, and processes it with the tools to build devices to commit the act to taking. The devices to trick people are central to a fraud case because they link the sources of information to the theft of items of value, which is often money.

This scene is a collaboration of benign scenes to make a crime scene. The scene parts function as tools to produce devices and documents containing information to trick people, like fake checks and credit cards. The tool production process also produces evidence.

The tools for this type of crime are mobile, and can escape notice as they have legitimate uses or are exotic to the point of being beyond an investigator's comprehension. Raw information makes the suspect vulnerable as explaining possession of other people's information is difficult. Investigators may not notice financial crimes and focus on the surface cases of stolen property, or drugs.

4. *Capacity and Interaction Points* The tools have the hosting capacity for DNA, fingerprint, and pattern marking evidence to prove presence, as well as information in the form of stored data to prove action.

All of the tools in this case require a person to touch them, depositing DNA and fingerprints. The embosser makes patterns, both physical and informational on the cars. The fake check has patterns of information.

Step 3. Evaluate the Evidence Potential

Evidence Decision How would the evidence work in this scene?

1. *Production* The credit card imprinter device makes patterns on the finished fraud tools of cards. DNA and fingerprints come from touching the items.

2. *Proof Ability* The scene provides a group of evidence items that are individually limited, but collectively strong. The identification evidence of DNA and fingerprints connects a suspect scene to the tools for fraud. The information about the tools show how they are used to commit fraud. The information in the form of documents in the suspect's possession show the raw material he used to produce the items for fraud. The suspect used fraud tools to produce more fraud tools.

3. *Quality* The tool evidence will probably be of high quality as they are from a protected location, both weather, and disturbance. Also, the suspect has a workshop or controlled hosting scene, which often contributes to a lot of contact with evidence in an unguarded manner. The evidence items combine to form a very unique connection between the tools and the person using them. The combination provides capabilities to the controller of the tools.

The tools are all relevant to commit the crimes because they are different forms of information carriers. Connecting at least one by fingerprint or DNA evidence cements the case, and prevents the claim of presence without action.

4. *Timeline* Information tool scenes or devices timestamp events in actual time. Relative time is robust in this case, because the suspect's tools are accounted for during the arrest. An investigator may be able to determine the actual time when he acquired them. The credit cards may also provide some indication of creation time, contributing to the overall production of fraud devices. Any computer or cellphone will provide accurate times.

5. *Resilience* The evidence is enduring.

6. *Collection* The priority for processing requires attention to a potential destruction of information. The devices appear stable.

Step 4. Work the Evidence

Evidence Decision How to obtain the evidence from this scene?

1. *Critical Thinking* The investigator thought about how the information tool scenes would have interacted with the other scenes, including the other information tool scenes, to create new tools which presented information in order to steal things. The investigator sought DNA and fingerprints to seek a physical connection of the tool scenes with person who were present, and taking action. The investigator also knew he needed to show the patterns the devices imparted on other tools, such as credit card imprinters, electronic information, and data belonging to other persons.

The real value is the information, and showing its path through the suspect controlled tools. Producing false credit cards requires specific devices. Information tools function as facilitation aids for financial crimes producing or handling information. Most of the tools create retrievable records with the proper equipment.

2. *Information* Proving presence and action challenge an investigator when suspects have built deception throughout the case, which compels an investigator to search for external information to corroborate or disprove the information from inside the case.

Fraud suspects often have lists of information for potential victims. They may disguise nine digit Social Security Numbers as ten digit phone numbers by adding another digit.

Identity theft includes a manufacturing operation requiring the application of raw information material to legitimate appearing instruments. The investigator must determine the real account owners as the suspect steals by producing fake credit cards with the real account numbers. Records often show the account owner listed as a victim of a predicate case, such as having a wallet stolen. Field access to the internet allows investigators to research victims and banks. The investigator must contact the bank's fraud department. Victims should review the evidence items such as documents with their signatures to determine their authenticity. A questioned document examiner provides expert testimony if needed.

3. *Photographs* Fraud cases have a lot of evidence and extensive photos with numbers helps keep evidence organized. Financial crimes suspects use

uncommon evidence artifacts for their crimes. Photography shows contextual information about the tools and their use in a way words cannot. Images also show the overall scene of an office dedicated to committing crimes.

4. *DNA* Biological evidence did not play a role in this case with the presence of persons with the evidence.

5. *Fingerprints* The embosser is the main tool to be connected with a person by fingerprints. The paper evidence is also a tool considering it stores information, and evidence to connect it to other scenes. Heptane ninhydrin processing the checks for fingerprints solidifies the case by confirming the suspect's presence and action. It prevents the argument of the suspect being a victim, with some other person doing the real crimes.

6. *Patterns* The embosser is a tool marking device which imprints credit cards with numbers and other information. Information is its own pattern and its use can reveal crimes.

7. *Artifacts* Suspects often retain large volumes of evidence artifacts. Scenes can include the following subcategories of artifacts:

a. Raw information and materials. Blank checks are legal. Showing the suspect has no blank paper removes the potential argument of working on school, etc.

b. Equipment and tools to handle or produce the fake items, including computers, memory sticks, printers, checks, identification, credit cards, and paper etc. Chemicals clean checks of handwriting ink and their presence at scene may indicate a check washing process. While suspects operate traditional tools in person, they may operate information tools from a distance, escaping investigator notice. An investigator should explain the credit card producing device and its significance in the report. Dual use equipment requires an explanation its crime nexus. A laser printer has its place for millions of legitimate consumers use every day.

c. Finished tools, like credit cards ready to be used, can show the depth of the activity.

8. *Report Production* The investigator structured this report by evidence in different stages of discovery of the case, which is also by location, with contents about identification and purpose.

Conclusion

Anyone can document a case by writing down what people said, and how the components looked. It takes an investigator to make decisions and solve cases with a disciplined process. The end goal is evidence to prove facts, but first the evidence must be found and collected. *Crime Scene Decisions* is a scene-based, evidence-centered approach to the investigative process. Finding evidence at scenes comes from a disciplined approach to analyzing the scene, making decisions, and using evidence skills.

The method starts when the investigator decides why something is a scene, and how it works. Then the investigator decides how the evidence works in the scene, and how to obtain it. The four main decisions divide into twenty two decisions. While the method works for today, what about tomorrow? Crimes and mysteries will continue to evolve in the future. New technology will flow in, and people will retain all the emotions and motives they have always had. Behavioral norms will change, and so will the laws. The world is getting smaller, and crime scenes are getting larger and more plentiful. Evidence and the scenes that produce evidence will present new cases without historical precedence because crime evolves too.

While the superficial aspects change, the foundations will remain steady. Solving a case will still rely on investigator decisions. Crimes will always be reflected at the scenes with evidence. Every case comes down to, *how to prove who did what.*

Start with scenes, end with evidence.

Glossary

Most of the concepts in *Crime Scene Decisions* are familiar to any investigator who has some knowledge of the field. However, there are several new presentations in this book warranting brief explanation.

Accessibility vs. restrictiveness of scene. How easily the scene is accessed. A park is more accessible than a person's skin beneath clothing.

Anonymous. Unknown person. This is used when someone's identity is unknown, and when a person has no connection to a scene.

Antiforensic. Actions or situations chosen to make evidence work more difficult. Burning a house down may not destroy all evidence in a murder, but it complicates the investigation. These are also functional tools.

Artifact. Evidence item. This can be traditional items like guns, but also microscopic trace evidence, such as skin cells, or chemicals.

Attributes of evidence. A way to look at evidence by features all evidence has.

Bias. (Cognitive) An investigator can have preformed ideas about a subject that then influences the way the case is investigated. An example of this counterproductive thought process is an investigator concludes a person was stabbed in the face by someone who he was close with. Since the investigator theorizes the crime was personal, there is a certain pool of suspects who the investigation will be focused on. By definition, this also shifts attention away from the evidence and other suspects.

Center of gravity. Where the action of the scene happened, and thus where the evidence is more apt to be found.

Chain of custody. Evidence must legally obtained, and include a trackable history of location, collection, manner of processing, and storage. If the chain is damaged, the evidence may not be usable in court.

Class characteristics. General facts of a thing. For instance, the specifications for a particular year of make and model of a car. (see individual characteristics).

Crime classification based investigation vs. scene based investigation. Classification based investigation centers on proving the cases as defined by law, such as a murder or burglary. Scene based investigation looks at the scenes to find evidence of presence and action. The two may end up in the same area of proving a set of elements, but scene based takes a path of discovery based on analysis.

Daubert Standard or Frye Standard. Daubert is the highest standard in the US, set by the Supreme Court, while Frye is the standard still used in some states. These are court standards for evidence. The point for investigators is to conduct evidence work in accordance with acceptable scientific practices. New styles of evidence work often gets reviewed by these standards.

Evidence Discipline. How much a person might exercise caution about preventing evidence production or remains. Wearing gloves and a ski mask at a robbery is evidence discipline.

Evidence production. Evidence is produced by the interaction of scenes. Evidence proves something. In some cases, this evidence can be exculpatory (clear a person by exclusion) or inculpatory (include a person).

Function scene or tool scene. A scene that does something for someone or thing. People, cars and tools do things, and varying parts of their existence is devoted to bringing about a change.

Geotagging. When a GPS enabled device records coordinates of an action. This is often with a smartphone photo.

Host scene or greater scene. The host scene holds the subscene(s). Hosting is the function. Traditional host scenes are public, private, and cars. A car is the greater scene holding the subscene of the person scene who drives it.

Identifiability. How much can something be identified. Fingerprints are unique to each person, and thus provide a potential absolute identification. Specific shoes, such as a size 10 running shoe are not unique, and have limited identifiability requiring support by additional evidence.

Individual Characteristics. Specific unique details of an item. For a car it would be the vehicle identification number, body damage, how the person kept the car, and accessorized it.

Inevitability of history. The dangerous concept of looking at a crime after the fact, and thinking every action and reaction were inevitable. This perspective leads to narrow considerations of possibilities and hinders investigations by limiting options. No matter how random things appear, they are the result of decisions with evidentiary consequences to be exploited by the investigator.

Locard's Exchange Principle. When two things interact their contact will leave a trace.

Medicolegal. The SART is a Medicolegal procedure. as it is a medical exam performed by trained medical personnel as coordinated by legal personnel. It combines the best practices of each for the court proceedings. For example, in normal situations, a medical person might assess a patient with closed questions about events and conditions, but for legal proceedings open questions where the patient explains what happed in his or her own words, without prompts are more preferred.

Object scene. An object scene receives the action of the subject scene when the two interact. A crowbar leaves a mark on the doorframe. The doorframe is the object scene.

Pattern matching. When scenes interact, one scene often leaves a mark on the other. In some cases there can be marks both ways. The marks can be physical like a brand on cattle, or a record of interaction such as on a website. Fingerprints, and even DNA are a part of the idea, but the science and logic behind it seeks to show the mark left on one scene can be linked to another scene.

Person Scene. The body is a scene like any other scene, and can hold evidence. Person scenes can serve many purposes, and are the center of investigations, as persons are accused of crimes in court.

Recency. Investigations rely on timelines to show what happened when. Recency emphasizes what happened last, especially with fragile evidence. Thousands of people visit a bar, but the fingerprints on glasses collected right after a shooting are presumed to be relevant to the crime, than a credit card bill for a patron three months prior.

Response Scene. The scene where the investigation begins is usually a hosting, and geographical scene. It is also where the event came to a point, and police were called.

SART. Sexual Assault Response Team. The SART is the medicolegal exam performed by nurses trained to investigate sexual assault. The examination by a nurse applied to a person scene. It can be for either role in the case, and by law anyone can be a victim. In practice the nurse typically treats females even if they are suspects. Male victims, and children are often processed by a SART nurse. Some jurisdictions have all parties processed by medical personnel, and others have male suspect processed by nurses.

Scene. Everything (noun) is a scene. This includes persons, places, and things. There are five scene types; public, private, car, person, and tool. The scenes differ on scale, function, and activity level. They share being able to interact with other scenes, and except for two immovable scenes, they all can leave their marks on the scenes they interact with.

Spatial Literacy. Recognizing the importance of measuring scenes for absolute dimensions, and relationships of items within the space.

Subject scene. A scene producing evidence or changing the object scene when the two interact. A crowbar leaves a mark on the doorframe. The crowbar is the subject scene.

Subscene. A component scene of a greater hosting scene. For a bank robbery, a person is a subscene of a robbery, as he was there in the bank. The person's smartphone is a subscene of the person. The person is a subscene of the car he drives.

Substrate. Literally, levels below. For evidence this is the material already present. The lining in a can brings chemicals into the testing process, therefor an investigator must send an unused can as a substrate, so it can be compared to the chemicals in the sample.

Tainting. To introduce anything into a scene that could jeopardize its use for investigation. This could take form by allowing suspects into the scene afterward, failing to secure the scene from outsiders, or bringing outsider evidence into the scene. A well-documented investigation answers the questions of tainting early.

Timeline and timestamp. Timeline is when events occur.

Tool scene. A functional scene used by a person to bring about a change. These scenes are usually portable, and leave patterns.

Tradeoff. Every scene has benefits and drawbacks for the persons involved in the case. Knowing how the tradeoffs work makes looking for evidence easier.

Transit scene. A scene with short-term occupancy, and not the primary scene, but has a connection to the crime. If a stabbing takes place in a bar scene, and the stabber runs through the kitchen only to escape, the kitchen is a transit scene, just as the roadway leading to a collision intersection is a transit scene.

Wi-Fi. The common name for local wireless communications for the Institute of Electrical and Electronics Engineers 802.11, sometimes the term *hotspot* is used.

Index

D

E

F

G

H

I

Q

R

S

T

V

W

About the Author

Eric Golembiewski has 15 years of investigative experience with a northern California law enforcement agency. He began his investigative career as a beat officer responding to crimes, graduating to crime scene investigator for five years, and detective for three. Along the way he has worked hundreds of cases from different perspectives. Before police work, he was a linguist in the US Army. Most of his time has been spent investigating something.

Eric believes in a renaissance of fundamental investigative work. In an era of explosive technological growth and evolving social issues everything comes back to a methodical application of the basics. The scene is bedrock of any investigation; the initial investigation sets the tone for the rest of the investigation. The evidence contained on those scenes proves how scenes and actions fit together to prove who did what.

Start with scenes, end with evidence. Evidence proves facts.

Made in the USA
Monee, IL
14 December 2023

49286590R00162